Contemporary Japan

Duncan McCargo

palgrave

Published by
PALGRAVE ™
Houndmills, Basingstoke, Hampshire RG21 6XS and
175 Fifth Avenue, New York, N. Y. 10010
Companies and representatives throughout the world

PALGRAVE is the new global academic imprint of
St. Martin's Press LLC Scholarly and Reference Division and
Palgrave Publishers Ltd (formerly Macmillan Press Ltd).

Outside North America
ISBN 0–333–71002–2 hardcover
ISBN 0–333–71001–0 paperback

Inside North America
ISBN 0–312–22741–8 hardcover
ISBN 0–312–22742–6 paperback

This book is printed on paper suitable for recycling and made from fully managed and sustained forest sources.

A catalogue record for this book is available from the British Library.

A catalogue record for this book is available from the Library of Congress.

10   9   8   7   6   5   4   3
10   09   08   07   06   05   04   03

Copy-edited and typeset by Povey–Edmondson
Tavistock and Rochdale, England

Printed in China

Contents

List of Figures, Tables, and Boxes

Figures

Tables

Boxes

Preface and Acknowledgements

I am an Asia specialist, but a Japan generalist; I have spent three years living and teaching in Japan, but I have no academically useful knowledge of the Japanese language. This book is a synthesis of English-language secondary sources, based mainly on several years of teaching Japanese politics to undergraduates at the University of Leeds. With a non-specialist readership in mind, I have taken a couple of contentious editorial decisions. Macrons (used to indicate vowel length) have been omitted from Japanese words. Japanese names have been written in the western style, with the family name second (for example, Ichiro Ozawa, rather than Ozawa Ichiro).

I am indebted to many people in Japan for their kindness and hospitality during my three extended sojourns there: my colleagues at Aichi Prefectural Chigusa High School and all my friends in Nagoya, 1986–88, especially Wayne Wilson; all those who befriended me during my stay at International Christian University, Tokyo, over the hot summer of 1994, especially Roger Buckley and Karen Shire; and, most recently, to Professors Hiroyuki Taniguchi, Eiichi Katahara and Masami Sato of the Faculty of Law, Kobe Gakuin University, who gave me a wonderful year as a Visiting Professor in 1997–98.

I could not have written this book at all without my two research assistants, Kanako Hiraoka and Jacqueline Hicks. I am very grateful for helpful comments on this manuscript from Cindy Daugherty, Penny Francks, Yoshie Ichinoe, Brian McVeigh, Mika Toyota, Caroline Rose, and three anonymous reviewers. Many thanks to Ian McCargo for compiling the index. Steven Kennedy has been a very supportive publisher throughout. The mistakes are all mine.

Duncan McCargo

List of Abbreviations

APEC	Asia Pacific Economic Cooperation
ASEAN	Association of Southeast Asian Nations
ASEM	Asia–Europe Summit Meeting
CM	citizens' movement
DLP	Democratic Liberal Party
DP	Democratic Party
DSP	Democratic Socialist Party
EAEC	East Asian Economic Caucus
EU	European Union
GATT	General Agreement on Tariffs and Trade
GDP	gross domestic product
IMF	International Monetary Fund
JCP	Japan Communist Party
JDP	Japan Democratic Party
JET	Japan Exchange and Teaching programme
JLP	Japan Liberal Party
JNP	Japan New Party
JRP	Japan Renewal Party
JSP	Japan Socialist Party
LDC	Less-developed country
LLDC	Least among less-developed countries
LDP	Liberal Democratic Party
LP	Liberal Party
MITI	Ministry of International Trade and Industry
MTDPE	Mid-Term Defence Programme Estimate
NAFTA	North American Free Trade
NDPO	National Defence Programme Outline
NFP	New Frontier Party
NHK	Japan's semi-governmental broadcasting agency
NIC	newly-industrialized country
ODA	Overseas development aid
PKO	peace-keeping operation
SCAP	Supreme Commander for the Allied Powers
SDF	Self-Defence Force
SDP(J)	Social Democratic Party (of Japan)

Map of Japan

1
Introduction: Themes and Debates

You are now entering contested territory. The nature of contemporary Japan is hotly debated by specialists and observers both inside and outside Japan. Whether the topic is Japan's domestic politics, international relations, or economic order, apparently simple questions such as 'Is Japan a liberal democracy?', 'Is Japan a superpower?', or 'Does Japan have a free market economy?' will provoke radically different answers from different scholars and analysts. Facts about Japan are often buried under different interpretations and perspectives. When reading books or articles about contemporary Japan, we need to be constantly alert to the biases and preferences of their authors. This book starts from the assumption that in order to understand much about contemporary Japan, we need to understand the alternative perspectives to be found in the literature on Japan.

Accordingly, this book will invite you to view Japan from three alternative perspectives which will be referred to regularly in each chapter: mainstream, revisionist, and culturalist. In reality, of course, there is a much wider range of perspectives which can be used to explain and to understand contemporary Japan, and many individual students of Japanese society and politics draw on elements of more than one. The three approaches presented here, however, provide a clear indication of the extent of debate and its range and character.

The Mainstream Perspective

The first perspective might best be described as the 'mainstream' perspective, and is generally the most common perspective to be found in the literature about Japan. Using methods derived from the sub-discipline of comparative politics, the mainstream perspective emphasises points of comparison between Japan and other societies. Indeed, some books written from this perspective explicitly compare Japan with one or more other countries, often including the USA. More commonly, however, the comparisons are implicit rather than explicit. Japan is treated as having economic, political and social systems that are broadly similar to those of other developed countries. Typically, Japan is seen by mainstream scholars as a fully functioning liberal democracy with a free market economy (albeit with minor variations).

Many scholars who adopt this perspective are based in the USA. This is unsurprising on one level, since the United States contains the largest concentration of Japan specialists outside Japan itself. At the same time the American Occupation of Japan at the end of the Second World War was an immensely important factor in shaping the course of Japanese history. The United States attempted to reshape Japan into something more closely resembling its own image, and American officials and scholars have consistently sought to emphasise the success of the Occupation project and the extent to which its goals have been realized. The mainstream perspective on contemporary Japan is partly a continuation of the philosophy and objectives of the US occupation. At the same time, the enormous differences between Japan and the United States raise serious questions about the utility of comparing the two countries.

There are strong arguments for comparing Japan with various European countries (which share such features as constitutional monarchies, parliamentary systems, multi-party systems, centralized education systems, capital city dominance, and economic interventionism by the state). Even more salient arguments exist for comparing Japan with other Asian territories such as South Korea and Taiwan (economies characterized by state-led development), or Thailand and the Philippines (political orders characterized by factionalism and structural corruption).

The scholars most closely identified with the mainstream approach have been affiliated with Harvard University. Their guru was the historian and former US Ambassador to Japan, Edwin O. Reischauer, author of numerous books including *The Japanese* and *The Japanese Today*. Reischauer promoted a positive image of Japanese society, politics and culture, and played an important role in maintaining the strong relationship between the two countries which persists to this day. He argued that although there were many differences between the Japanese political system and the politics of western countries, Japan 'appears to measure up quite well as an effective system of democratic rule' (Reischauer, 1977: 327). In *Japan as Number One*, his colleague Ezra Vogel sought to present Japan, not simply as a successful imitator of American values and systems, but as a state which was succeeding in displacing the USA from a position of industrial and political dominance (Vogel 1979).

Many American political scientists (for example, Ellis Krauss, Bradley Richardson, Scott Flanagan, Gerald Curtis, and John Creighton Campbell), have adopted a broadly positive view of Japan which could well be characterized as mainstream, and the themes of their work are shared by well-known Japanese counterparts such as Takashi Inoguchi. They see Japanese politics as pluralistic, characterized by free elections, genuine political parties and open public debate. Japanese society is typically seen as meritocratic, stable and characterized by limited class conflict. Vogel and others have even argued that other countries need to 'learn from Japan' in order to increase their levels of economic productivity, to limit social inequalities, and reduce problems such as drug abuse and crime. The mainstream approach reached its zenith of popularity during the 1980s, when Japan's extraordinary economic growth seemed to pose a real challenge to the global hegemony of the West, and especially the position of the United States. However, some mainstream analysts have been guilty of exaggerating the successes of Japan, glossing over the shortcomings of the Japanese system.

The Revisionist Approach

Chalmers Johnson – a leading 'revisionist' – argues that the majority of American Japan experts:

> spend their time not studying the Japanese state itself but looking for candidates within the Japanese political system who, they hope, might one day assume political direction over the activities of the state. If they could find such a person or group, this would help confirm the American proposition that democratic politics inevitably conforms to the pluralist paradigm. (Johnson, 1995: 14)

If the mainstream perspective sometimes fails to see the darker side of Japan, the revisionist perspective often concentrates on little else. Revisionists typically see Japan as a very different kettle of fish from western liberal democracies. They view Japan as operating according to distinctive principles of its own: typically, they regard it as undemocratic, and as characterized by a deeply flawed political system that features a considerable degree of structural corruption.⎤ They view Japan's economic system as far more state-led and far less open to outside competition than mainstream analysts typically acknowledge. Some revisionists go so far as to see Japan as a kind of 'soft authoritarian' state, characterized by repressive elements of social and political conformity. Revisionists typically view Japan's relations with the rest of the world with a sceptical eye, arguing that Japan cynically manipulates its trade, aid and defence policies for its own advantage. Indeed, the revisionist view of Japan became popular during the intense trade frictions between Japan and the USA in the 1980s. Pro-Japan commentators labelled revisionist scholars and analysts 'Japan-bashers', and some revisionist themes were taken up by American politicians who sought to play to domestic electorates (such as the congressman who put a sledge hammer to various Japanese appliances).

Nevertheless, most revisionists themselves reject the 'Japan-basher' label, and it is difficult to generalize about the perspectives of so-called revisionists, who constitute a heterogenous group with divergent views. They range from Chalmers Johnson, a political economist and Asia specialist, to Karel van Wolferen, a Dutch journalist, former US trade negotiator Clyde Prestowitz, and James Fallows, an American journalist. They also include scholars who have arrived at similarly critical views of Japanese society from a Marxist-influenced perspective, including Gavan McCormack and Yoshio Sugimoto. Stockwin lumps these (and other) critical scholars together under the catch-all category of 'controversial approaches' (Stockwin, 1999: 34–5; 260).

A common feature of the revisionists is their collective exasperation with what they see as the successful public relations of the Japanese government, and the unduly sympathetic line on Japan adopted by mainstream writers and academics. Partly because of their sense of adopting a minority position that challenges academic orthodoxies, the revisionists have sometimes been unnecessarily combative and provocative in their writings. At the same time, writers such as Johnson and Wolferen produce books and articles which are far more readable than the relatively turgid output of some mainstream scholars, and their work is often highly persuasive.

The Culturalist Perspective

To paraphrase L. P. Hartley: 'Japan is a foreign country: they do things differently there'. To study Japanese politics (or, indeed, the politics of any Asian country) it is necessary to understand that what people raised in a western society take to be the normal rules of social behaviour do not necessarily apply. Adherents of the culturalist perspective typically seek to explain the nature of Japanese politics, economy and society primarily by reference to cultural differences. Many of the originators of this perspective were American anthropologists (such as Ruth Benedict and John Embree); however, their arguments have been elaborated and developed by numerous Japanese scholars, giving rise to a vast literature on 'Japaneseness' which typically accentuated the supposedly distinctive and even unique character of Japan. Dale has strongly criticized this approach, which he reduces to three core assumptions: a belief that the Japanese possess 'a culturally and socially homogeneous racial identity' which has not changed since prehistoric times; that the Japanese are entirely different from other peoples; and that they proceed from an intensely nationalistic basis which is hostile to non-Japanese sources (Dale, 1986: i). This approach is more difficult to grasp than either the mainstream or the revisionist approaches. At the core of the culturalist perspective is a stress on the Japanese as 'groupist' rather than individualist, an approach often referred to as the 'group model' of Japanese society.

A problem with the so-called 'group model' is that it can suggest a simplistic image of a harmonious, virtually conflict-free Japanese society. Many works by Japanese scholars – a genre known as '*nihon(jin)ron* literature' – emphasise the supposedly 'unique' nature of the Japanese 'miracle'. Among the most notorious is Tadanobu Tsunoda's *The Japanese Brain: Uniqueness and Universality* (which argues that Japanese brains function differently from those of non-Japanese) (Tsunoda, 1985). Other books 'explain' Japaneseness by reference to characteristics such as the Japanese 'non-carnivorous' diet, and (a very widely believed argument) the rice agriculture theory of Japanese society. Although these examples of *nihon(jin)ron* literature differ in their answers to the enigma of Japaneseness, they belong to the same strain of popular scholarship, a scholarship of admiration for Japan.

The assumptions behind this 'group model' literature need to be teased out and questioned. Harumi Befu has argued that Japanese groups are not nearly so internally harmonious as has been suggested. In particular, Japanese education is ruthlessly competitive, especially at senior high school level when pupils prepare to take entrance examinations for the prestigious universities (Befu, 1980). Befu also challenges the idea that there is no class conflict in Japan, arguing that the Japanese have their own 'native concepts' of social classes, which testify to the existence of horizontal strata in Japanese society.

Mainstream and revisionist scholars sometimes make use of culturalist arguments: some mainstream scholars refer to Japanese culture as one of the sources of Japan's political, social, and economic virtues. Revisionist scholars are typically more critical of culturalist interpretations. Yoshio Sugimoto has argued that what he calls the 'learn from Japan' school has a built-in elite bias, concentrating on examples from government and big business, while neglecting less impressive areas of the Japanese order. Sugimoto questions whether Japan really is a consensual society, asking firstly 'Who defines the content of consensus?', and secondly 'In whose interests is consensus formed?' He suggests that:

> Groupism is itself an explicit ideology directly communicated to subordinate groups in an attempt to routinise the obedience of individuals to the so-called needs of the company, school, or state. (Sugimoto, 1986: 68)

Whilst such criticisms of the group model challenge over-idealistic views of Japan, the existence of a potential for competition and conflict between individual Japanese, between employees and employers, and between different social classes, offers the possibility of more dynamic interpretations of Japanese politics. Instead of a static, harmonious, and self-sustaining system, Japanese politics is seen as a system of competing interests.

At the same time, some revisionists have flirted with cultural explanations in their analyses of contemporary Japan: Karel van Wolferen, for all his criticisms of the Japanese order and his emphasis on the political origins of culture, appears to regard Japan as a unique country, distinctively characterized by a multi-tentacled 'System', rather than a conventional state. Although it is possible to differentiate between mainstream, revisionist and culturalist approaches, there are numerous points of intersection, overlap, and cross-over between these three perspectives.

The Country and its People

What is Japan? Our images of other countries are shaped by a variety of sources, including popular culture, consumer goods, art, music, literature, and our (often hazy) understandings or misunderstandings of history. Japan is often seen as remote and rather mysterious. Picturesque scenes of *geisha* and Mount Fuji are typically mixed up with high-tech images of robot-like factory

---

Box 1.1 Key Facts about Japan

Government type	Constitutional monarchy
Capital	Tokyo
Currency	Yen
Highest point	Mount Fuji, 3776 metres
Population	126 310 000 (est. 1998)
Population growth rate	0.23%
Urban population as a % of total population	78%
Land area	374 744 sq. kilometres (nearly 1.5 times the land area of the United Kingdom or slightly less than that of California)
Land use	Agricultural land 14% Forests and fields 67% Others 19%
Natural resources	Negligible mineral resources, fish
Labour force	67.23 million
GDP composition by sector	Agriculture 2% Industry 41.5% Services 56.5%
Major cities	Tokyo (8 m), Yokohama (3.3 m). Osaka (2.5 m), Nagoya (2.1 m), Sapporo (1.8 m), Kyoto (1.5 m), Kobe (1.4 m), Fukuoka (1.3 m)

Source: CIA (1998), *CIA Factbook;* Japan National Statistical Office; Kawai, Nobukazu (1996) *Asahi Shimbun Japan Almanac 1997,* Tokyo, Asahi Shimbun Publishing Company; Keizai Koho Center (1997*), Japan 1998, An International Comparison,* Tokyo, Keizai Koho Center.

workers, and bullet trains. Whilst these images contain elements of truth, they are also stereotypes. Westerners typically view the disparate facets of Japan as highly bizarre and contradictory: a favourite image is the salesman in the electronics store, totting up a customer's bill on a wooden abacus. Japan is seen as a place where tradition and novelty, the ancient and the modern, the very simple and the highly sophisticated, exist side-by-side in a kind of profound contradiction, which the Japanese are uniquely able to create and to comprehend. Bemused western visitors are always writing books and articles about the deep paradoxes of Japan, writings that often tell you more about the deep ignorance of their authors than anything else. Serious students of Japan need to pass quickly through this phase of initial bafflement and awe. To see Japan primarily in terms of 'otherness' and to be preoccupied by its difference from the West, exemplifies what Edward Said calls 'orientalism' – a tendency to make essentialist and patronizing generalizations about non-western societies.

It is important to remember that Japanese people are not defined by their Japaneseness: they are human first, and Japanese second, not the other way around. A European country such as Britain, with its ancient monarchy, often fusty traditions and its long history, displays many of the same discrepancies and overlaps between the new and the old which are evident in Japan. If you compare Japan with other Asian countries such as India, Thailand or Singapore, you will see that there is nothing at all unusual about mixing the ancient and the modern in a single country.

The origins of the Japanese people are obscure and controversial. Reischauer argues that there was 'a broad flow of peoples from Northeastern Asia through the Korean peninsula into Japan, especially during the first seven centuries of the Christian era' (1977: 35). However, other accounts emphasise the continuities between prehistoric settlements and modern Japan, implying that the Japanese have existed in some form for many thousands of years. Certainly, many Japanese people are resistant to the idea that they might be of Chinese or Korean origin.

Japan is an island nation, perhaps in more ways than one. There are four main islands in the Japanese archipelago; most of the major cities (and much of the heavy industry) are on the central island of Honshu. Japan's island identity has significant psychological and political implications. Although non-Japanese think of Japan primarily as one country in Asia, the Japanese for the most part tend to

Figure 1.1   Population density (1995)

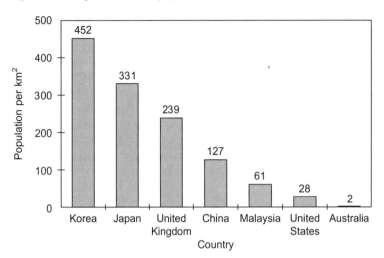

Original Sources: Nihon Kokusei Zue 1997/1998, Kokuseisha; UN (1994) *World Population Prospects.*
Secondary Source: Keizai Koho Center (1998) *Japan 1998: An International Comparison,* Tokyo, Takeo Kurita

feel that they are a distinct civilization in their own right. There is an obvious comparison here with Britain's ambiguous relationship with the rest of Europe. Japan is a very sizeable country in population terms, with around 126 million people in 1997: the population is concentrated in urban areas, since many parts of Japan are mountainous and largely uninhabitable. Japan's population density in comparison to other countries is shown in Figure 1.1.

Less than a fifth of Japan's land area is sufficiently level for agriculture or other economic activity, and apart from the tiny city-states of Singapore and Hong Kong, Japan has the world's highest population density per square mile of habitable land. Japan's mountains are steep, but not especially high. Japan consists largely of 'long stretches of forest-covered hills interlaced with narrow valleys that form slim strips of agriculture and habitation' (Reischauer, 1977: 5). Central Honshu contains several ranges of mountains known as the Japan Alps, which reach heights of around 10 000 feet. Mount Fuji, at 12 389 feet, is Japan's highest mountain. The only sizeable plains area in Japan is the Kanto area, around Tokyo. Before the construction of modern roads and railways, sea transportation was widely used to move goods and people around different parts of the country. Japan's difficult terrain probably contributed to the emergence of a medieval feudal order controlled by local warlords. Apart from an abundance of water, Japan is singularly lacking in natural resources, and very reliant upon imported raw materials (though there is a significant domestic timber industry). All in all, Japanese topography would seem to be singularly unsuitable for the task of building a powerful and centrally-managed industrial economy.

The relationship between Japanese people and nature is a complex one. On the one hand, the Japanese have been very destructive of the natural environment in their quest for rapid industrialization. Yet at the same time, they retain a close affinity with the idea of nature, and constantly celebrate nature's transient beauties. The Japanese are probably more conscious of the changing seasons than any other people: there are numerous special foods, festivals and social rituals marking the arrival of different seasons. Certain places are renowned as beauty spots at particular times of the year, and may receive hundreds of thousands of visitors within a given two-week period. According to convention, all personal letters open with a reference to the season, a practice which sometimes even extends to e-mail correspondence. Japan has four seasons, roughly corresponding to the climate of the East Coast of the United States: a hot, humid summer, a beautiful autumn, a winter which can be surprisingly severe (especially on the Japan Sea coast of Honshu, where snow-filled winds blow in from Siberia), and a short, spectacular spring (symbolized by the famous *sakura*, or cherry blossoms), which is over almost as soon as it has begun. Some observers argue that Japan has five seasons, since June and July typically see intense spells of heavy rain, followed by a wave of typhoons in late summer and early autumn. Destructive typhoons and devastating earthquakes (such as those which struck Tokyo in 1923, and Kobe in 1995) are an accepted fact of life for the Japanese, who often see themselves pitted in a sort of cosmic struggle with potentially hostile natural forces.

Japan's four main islands comprise: the central island of Honshu – by far the most important – which contains the great cities of Tokyo, Osaka and Nagoya, the ancient capital of Kyoto, and the three largest urban regions (Kanto, Kansai and Chubu); Kyushu, to the South, home to Nagasaki, Kagoshima and Fukuoka; Shikoku, the smallest of the main islands, to the East of Southern Honshu;

and Hokkaido (sometimes referred to as 'the Japanese Scotland'), a far less densely populated island to the North. In terms of size of population and economic importance, Japan is dominated by the urban centres along the Pacific Coast of Honshu: especially Kobe, Osaka, Kyoto, Nagoya, Tokyo, Yokohama and Kawasaki. The country is divided into 47 prefectures for administrative purposes. Politically, Tokyo rules supreme: despite the existence of elected politicians at prefectural, city and municipal level, purse strings are controlled largely by ministries in the capital. There are big disparities in income between urban and rural areas.

For most visitors to Japan, their first impressions are of ugliness and urban sprawl. The expectant traveller who longs to explore Japan's ancient beauties and arrives for the first time at the newly-refurbished Kyoto JR Station, will then be confronted by the Kyoto Tower, a looming monstrosity of staggering tackiness. There is considerable beauty in Japan, but you have to look for it. The Japanese have a very highly developed aesthetic sense, but to appreciate the beauty of Japan often requires a literal or figurative 'zoom lens'. Japanese people may see the beauty of a flower in the shadow of a temple gate; in doing so, they can simply 'shut out' the ugly concrete buildings which have sprouted up around the gate, the garish soft-drink vending machines just inside, and the pylons and power gables just above. Most of urban Japan is a hideous mess, which repeatedly violates every basic principle of town planning and conservation: the result of *ad hoc* redevelopment after the war, coupled with the all-pervasive (and largely malign) influence of construction companies and their powerful political allies. Yet away from urban regions, particularly in the mountains, in Hokkaido, and on the Japan Sea coast, there are many areas of considerable natural beauty.

Traditionally, most Japanese people lived from farming (especially rice farming) and fishing. It has been argued that the co-operative efforts involved in rice production and harvesting fostered a group culture among the Japanese, an argument which revisionists find far-fetched. Nevertheless, the Japanese have an emotional attachment to the idea of themselves as an agricultural people, and during the postwar period farmers have been the recipients of considerable government largesse. The word for rice *(gohan)* is synonymous with the word for meal. The Japanese like to claim that they eat everything produced by the sea, from whalemeat, fish, shrimps and shellfish, to seaweed. A typical Japanese meal consists of rice, vegetables and fish. Unlike most other Asian foods, Japanese food is not spicy, but is served with side dishes of sauces and pickles. Great importance is attached to the visual impact of a meal, which is often exquisitely presented. Whereas most Chinese and Southeast Asian food is served in a collective manner, with various dishes placed in the centre of the table, Japanese food is individually prepared, and typically served in lacquered containers or ceramic dishes.

Japan is singularly rich in terms of culture. The Japanese passion for detail is revealed in innumerable wonderful artworks, such as the many wooden carved Buddhist images to be found in temples, beautifully painted scrolls and screens from various periods, and very fine ceramics. Outside Japan, Edo-period *ukiyoe* prints showing famous landscapes, beauties and actors are widely appreciated and collected, though for most Japanese these prints are ephemeral works rather than high art. Japan has an outstanding literary tradition, as evidenced in genres such as *haiku* poetry, and in the novels of internationally-renowned twentieth-century writers such as Natsume, Kawabata, and Mishima. Traditional Japanese drama, such as *kabuki* and *noh,* continues to be widely performed, and is gaining increasing interest outside Japan.

Other important aspects of Japanese culture are the traditional cultural pursuits favoured by many women: the tea ceremony with its combination of the simple and elaborate, *ikebana* or Japanese flower-arranging, and playing musical instruments such as the harp-like *koto.* In contrast with many other societies, cultural matters are taken very seriously, and attract considerable attention. Special exhibitions of western painting (often at department stores) or some rarely displayed Japanese screens (often at a temple or museum) can draw huge crowds. Certain objects of historical or artistic significance are designated 'national treasures', while outstanding artists may be given the status of 'living national treasures'. Japan also has a rich and thriving world of popular culture, ranging from sumo wrestling and pop music, to comic books and television game shows.

Conclusion

Contemporary Japan is one of the world's most fascinating, important and complex nations. Understanding Japan is an important task for everyone who studies modern economic, social and political systems. Yet gaining an accurate understanding is often hindered by the extensive debates and disagreements among Japan scholars themselves, disagreements which permeate most of the available published literature. When reading and studying about Japan, it is very important to be aware of being constantly in disputed territory, caught in the crossfire between mainstream analysts, revisionists, and culturalists. To start to understand Japan, we need to begin by adopting a critical, sceptical and questioning attitude to everything we hear and read – including, of course, this book.

2
Historical Background

After a long period of relative isolation from the beginning of the seventeenth century, in the mid-1800s Japan began a process of extraordinarily rapid industrialization and social change, making the transition from an essentially feudal society to a modern nation-state within a couple of decades. Following its successful defeat of a western power in the Russo–Japanese war, Japan increasingly turned towards imperialism, and eventually to the militarism which culminated in the disastrous Pacific War. Following the Japanese surrender in August 1945, Japan again recreated itself, this time as an economic giant. By the 1980s, Japan was challenging even the United States in trade and manufacturing. Yet as the twentieth century drew to a close Japan faced new challenges, as its political and economic systems appeared to be losing direction. Many aspects of this history are highly contentious.

The Tokugawa Period (1603–1868)

During the Tokugawa period, Japan was unified following the period of the warring states, a long spell of civil conflict. By defeating their rivals militarily, the Tokugawa family achieved hegemonic control of Japan, bringing under their control the numerous local feudal lords. During this Edo (an earlier name for Tokyo) or Tokugawa period, Japan was relatively removed from foreign influences. Under the policy of national isolation, the Tokugawa *shogun* expelled all Europeans from Japan, with the exception of a small Dutch trading community that was confined to an island in the port of Nagasaki. Christianity was outlawed. It was only with the arrival of the famous 'black ships' – an American fleet commanded by Commodore Matthew Perry – in 1853, that Japan was compelled to re-open to international trade.

However, the image of Japan as a 'closed country' has been somewhat exaggerated, leading to an overemphasis on the distinc-

14

tiveness and uniqueness of Japanese culture (Pyle, 1996: 57–9). In practice, there was substantial foreign trade throughout this period, especially with China and Korea, and through the Ryukyu Islands (which provided a staging post for trade with China and Southeast Asia). Dutch traders were presented to the *shogun* in Edo, western books other than Christian tracts were allowed to circulate in Japan after 1720, and Japanese experts in 'Dutch studies' (knowledge about the West) were engaged in translating and assimilating information from abroad, especially material relating to advances in science and technology. It was only during the final decades of the Tokugawa period that the seclusion policy took on a xenophobic character.

During the two centuries when Japan was a relatively closed country, real political power lay in the hands of the Edo *shogun* (or 'generalissimo'), while the emperor lived in seclusion in Kyoto. Although notionally subordinate to the Emperor, the *shogun* was effectively a ruler to whom other lords swore allegiance. The country was tightly regimented: firm action was taken against subversive elements, and even members of the elite were subject to considerable control. The *shogun* directly controlled around a quarter of all lands, while the remaining three-quarters were administered by the 260 or so *daimyo*, or great landowning aristocrats. Although Edo Japan is often loosely termed 'feudal', a combination of central military power and local devolution to the *daimyo* amounted to a 'feudal-central hybrid'. *Shogun* could rearrange or reassign the domains of *daimyo* at will – and often did so during the first century of Tokugawa rule in order to establish their own power and control. The *daimyo* were also forced to divide their time between Edo and their home estates through a system of 'alternate residence' (see Waswo, 1996: 9–17). Maintaining two lavish residences encouraged many *daimyo* to live beyond their means, engaging in patterns of conspicuous consumption which concealed growing indebtedness: under these conditions, the merchant class was able to amass considerable wealth. This gradually had the effect of shifting power away from the *samurai* (retainers of the *shogun* and *daimyo*, who made up some 6–7 per cent of the population) and towards the emerging commercial sector. This shift was symbolized by the rise of the trading city of Osaka.

The pace of change in late Edo Japan produced numerous sources of social discontent. *Samurai* became jealous of the higher incomes and better lifestyles enjoyed by the more well-to-do merchant

Box 2.1   Key dates in modern Japanese history

1603	Tokugawa shogunate established.
1635–9	Seclusion policy adopted.
1774	Rise of so-called 'Dutch studies'.
1853	Commodore Perry's 'black ships' arrive in Tokyo Bay.
1868	Meiji Restoration (reversion to imperial rule).
1889	Meiji Constitution
1890	Imperial rescript on education, beginning of parliamentary government.
1894	Sino–Japanese war, extraterritoriality abolished.
1895	Annexation of Taiwan.
1902	Anglo–Japanese alliance.
1904	Russo–Japanese war.
1910	Annexation of Korea.
1918	First party government formed; 'Taisho democracy' begins.
1923	Tokyo earthquake.
1925	Universal manhood suffrage.
1931	Manchurian incident.
1932	Puppet state of Manchuko established in Manchuria; assassination of Prime Minister Inukai by rightist naval cadets.
1937	Invasion of China begins.
1940	Japan signs Tripartite Pact with Germany and Italy.
1941	Attacks on Pearl Harbour and the Malay peninsula; United States enters the war.
1942	Philippines taken; Allied victory at the Battle of Midway.
1944	Allies recapture the Philippines.
1945	Atomic bombing of Hiroshima and Nagasaki; surrender, beginning of Allied Occupation and reforms.
1946	Political purges begin.
1946–8	Tokyo war trials.
1947	New Constitution and major political reforms; Socialist government takes office.
1948	'Reverse course' begins.
1949	'Dodge line' implemented.
1950	Korean War breaks out.
1951	San Francisco peace treaty; US–Japan security pact.
1952	End of Occupation.
1954	Self-Defence Forces established.
1955	Liberal Democratic Party is formed and takes power; industrial production back to 1942 levels.
1956	Diplomatic relations restored with Soviet Union; Japan admitted to the United Nations.

1959	Minamata disease first confirmed.
1960	Mass protests against renewal of US–Japan security treaty; income-doubling policy announced.
1964	Tokyo Olympics held.
1967	Incomes successfully doubled after seven years; first anti-pollution legislation passed.
1971	Environment Agency established.
1972	Okinawa reverts to Japanese administration; diplomatic relations restored with China.
1974	First oil shock.
1976	Ex-Prime Minister Tanaka arrested over Lockheed scandal; National Defence Programme Outline announced.
1977	Fukuda doctrine announced.
1978	Narita airport protesters destroy control tower; airport finally opens.
1979	Second oil shock.
1983	Prime Minister Nakasone takes office with a conservative agenda.
1987	New union federation Rengo formed.
1988	Japan attains record trade surplus with the US. US–Japan trade disputes peak.
1989	Death of Emperor Hirohito; Showa period ends, and Heisei era begins. Many leading politicians involved in Recruit-Cosmos scandal.
1990	End of 'bubble' economy based on land and stockmarket speculation.
1991	Gulf War raises questions about Japan's defence policy.
1992	Economic downturn sets in; Hosokawa forms Japan New Party. Sagawa Kyubin scandal breaks.
1993	Ozawa and Hata form Japan Renewal Party and break away from LDP. LDP loses power in 1993 general elections, replaced by a coalition led by Hosokawa.
1994	Electoral reform legislation implemented. Anti-LDP coalition collapses, and a hybrid alliance based on the LDP and the Socialist Party takes over.
1995	Kobe earthquake; sarin attack by Aum Shinrikyo cult in Tokyo.
1996	LDP leader Hashimoto becomes prime minister. First general election under the new electoral system sees little substantive change.
1997	Asian financial crisis has an adverse impact on Japan's economy.

families: social class alone no longer determined wealth. Peasant protests over harsh taxes or local abuses were common, their violence often directed at oppressive village leaders rather than the *samurai* class (Sato, 1990: 59). Another source of dissatisfaction was that the Edo bureaucracy was not meritocratic, but reserved higher positions for the well-born, blocking career prospects for lower-ranking but more able young *samurai*. Tensions within the *shogunate* were well-established long before the challenge of the West hit home in 1853. Doubts about the effectiveness of *samurai* rule undermined the hierarchical ideology of Tokugawa Japan. Yet to see the Edo period as essentially feudal, static and backward would be much too simplistic: the tensions which emerged during these two and a half centuries reflected vast social and economic changes, which had an enormous impact on early modern Japan.

The Meiji Period (1868–1912)

The economic and political crisis brought about by the arrival of the Americans precipitated the collapse of the *shogun* system. In agreeing to 'open up' Japan to foreign trade, the ruling elite saw this as a strategy to create a strong Japan, capable of mastering western science and technology, and thereby emulating western power. At the same time, the external challenge from foreign powers offered new solutions to the social problems that had afflicted late-Tokugawa Japan. In 1867, the Emperor Meiji was 'restored' to head a new government. This 'restoration' meant that after many centuries without any effective power, the Japanese Emperor regained a central political role. The significance of the restoration is contested: some historians see it simply as an elite manoeuvre on the part of a small group of ambitious *samurai*, whereas more recent scholarship has supported the view that it reflected a growing social movement for revolutionary change, which dated back to the eighteenth century. As Pyle explains: 'The role of the foreign crisis was to bring into sharp focus the impotence of the old system and to prompt revolutionary action to create a new order' (Pyle, 1996: 74).

A period of rapid modernization followed, as Japan sought to 'catch up' with the West. Seeing the imperial powers as a serious threat, Japan sought to learn from western countries, partly in order to fend off the dangers of colonization. Missions were sent to study western states and societies (particularly those of Britain, France,

Germany and the United States), and to identify models that Japan could adapt. During the early Meiji period, Japan established a wide range of new institutions, including a British-style navy and postal system, a French-style police and judicial system, American-style banking and primary school systems, and a German-style army (Pyle, 1996: 79). More than 3 000 foreign advisors were employed in Japan during the Meiji period, many of them engineers and technologists: Japan did not become reliant on these expatriates, however, but sought to replace them with Japanese personnel as soon as these had been trained.

Over 11 000 Japanese people were sent to study abroad during the Meiji period, primarily to the USA and Germany. Japan benefited from a relatively young leadership; importantly, the ruling elite were urban-dwellers who derived their power from their formal positions, not from landed estates; this made them far more open to change, since they did not have to fear that they might lose property and wealth under new social arrangements (Pyle, 1996: 79–80). Under these conditions, the 'Japanese enlightenment' took place during the Meiji period. Salient features of this enlightenment included a negative view of Japan's traditions, considerable optimism about the prospects for Japan to catch up with the West, a belief in the inexorability of progress by emulating western examples, and 'a wholehearted commitment to science, technology, and utilitarian knowledge' (Pyle, 1996: 93).

During the Meiji period, Japan emerged as the first non-western industrial power. The government gradually developed a state-led industrial policy emphasising the establishment of heavy industries such as mining, steel and railways; pursued a strategy of import substitution, coupled with the purchase of the best available western industrial technology; and established a dynamic export sector. Foreign debt was avoided wherever possible. By the end of the Meiji period, Japan was successfully competing with Britain as a leading exporter of textiles. At the same time, some scholars argue that the role of the state in fostering Japan's industrialization should not be overplayed: individual entrepreneurs were also central to this complex process, which government could facilitate but not implement without the active participation of the private sector (Pyle, 1996: 108–12).

Various steps were taken during the Meiji period to forge a more powerful and effective state, and to establish a strong sense of national identity. Conscription was introduced in 1873 for all men over 20. The monarchy was used as an important symbol of the nation, not just to the outside world but also to the Japanese population at large (Waswo, 1996: 26–33). This was seen in new national holidays associated with imperial dates, the use of impressive Imperial edicts and proclamations, and an emphasis on the idea of serving the Emperor. School textbooks were controlled – and later directly written – by the Ministry of Education, and came to emphasise 'moral' themes such as loyalty to the throne and filial piety. Another important step entailed incorporating traditional localities into a national administrative structure. At the same time, the bureaucracy was made more open and meritocratic.

The most significant political development of the Meiji period was the promulgation of the 1889 constitution, which symbolized the forging of the first modern nation-state in Asia (for the best discussion, see Gluck, 1985: 42–72). The document was heavily influenced by German political and legal ideas, and established a bicameral legislature resembling those of European countries. There was an unelected upper house dominated by the nobility, and an elected lower chamber – though suffrage was limited to around 1 per cent of the population. These representative institutions were seen as instruments of nation-building and unity, and as 'safety valves' for popular discontent, rather than as instruments for establishing or managing democracy (Gluck, 1985: 49–50). In theory the 1889 constitution enshrined certain civil liberties, though in practice these provisions made little impact. This was a constitution imposed from above, rather than one that reflected any sense of broader political demands (unlike the western constitutions on which it was modelled). A central feature of the 1889 constitution was its definition of the Emperor as the sovereign source of supreme authority. In practice, however, real power belonged to a group of influential leaders. Ministers were appointed by the Emperor, and cabinets were accountable to him rather than to parliament. The elected assembly – which featured political parties – was intended to play a merely consultative role (for a discussion, see Gluck, 1985: 64–7). Despite all these limitations and shortcomings, the 1889 constitution was a great step forward for Japan, establishing the political foundations of a modern nation-state. Following the formal promulgation of the constitution, it took roughly a decade for the constitutional system to be thoroughly institutionalized and established as a working entity (Banno, 1992: 200).

Taisho Democracy

In practice, the political system inaugurated by the Meiji constitution was one of competing elites. As Stockwin puts it:

> Cabinets, political parties, senior government bureaucrats, the House of Peers, the Privy Council, the *tenno's* [Emperor's] personal advisers in the Imperial Household Ministry, the chiefs of staff of the armed forces and directors of certain big business combines were all jockeying for power in a situation where it was unclear where power really lay. (Stockwin 1999: 20)

This sense of contending forces reached its peak during the period of 'Taisho democracy' (corresponding to the reign of the weak and mentally-ill Emperor Taisho from 1912 to 1926), when political parties grew in importance and there was greater political freedom than previously. From 1918 to 1932, parties were especially powerful, and prime ministers were generally selected from among the party leaders. Nevertheless, the political parties that existed were elite organizations, rather than mass-based ones (see Pyle, 1996: 159–71). Party politicians were obliged to work in close collaboration with the court, the bureaucracy, and the military. However, the political system did seem to be moving in a democratic direction, though substantive change was limited by the nature of the Meiji constitutional order. Outside the elite, popular political consciousness was growing rapidly: unions flourished (including militant unions of tenant farmers), students became politically active, and a wide range of liberal and even radical reform movements emerged. One important political change occurred in 1925, when universal male suffrage was introduced, increasing the size of the electorate fourfold to more than 12 million.

Imperialism, Militarism and War

The Meiji leadership placed considerable emphasis on military strength, recognizing that only a well-armed Japan could deal with the West on an equal footing. The success of its policies was first seen in the Sino-Japanese War of 1894–95, in which Japan destroyed China's navy and overwhelmed her army. Japan was then able to dictate the terms of a highly favourable treaty: China ceded the

Pescadores, Formosa (later Taiwan) and the Laiotung Peninsula to Japan. The reality of China's weakness was exposed, and the war precipitated a 'scramble for China' among the imperial powers. However, the western powers were unwilling to see Japan reap the full benefits of her aggressive action, and in April 1895, Germany, Russia and France forced Japan to renounce the Peninsula. Japan then concentrated on building up sufficient forces to take on Russia, and succeeded in defeating the Russian navy in the Russo–Japanese War of 1904–5.

The defeat of a western great power by an Asian nation was a major turning-point, greatly emboldening Japan's leadership for the pursuit of further imperialist adventures. At the same time, the victory over Russia had been hard-won, leaving Japan feeling vulnerable and insecure. This persistent sense of insecurity was one of a compound of forces which drove Japanese foreign policy over the following decades. Japan annexed Korea in 1910, and took advantage of the global upheavals of the First World War to seize German territories in Asia, and to increase pressure on China. The rise of militarism in Japan during the 1920s empowered the armed forces at the expense of other political institutions, leaving the military in a strong position to help shape Japan's domestic and overseas agenda.

Japan acted as an imperialist aggressor during the 15 years from the September 1931 Manchuria Incident (in which the Japanese Army used the pretext of a small explosion to invade the whole of Manchuria, subsequently establishing the puppet state of Manchukuo) to the August 1945 surrender. During this 'Fifteen-Year War', Japan terrorized the population of China, carried out a surprise attack against the US Navy at Pearl Harbor in December 1941, invaded and conquered most of Southeast Asia, and fought a brutal war against the allies. Japanese aggression only ceased following the terrible use of the atom bomb on Hiroshima and Nagasaki. The Fifteen-Year War was one of the darkest episodes in Japanese history, and any discussion of that history readily invokes intense emotions. Many of the actions of the Japanese forces – rapes and massacres of Chinese civilians, or dreadful treatment of prisoners of war, for example – are difficult to comprehend, let alone to explain. But Japan's decision to pursue the imperialist policies that culminated in war with the Allies can be understood by reference to considerations of domestic and international politics.

One leading Japanese historian describes Japanese actions during the Pacific War as 'an imperialist war after the age of imperialism'

(Nakamura, 1998: 248). The Versailles and Washington treaties signed at the end of the First World War had been intended to put an end to imperialist rivalry. However, the order they sought to define was one that greatly favoured the victors in that war, such as the United States, Britain and France. The rise of fascism in Germany and Italy reflected the attempts of the defeated nations to turn the tables on their victors. In Japan, the situation was both similar and different. The similarity was that Japan also numbered among the have-nots in the Anglo–American dominated global order. The difference was that unlike the countries of western Europe, Japan had not had the opportunity to form a great overseas Empire, a ready source of natural resources and raw materials to fuel rapid industrialization. In some respects, Japan had achieved its Meiji goal of 'catching up' with the West, transforming itself into a modern industrial society. Yet Japan had not gained the prestige and advantages of imperialist status. As Nakamura argues:

> The Allies were the 'haves', trying to preserve the post-World War I, post-imperialist order, and the Axis countries were the 'have-nots', envious of the Allies' vast territories and overseas possessions and eager for a redistribution of global wealth and power. (Nakamura, 1998: 249)

Although Japanese apologists for the war have sought to represent it as a war of liberation, designed to free Asia from colonialism and establish a 'Greater East Asian Co-Prosperity Zone', the reality was that the Fifteen-Year War reflected attempts by Japan to emulate western patterns of imperial domination and exploitation. In doing so, Japan singularly failed to recognize that the tide was already turning against imperialism. Nationalist movements were sweeping Asia, in India, in the Dutch East Indies (later Indonesia) and above all in China. Imperialism of the kind that Japan sought to export was already past its sell-by date, and Japan's claims that it wanted to nurture Asian independence movements were highly suspect.

Questions concerning how and why Japan decided to invade Manchuria and later China, to sign a military pact with the Axis, and to launch attacks on US forces and British colonies in 1941, require long and careful answers. Significantly, throughout the 1931–45 period, the military was largely beyond the reach of civilian control. China policy was not primarily determined by the cabinet, but by the military. The prime minister and foreign ministers of the day often found themselves reacting to situations over which they had little control or influence. The tenure of civilian leaders was usually short-lived: there were 13 cabinets and 11 prime ministers between 1932 and 1945. When politicians sought to rein in or to dissent from military actions, they were literally taking their lives in their hands: prime minister Tsuyoshi Inukai (who advocated a peaceful solution to the Manchuria dispute) was shot dead by uniformed naval cadets in his official residence on 15 May 1932 (Ienaga, 1978: 42–3). Several other prominent civilian leaders were also killed in plots hatched by young military officers, including the highly influential Finance Minister Korekiyo Takahashi in 1936.

The military insisted on vetoing cabinet appointments, and often completely refused to account for their actions. In making the decision to embark on war with the United States, 'the opinion leaders were the officers of a few key departments in the army and navy' (Nakamura, 1998: 252), not the prime minister or other members of the cabinet. During the war, the cabinet was not always kept informed of developments at the front: when several Japanese warships were lost at the disastrous Battle of Midway, Hideki Tojo (who was then prime minister and army minister, as well as a serving general) was not told for a month (Ienaga, 1978: 39). Nor was the military hierarchy itself capable of imposing discipline; Ienaga cites the Manchuria campaign as evidence that the armed services could not control their own officers and men (Ienaga, 1978: 44). The role of the Emperor in the war remains highly controversial: some scholars see Hirohito as a rather peace-loving man, 'the unwilling symbol' of war (Large, 1992: 216), whereas others have denounced him as a war criminal. Bix argues that the military never completely controlled the political process: the Emperor and those around him also played important roles, especially in the final stages of the Pacific War, and must be held responsible for not bringing the war to a speedier end (Bix, 1995: 223).

An expansionist military abroad was backed by political repression at home; the notorious Kempeitai secret police, supported by extensive legal powers, monitored the civilian population closely for signs of dissident views or behaviour, and acted swiftly and effectively against offenders. However, the same Keynesian policies of state-supported economic stimulation which helped pull Japan out of recession did provide significant economic benefits to much of the population during the late 1930s. Allinson argues that a combination of economic recovery and 'a more bellicose' nationalism helped ensure that the Japanese people accepted the expansionism in China, and later the Pacific War itself (Allinson, 1997: 26). This economic recovery helped forge a strong industrial sector led by a small number of powerful conglomerates, and so paved the way for the reconstruction of Japanese economic power after the war. Dower calls the conflict 'the useful war', arguing that war put into place the basic infrastructure for Japan's postwar economic ascendancy, building a strong capitalist state brokered by conservative interests (Dower, 1992: 49–70).

The American decision to drop atomic bombs on the Japanese cities of Hiroshima and Nagasaki was one of the most controversial issues of the Second World War (for a discussion, see Bernstein, 1995: 227–73, and other articles in the Spring 1995 special issue of *Diplomatic History*). Officials in the Truman administration claimed that dropping the bombs had foreshortened the war, rendering an invasion unneccessary, and so saving up to half a million American lives. Revisionist historians have argued that Japan was already on the verge of surrender, and that the nuclear bombing served little military purpose: Truman's real aim was to demonstrate US superiority over the Soviet Union. The official projections of American fatalities for the planned invasion were 25 000 to 46 000 – not hundreds of thousands. The bombs themselves eventually killed as many as three hundred thousand people (see Dower, 1995: 282), the great majority civilians. There is plenty of middle ground between the official and the revisionist views: arguably, a Japanese surrender might have been achieved without either the atom bombs, or a full-scale invasion. And while a case can be made that the Hiroshima bomb expedited the Japanese surrender, the dropping of a second bomb on Nagasaki is much more difficult to justify.

Despite the fact that the rest of the world has always regarded Japan as an aggressive power during the 15 year period from 1931–45, within Japan there has often been a dominant perception of Japan as a victim of war. Not only was Japan uniquely victimized as the target of two atomic bombs, but the Japanese people saw themselves as the victims of militarism. Blame was shifted away from the nation as a whole, and onto the military and their elite supporters, especially the 28 leaders tried at the Tokyo War Crimes Tribunal. Tanaka writes:

. . . popular thinking in Japan remains strongly linked to the feeling that responsibility for the war lies overwhelmingly in the hands of the war leaders who deceived a gullible populace and led citizens into a war no-one would want to see repeated. Consequently people at large were made to feel they were victims. (Tanaka, 1996: 214)

Tanaka believes that in actual fact 'citizens at large eventually supported the war and as such bear responsibility' (Tanaka, 1996: 215). Many of Japan's leaders in turn claimed to be victims: they were only acting on behalf of the Emperor, who was not put on trial. As Gluck puts it 'neither the people nor the Emperor were arraigned' (Gluck, 1992: 13). As a consequence, many ordinary Japanese people were able to feel in retrospect that the war had little to do with them, whereas actually the kind of 'total war' in which Japan engaged involved the active or passive complicity of virtually the entire population. Far more than the Germans, the Japanese people have engaged in collective denial of their wartime responsibility and culpability. Japanese memories of the Pacific War – the conflict with the United States and the Allies – loom much larger than the darker attacks on Manchuria and China from 1931 onwards; yet Japan began the Pacific War precisely to consolidate and build upon those conquests.

The American Occupation

Much of the difficulty involved in evaluating the present-day Japanese political system hinges on the fact, that outwardly, the system appears to be a western one. The reason for this misleading impression is the historical fact that the Japanese constitution was imposed upon the country during the American Occupation, which lasted from 1945 to 1952. An understanding of the conflicting views and interpretations of the American role in postwar Japan is central in obtaining a sense of subsequent Japanese politics.

At the end of the Second World War, there was considerable disagreement in allied circles over how Japan should be dealt with. Whilst Australia, for example, advocated punitive treatment of the Japanese, including the abolition of the Emperor system, many in the United States (such as Secretary of State Stimson) favoured an extremely limited intervention in Japan's affairs, confined to a programme of demilitarization and the trial of war criminals. In the event, General Douglas MacArthur, the American who was assigned the task of implementing post-surrender arrangements, was given a more ambitious brief: to introduce a system of 'democratic self-government' in Japan. MacArthur was also instructed, however, not 'to impose upon Japan any form of government not supported by the freely expressed will of the people'. In other words, Japan was to become a democracy whether it wanted to or not, so long as everyone agreed.

The American-drafted 1947 constitution was a very different matter from the Meiji constitution, imported virtually lock, stock and barrel from an alien political culture. The Emperor was stripped of all powers, and designated the 'symbol of state, rather than head of state (for the full text, see Hayes, 1992: 282–93). Sovereignty now rested with the Japanese people, who elected a parliament (known as the Diet) to which the Cabinet was answerable. The authority of the legislature was greatly enhanced, and women's suffrage was introduced for the first time. 'Local autonomy' was adopted as a central principle for local and prefectural government; a range of human rights was to be protected; an independent judiciary was established; and, most controversially of all, Article 9 decreed that Japan had forever renounced the sovereign right to wage war.

In addition to the constitution itself, the Occupation forces also implemented a range of secondary reforms aimed at broadening and democratizing participation in politics. One of the most important secondary reforms was the re-establishment of the right to form unions and other interest groups, including left-wing political parties (communists had been jailed since the 1920s). Another was an extensive programme of land reform; no individual was allowed to hold more than about 7.5 acres of land, which had the effect of bringing rural landlordism to an end. A further reform gave new powers to local government in place of the old centralized system. Education was also reformed: nationalist textbooks were rewritten, the education system was decentralized, and many new degree-granting institutions were created. Many scholars have regarded the great majority of these reforms as highly successful.

Another significant aspect of the Occupation was the 'purging' (meaning, for the most part, forced retirement) of individuals held to have been important supporters of the war, including members of the secret police, religious officials and members of militaristic organizations, as well as military officers, ex-bureaucrats, around 3 000 prominent members of the business community, and about 300 national-level politicians. Twenty-eight men were tried at the Tokyo war trials from 1946–48: seven were executed (including two former prime ministers), and 18 received long prison sentences (Allinson, 1997: 52–5).

Nevertheless, the American Occupation did not pursue the same goals throughout: while there was considerable zeal for 'New Deal' style social and political reform during the period 1945–47, by 1948 the dawning realities of the Cold War led to a change in US policy towards Japan, popularly known as the 'reverse course'. Democratization was downgraded as a priority: instead, Occupation policies concentrated on forging an economically strong and self-sufficient nation, which would form a robust bulwark against communism in Asia. MacArthur's early enthusiasm for building up countervailing left-wing forces in Japan was now reversed. The main emphasis during the latter part of the Occupation was on reviving the Japanese economy, a task overseen by the American banker Joseph Dodge. The Occupation formally ended in April 1952.

A number of analysts have emphasised the limited achievements of the American Occupation. In particular, they note the failure of MacArthur to purge the Japanese bureaucracy of those who had held key positions before the war – only a few score were removed, and many of these later regained important posts (see Pempel, 1987: 157–87) – and his parallel failure to break the dominance of prewar large companies in the business sector, despite token attempts to reform the *zaibatsu,* or great conglomerates (Allinson, 1997: 74–5). If the Occupation did not displace old concentrations of power, it is difficult to see postwar Japan as a dramatically more democratic and open society than prewar Japan.

How could a country such as Japan embrace a constitution apparently so different from its previous political direction? An answer favoured by some scholars is that the 1889 constitution marked the beginnings of more widespread political participation in Japan; something not dissimilar to the 1947 constitution was already evolving. Reischauer claimed that:

> An aversion to dictatorial power, or even to charismatic leadership, and a strong tendency to group co-operation were pronounced features of Japan's political heritage, and in my view they still constitute great political assets for Japan today. (Reischauer, 1977: 240)

Reischauer also cites universal literacy and a strong entrepreneurial spirit as reasons for Japan's successful creation of a 'mass democracy'. He suggests a continuity between the 1889 and 1947 constitutions; by implication, the period of Japanese militarism during the 1930s, which culminated in the Pacific War, was an aberration from a gradual process of democratization. Support for this argument may be drawn from an analysis of the workings of the post-1889 political system. Although the Meiji constitution was doubtless intended to keep political participation under control, in practice MPs and political parties did not prove as docile and ineffectual as had been hoped. Although the Great Depression of 1929 saw the military return strongly to the political ascendant, scholars such as Reischauer have argued that during the Taisho era Japan was evolving into a modern democratic state: the American-imposed 1947 constitution simply cut short a process of evolution which was already under way. Reischauer's view is disputed by other scholars, who argue that the Japanese elite were forced to make the best of a postwar political settlement which was little to their liking.

Considerable debate centres around the importance of the Occupation and 1947 constitution. For many American scholars, who suffer from what might be termed a 'constitution complex' reflecting the US historical experience, the new Japanese constitution was of the utmost significance. The Occupation has received more mixed reviews from non-Americans. Van Wolferen has forcefully questioned the assumptions of many Japan specialists. He calls the idea that Japan made a break with its political past after losing the Pacific War 'a major hindrance to an accurate assessment of the Japanese system' (van Wolferen, 1989: 347). Like Reischauer, van Wolferen sees a great deal of historical continuity in the Japanese political order. But whereas Reischauer sees that continuity in terms of democratic tendencies, van Wolferen describes a continuity of bureaucratic control, a persistent pattern of curtailing opposition.

For van Wolferen, the militarism of the Pacific War seems a logical development from the repressive, centralized nature of the Japanese system. He supports his argument by looking back at the Meiji period, arguing that bureaucrats in late-nineteenth-century Japan practised a system of 'thought guidance', trying to prevent the growth of the dissident social forces which had emerged in Europe. Both the highly efficient Meiji era police force and the introduction of conscription were measures designed to enforce 'order': in other words, to prevent dissent.

Kawai argued that there were three main hypotheses about Japanese modernization – and, by analogy, Japanese political development (Kawai, 1960: 234–48). According to the 'conservative hypothesis', in order to modernize successfully, Japan needed to preserve its cultural traditions as much as possible. The 'liberal hypothesis' contended that Japan needed to introduce all the changes which western societies had experienced so as to achieve the same degree of modernization. A third approach was expressed in Kawai's 'pragmatic hypothesis' – Japan needed to use a mixture of traditional values and imported western ideas in achieving modernization and political development. Culturalist scholars have argued that Japan's successes since the Occupation represented substantial vindications of the conservative or the pragmatic hypotheses. Revisionist critics of Japan's political system, on the other hand, have continued to find Japan wanting, usually for failing to measure up to liberal democratic ideals. Mainstream scholars, by contrast, (using the same 'liberal hypothesis' as their baseline) have tended to see Japan as 'converging' with western liberal democracy.

It can be difficult to establish exactly what was – and was not – the result of the Occupation: for example, was Japan's political stability in the post-Occupation years a result of the reforms introduced by the Americans, or the economic growth during this period? Much of the academic work written on the American Occupation suffers from bias; many accounts are attempts either to vindicate the Occupation, or to repudiate it. Outwardly, Japan accepted the American liberal democratic values contained in the 1947 constitution, but the deeper realities were more complex.

3

The Changing Political Economy

The phoenix-like emergence of Japan from the ashes and rubble of the 1945 defeat to become one of the world's most powerful industrial economies by the 1980s, has often been casually characterized as a 'miracle'. Yet, as with other aspects of contemporary Japan, both the origins and the nature of that 'miracle' are highly contested. For some scholars, Japan's success represents the triumph of market forces: they see Japan as engaged in a process of convergence, becoming more and more like the West. Other interpretations stress the special circumstances of Japan's economic rise, notably the external agency of the United States – with its technical assistance and know-how – and the fortuitous outbreak of the Cold War (and especially the Korean conflict) which provided the Americans with a compelling rationale to bolster the Japanese economy. Revisionists (led by Chalmers Johnson) emphasise the degree to which Japan's accelerated postwar industrialization was a state-led process, coordinated by key agencies such as the Ministry for International Trade and Industry. Johnson describes Japan as a 'developmental state', a view opposed by mainstream American scholars (who are generally uncomfortable with statist explanations for ideological reasons). Other explanations centre upon the quality of the Japanese workforce (based on high levels of education and training); culturalists take this view a stage further, arguing that Japanese cultural norms of diligence, teamwork and deferred gratification were the root cause of the country's economic transformation.

The Occupation and After

As American warships enter Tokyo Bay, Japan faces an economic, political and social crisis. The old political order is about to be dismantled, and replaced with an imported imitation of western models. In order to compete with the West, Japan needs to overhaul its economy, and engage in a rapid process of industrialisation. Yet within a few decades, Japan will pose a vigorous challenge to the hegemony of the West.

The four sentences above are deliberately ambiguous: they could refer either to the Japan of 1853, or to the Japan of 1945. In many respects, the challenges faced by Japan after the end of the Pacific War replicated the challenges previously faced in the Meiji period. In both cases, the ruling order was largely bankrupt, and had capitulated in the face of overwhelming foreign pressure. Yet, in both cases, far-reaching socioeconomic changes that had taken place during previous decades laid the basis for Japan to tackle the challenges ahead. Despite the staggering destruction of Japan's cities and industrial capacity by American bombing, the task of reconstruction began almost immediately: once again, the imperative was to 'catch up' with the West. While much of the physical infrastructure of Japan's industrial economy had been destroyed (and some plant was confiscated as war reparations), the technical expertise to operate heavy industries such as steel and shipbuilding still existed.

The Occupation administration set out to 'democratize' the Japanese economy, by promoting unionization, breaking up the big *zaibatsu* (or conglomerates) – 10 holding companies, 26 industrial companies and two trading companies were dissolved – selling shares to the public, and instituting a land reform programme. Only the last of these reforms was substantially successful: in practice, the big companies which had formed the industrial core of Japan's war machine largely succeeded in recreating and reinventing themselves in the postwar era. This was especially true of the banks, which were barely touched by the dissolution programme: four of the biggest banks in the postwar period – Mitsui, Mitsubishi, Sumitomo and Fuji – had their origins in prewar banks. *Zaibatsu* reform was criticized as a policy with no clear beneficiaries, and was controversial even within SCAP ('Supreme Commander for the Allied

Powers', a common abbreviation for the Occupation administration) (Allinson, 1997: 74–5).

Dower has argued that the Fifteen-Year War was a 'useful war', since 'modern Japanese capitalism was created in the crucible of conflict' (Dower, 1992: 49). During the war, Japanese industry underwent enormous expansion, and Japan was one of the world's fastest growing economies by the time of Pearl Harbor. Japan was already capable of building its own plants, and producing many of its own chemical products: it was the world's fourth largest exporter. The period from 1937–41 had seen colossal increases in production, including a 252 per cent increase in machinery production, and by 1942 68 per cent of the industrial workforce was employed in heavy industry. In other words, Japan's economic recovery during the late 1940s and early 1950s began literally as a reconstruction, a programme to bring Japan back to the levels of industrial output which had been attained prior to 1942. Viewed in this light, what took place in the immediate postwar period was no 'miracle', simply the continuation of a longstanding process which had been interrupted by the wartime defeat.

Dower argues that industrial technologies developed primarily for military purposes – ranging from automotive engineering and shipbuilding to optical equipment – formed the basis of many of Japan's most successful postwar businesses (Dower, 1992: 54–6). The industrial revival of the postwar period also capitalized on changes in the labour market during the war years, including a great increase in technical school graduates. Another important factor was the existence of a strong core banking structure based on a relatively small number of sizeable banks. At the same time, not all businesses were large. Japan had a two-tier economic structure, in which large companies farmed out parts of their activities to subsidiary companies and subcontractors, giving rise to vast numbers of small and medium-sized enterprises. This dualism gave added flexibility to the economy, enabling the conglomerates to control costs, and inevitably weakening the bargaining position of workers.

During the early period of SCAP, the emphasis was on 'reform, revenge, and reparations' (Allinson, 1997: 76), an approach which did not bode well for Japan's economic recovery. During the later years of the Occupation, however, the USA became increasingly interested in building up a strong capitalist democracy in Japan, especially in the light of the rise of communism in China. Joseph Dodge, a Detroit banker, was sent to Japan in 1948 to devise a programme of measures aimed at securing financial stability. His nine-point 'Dodge Line' package of 1949 imposed an austere fiscal regime, involving cuts in spending and job losses, but thereby controlling credit and inflation.

The outbreak of the Korean War in 1950 provided a much-needed boost to Japan's economy, producing huge orders for uniforms and equipment which Japanese concerns were eager to fulfil. Japan was able to establish itself as the Asian powerhouse of the Cold War, and Japanese economic recovery was seen as an important element in US strategy to create bulwarks against communism in Asia. This role later continued during the Vietnam conflict: whilst the 'peace constitution' imposed by the Occupation rendered Japan conveniently *hors de combat,* Japan was able to reap considerable economic benefits from these surrogate 'hot wars' prosecuted in Asia by the superpowers and their local allies. The Korean War orders helped kickstart the Japanese economy at a crucial moment, boosting employment levels and wages, and helping to generate domestic consumer demand. Well-known companies such as Nissan, Toyota, Toshiba and Hitachi were among the leading beneficiaries, and by 1955 Japan's industrial output was back to prewar levels (Allinson, 1997: 78–9).

The same was true of agricultural output; during the 1950s, government subsidies for infrastructure and irrigation helped farmers, who also began diversifying from rice growing into other areas such as fruit and vegetable production. In terms of contribution to gross domestic product, however, primary industries (mainly agriculture, forestry and fisheries) were in long-term decline relative to the manufacturing sector. Primary industries accounted for 26 per cent of GDP in 1950, only 12.9 per cent by 1960, and 6 per cent by 1970 (Lincoln, 1988: 85). Thereafter the decline of the primary sector slowed somewhat, but new growth was mainly in the tertiary sector at the expense of heavy manufacturing. By 1990, 2.9 per cent of the workforce was employed in agriculture, while agriculture accounted for only 6 per cent of GDP (Argy and Stein, 1997: 257).

Despite their limited contribution to the economy, farmers remained politically quite important: they were the recipients of sizeable government subsidies, administered through an arcane 'food control system' which supported large numbers of small-scale – often part-time – farmers (Yayama, 1998: 102–4) and limited

---

Box 3.1 Shigeru Yoshida (1878–1967)

Yoshida was a former diplomat from a prominent political family. He played a crucial role in shaping the direction of Japan during the early postwar period, when he served as prime minister for a total of seven years (1946–47, and 1948–54). Yoshida excelled at dealing with MacArthur and the American occupiers, satisfying their demands whilst securing favourable terms for his country. The 'Yoshida doctrine' formed the basis of Japanese foreign policy: Japan relied on the United States to provide for its national security needs, concentrating instead on economic growth and national reconstruction. In other words, Japan integrated itself into the economic and political international order created by the USA.

---

imports. Rice production accounted for 40 per cent of Japan's agricultural land by 1990, but it was estimated in the late 1980s that over half of Japanese rice farmers' income derived from actual or *de facto* subsidies by the taxpayer and consumer (Argy and Stein, 1997: 268). Despite the generous rates of subsidy provided to Japanese farmers, and an increase in aggregate agricultural production of 43 per cent from 1960 to 1985, Japan's food self-sufficiency rate fell from 90 per cent in 1960, to 67 per cent in 1990 (Argy and Stein, 1997: 269–70). Faced with considerable foreign pressure, especially from the United States, Japan has been gradually liberalizing the import of agricultural products.

Consolidating Growth

1955 can be considered something of a turning-point for Japan: ten years after the momentous wartime defeat, the economy was back to 1942 levels of production. The merger of two conservative parties to create the Liberal Democratic Party (LDP) in 1955 marked the beginning of a period of one-party dominance (popularly known as the 1955 system) which lasted almost four decades. The emphasis was now on a remarkable degree of economic growth, which brought vastly increased living standards and elevated Japan to economic superpower status. Indeed, some analysts have argued that Japan was driven by 'economism', a quasi-ideological preoccupation with economic success. McCormack describes the postwar

Japanese state as 'a kind of joint venture by General McArthur and Yoshida Shigeru' characterized by an economist orientation and a weak, subordinated nationalism (McCormack, 1986: 39–40). Critics described the Japanese as 'economic animals' who had abandoned their culture, their principles, and (implicitly) even their humanity in the pursuit of material gains. French President de Gaulle famously remarked after the visit of a Japanese prime minister in 1963 'who was that transistor salesman?' (Horsley and Buckley, 1990: 64).

In reality, the late 1950s and much of the 1960s were characterized by intense ideological conflict in Japan. During the 1950s, there was a wave of crippling strikes organized by militant unions, and 1960 saw huge demonstrations against the renewal of the Security Treaty with the USA. Rapid economic growth offered a means of buying off dissent, an implicit bargain offered to the populace by the Japanese state. Never was this more apparent than when Prime Minister Hayato Ikeda announced his 'income-doubling plan'. Unveiled shortly after the Security Treaty demonstrations, the plan (politically inspired, and based on dubious statistics) called for Japan's GNP and the personal incomes of the Japanese to be doubled in the next 10 years (Masumi, 1995: 67). In other words, people should keep their heads down, work hard, and watch their salaries grow, rather than engaging in political protest or industrial disputes: it was 'a social contract on a grand scale' (Horsley and Buckley, 1990: 62). Contrary to many predictions, the plan proved a great success, and average incomes actually doubled within seven years rather than ten.

In the years that followed, consumer demand increased considerably, as most families sought to equip themselves with the 'three sacred treasures' (television, fridge and washing machine): by 1964, 90 per cent of households possessed all three items (Horsley and Buckley, 1990: 76), and many new blocks of flats were constructed to accommodate workers in rapidly-expanding urban areas. Not all the extra income generated by rapid growth was spent on consumer goods or housing, however: small savers were a crucial source of the funds lent out by Japan's banks and financial institutions. An average Japanese family was saving 25 per cent of its disposable income by 1974, which represented a 'savings-doubling' since 1955 (Allinson, 1997: 101). Japan's new postwar affluence was aptly symbolized by the 1964 Tokyo Olympics, which marked the first ever Olympics to be held in Asia. It was accompanied by showcase infrastructure and technological projects, notably the inauguration of the first high-speed 'bullet train' (*shinkansen*) route, from Tokyo to Osaka.

Several factors drove Japan's high-speed growth during this period. One was the high rate of investment: the contributions of small savers were matched by those of industry itself, which reinvested a large proportion of national gross national product in productive capacity, especially capital goods industries (Pyle, 1996: 245). Another factor was a well-educated labour force, boosted during the 1960s by postwar baby boomers. The population rose from around 72 million in 1945 to 93.4 million in 1960, 103.7 million in 1970, and 117 million in 1980; thereafter, population growth began to level off (*Japan Almanac 1999*: 286–7). There was a large shift of labour away from agriculture and into manufacturing (see Figure 3.1), accompanied by sizeable migration into urban areas, especially the Kanto (Tokyo–Yokohama–Kawasaki), Chubu (Nagoya), and Kansai (Osaka–Kyoto–Kobe) regions on the Pacific coast of Honshu. Japan's workforce was widely seen as highly-

Figure 3.1   Employed persons by industry (1996)

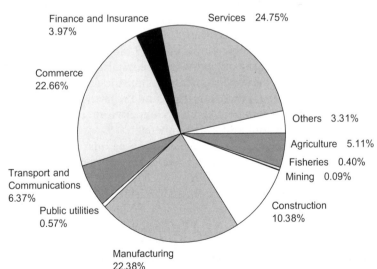

Original Source: Management and Coordination Agency (May 1997) *Monthly Statistics of Japan*.
Secondary Source: Keizai Koho Center (1998) *Japan 1998: An International Comparison*, Tokyo, Takeo Kurita, p. 88.

motivated, preoccupied by the imperatives of economic recovery and growth.

A further factor driving increased productivity was widespread technological innovation, as a large contingent of engineers and specialists sought to regain the competitive edge that Japan had lost because of the war. A great deal of foreign technology was bought in by Japanese concerns (often at bargain prices, from western companies that saw no competitive threat from Japan), though some foreign products were simply copied (Pyle, 1996: 245; Horsley and Buckley, 1990: 63). Japan gradually moved away from labour-intensive textile production, and into heavy industries. Japanese electronics companies first vacuumed up global markets for consumer electronics such as televisions, radios and hi-fis, while their American counterparts were concentrating on pioneering large-scale capital goods for the space programme and the military-industrial complex (Horsley and Buckley, 1990: 144–50).

During the 1970s, companies such as NEC and Fujitsu concentrated on acquiring and developing cutting-edge integrated-circuit technology and semiconductors, spearheaded by a MITI (Ministry of International Trade and Industry) 'national plan' for the semi-conductor industry from 1972, later organizing a consortium of five leading Japanese computer firms which succeeded in developing their own 64k-RAM superchips by 1979. In 1971, MITI had published a report setting out a new technological agenda for Japan, based on a shift to 'knowledge-intensive' industries, a 'vision' which formed the basis of Japan's industrial strategy in the decades that followed. Japan's commercial banks underwrote the necessary investment with low-interest long-term credit.

Aside from domestic factors such as these, broader international conditions played a part in Japan's remarkable economic rise. After the war, trade restrictions were reduced, world markets were opened, and international trade entered a highly expansionist period – so providing a favourable climate for Japanese exports. Japan joined the newly-established GATT (General Agreement on Tariffs and Trade) in 1955, and membership helped Japan gain access to export markets. The establishment of the International Monetary Fund (IMF) in 1945 helped create a stable international currency regime, and Japan was able to obtain secure supplies of raw materials for its industrial output (Allinson, 1997: 98–9). Given the limited domestic sources of raw materials, Japan was exceptionally dependent upon such supplies, and highly vulnerable to external pressures in consequence. Japan's exports increased by an average of 17 per cent from 1953 to 1965 (Pyle, 1996: 246), reflecting a growing world demand for manufactured goods. The total global volume of manufacturing exports increased sixfold from 1953 to 1973, while the dollar value of Japanese exports increased by 25 times from 1955 to 1974 (Allinson, 1997: 99). Japan became a leading supplier of goods ranging from steel and ships, to cars, and audio and video equipment. At the same time, 90 per cent of what Japan produced from 1955 to 1974 was for the domestic market (Allinson 1997: 100): huge consumer demand at home was the primary engine behind the growth of Japan's industrial capacity. Table 3.1 shows a comparison of Japan's exports and imports in 1985 and 1997.

Table 3.1   Japan's principal exports and imports by commodity

Exports *(yen billions)*	1985	1997	*Imports* *(yen billions)*	1985	1997
Foodstuffs	315	267	Foodstuffs	3719	5579
Textiles	1496	1003	Raw materials	4343	3557
Chemicals	1843	3623	Mineral fuels	13386	7542
Non-metallic mineral products	515	629	Chemicals	1939	2841
Metals and metal products	4430	3246	Textile products	933	2708
General machinery	7040	12130	Non-metallic mineral products	303	623
Electrical machinery	7102	12041	Metals and metal products	1451	2161
Transport equipment	11732	10969	Machinery and equipment	2971	1147
Precision instruments	n/a	2427	Other	n/a	4467
Other	3237	4603			
Total	¥41956	¥50938		¥31085	¥40956

Source: Ministry of Finance, Japan.

Savings

Like the importance of domestic consumer demand, the importance of savings in the Japanese economy can hardly be understated (see Table 3.2). Savings rates are very high, and rose steadily during the 1960s to peak in the 1970s (for a technical discussion, see Ito, 1992; 259–77). Levels of savings are consistently high across different parts of the country, and among the various age groups. Explanations offered for these high savings rates include culturalist interpretations ('Confucian' thriftiness), deficiencies in the social security system, the bonus system (whereby employees receive a sizeable proportion of their annual pay in the form of half-yearly bonuses), tax incentives, the need to save for the high costs of purchasing a home, and the desire to pass on inheritances to relatives. Garon argues that high levels of savings reflect systematic government promotional efforts led by the Central Council for Savings Promotion, which used radio, television and poster campaigns in a sophisticated programme of moral suasion (Garon, 1997: 153–7).

In the recent period, another factor supporting high levels of savings has been popular concern about the ageing society and falling birth-rates: with fewer children to take care of the elderly, many Japanese people want to be assured of financial security in their old age. One very important form of savings is the postal savings system, which offers tax-free savings accounts, and by 1980 this system held deposits four times larger than the Bank of America, the world's biggest commercial bank (Johnson, 1982:

Table 3.2   Net household saving as a percentage of disposable household income

	1960	1975	1985	1990	1997
United States	7.2	8.9	6.6	4.9	5.0
Japan	14.5	22.8	15.6	14.1	13.1
United Kingdom	4.5	11.4	5.4	4.4	7.4
Germany	8.6	15.1	11.4	13.9	11.6
Italy	16.5	26.9	17.8	15.6	14.5
Canada	3.8	12.7	13.4	10.5	4.7

Sources: OECD Economic Outlooks; OECD (1989) *Historical Economic Statistics 1960–1990*; Bank of Japan (1997) *Comparative Economic and Financial Statistics*.

210). High levels of savings in Japan have provided a ready source of capital for industrial development.

The Developmental State?

Just as scholars of Japanese politics are constantly debating whether politicians or bureaucrats have the upper hand in governing the country, so scholars of the Japanese economy often disagree profoundly about the relative degrees of state and market influence in shaping the country's economic and industrial policies. Many mainstream American scholars display a touching faith in the primacy of democracy, the constitution, and the free market: they typically seek to portray the politics and the economy of Japan as resembling those of the United States. Such views were robustly challenged in one of the most important and controversial books ever published about Japan: Chalmers Johnson's *MITI and the Japanese Miracle: The Growth of Industrial Policy, 1925–1975* (Johnson, 1982). Johnson identified four core elements in his model of Japan's 'developmental state':

1. a small, inexpensive, but elite bureaucracy staffed by the best managerial talent available in the system;
2. a political system in which the bureaucracy is given sufficient scope to take initiative and operate effectively;
3. the perfection of market-conforming methods of state intervention in the economy;
4. a pilot organisation like MITI (Johnson, 1992: 315–19).

He argues that the powerful bureaucracy in Japan served as an 'economic general staff', planning and directing Japan's industrial policy through direct and indirect forms of administrative guidance. Japan's shift from labour-intensive declining industries such as textiles, to new high-growth areas such as shipbuilding, machinery, and later electronics, was superintended by MITI, while the restructuring of companies and industries was carried out by MITI and the Ministry of Finance. These same ministries also established the Japan Development Bank in 1951, a bank with access to the resources of the country's postal savings system (Johnson, 1982: 210) and which offered inexpensive capital to selected industries, thereby bankrolling long-term growth. The Japanese government practised 'preferential credit allocation', turned a blind eye to monopolistic practices, coordinated investment strategy, and created a variety of non-tariff barriers (Pyle, 1996: 248). Gibney argues that economic growth replaced war as Japan's national preoccupation:

> Practically speaking, the economic ministries – principally the Finance Ministry and MITI – were to serve as Japan's Pentagon; and bureaucrats, rather than politicians, were to be its generals. (Gibney 1998: 70)

Johnson has extended his arguments about Japan to account for the rapid industrialization of other economies in the region, including Singapore, South Korea, and Taiwan (Johnson, 1987), views which have been elaborated by other authors. These economies are held to have pursued similar policies of 'developmentalism', characterized by features such as strong government, a close public/private sector relationship, foreign direct investment, 'deferred gratification', and the US security umbrella (see McCargo, 1998: 130–7). These ideas reflected an important 'developmentalist' school of thought concerning the rise of East Asian economies.

Since Johnson's arguments directly contradict analyses that stress the preeminence of the market, they have met with considerable criticism. The 'market school' stresses different factors to account for Japan's industrial success, arguing that private enterprise in Japan was able to take advantage of:

> the rates of savings, investment, and taxation; the high level of skills and education in Japan; the huge stock of advanced Western technology; the unparalleled export opportunities created by the expansion of world trade, and the availability of capital. (Pyle, 1996: 248)

Johnson himself counter-argues that:

> American economic theory and Cold War strategy interacted to produce an environment of condescension toward and self-delusion about the Japanese economy. (Johnson, 1994: 56)

There is a considerable (and often rather arcane) literature discussing the relative importance of state agencies, private sector bodies, and market forces in Japanese and East Asian economic development. Nevertheless, even the normally firmly neo-liberal World Bank recognized in an important 1993 report that the industrialized economies of East Asia employed 'a principle of shared growth' underpinned by 'a cadre of economic technocrats insulated from narrow political pressures', coupled with 'institutions and mechanisms to share information and win the support of business elites' (World Bank, 1993: 157–8). This was the closest the World Bank came to accepting that Japan might possess a capitalist developmental state.

Much recent debate has been less concerned with the rights and wrongs of Johnson's original argument (which covers the period to 1975), and more concerned with the degree to which the 'developmental state' model holds true for the last quarter of the twentieth century. During the 1980s and 1990s, the Japanese economy underwent a rapid transition away from traditional heavy manufacturing ('smokestack industries') and towards cleaner, high-technology industries such as information technology and electronics. At the same time, there was a parallel shift away from manufacturing and into the service sector. With the decline of those industries traditionally shepherded by MITI, the developmental state model became gradually less appropriate. Writers such as Okimoto (1989) and Callon (1995) argue that MITI has gradually declined in influence, as have private sector bodies such as the employers' organization *Keidanren*.

The result has been a more flexible and complex set of relationships between the public and private sectors, rather than the relatively fixed pattern described by Johnson. A common view is that Johnson may have been broadly correct about the 1950s and 1960s, but his ideas are not as helpful in explaining the 1980s and 1990s. Calder, taking the developmental state model as a starting-point, argues that Japan has evolved a hybrid public–private system of 'corporate-led strategic capitalism' especially after the 1973 oil shock (Calder, 1993: 268). This system is characterised by higher levels of clientelism than the purely technocratic developmental state model acknowledges, and partly arises from the hollowing out of state capacity resulting from: 'the globalisation of industry and finance, combined with escalating research costs, risk factors, and market-scale economies' (Calder, 1993: 268–9). The result is a continuing tendency for 'systematic partnerships' between Japanese enterprises, which may involve some secondary collaboration with government agencies. Calder emphasises the importance of *keiretsu,* industrial and business networks which generate 'private-sector-dominated strategic capitalism'. He stresses that the Japanese state is rather risk-averse; the shortcomings of statism are offset by 'a creative, organized private sector, with a powerful sense of long-term objectives' (Calder, 1993: 277). Johnson himself has more recently described Japan's 'Asian capitalism' as a combination of 'a strong state, industrial policy, producer economics, and managerial autonomy' (Johnson, 1993: 68), a description which offers some concessions to his critics.

The Structure of Japanese Business

The most popular international images of Japanese business centre on major industrial giants such as Toyota or Sony. Japan is often portrayed as an economy dominated by large trading companies with huge workforces and complex structures, which are engaged in a diverse range of activities. Although big companies are very important players in the Japanese economy, most Japanese companies are small or medium-sized, and many have very limited operations. Small family concerns, ranging from mum-and-dad shops to tiny factories, abound in Japan. There are elaborate networks of relationships between larger companies and the sub-contractors which supply them.

Much of the academic research on Japanese business has focused on big firms, which make use of interlocking alliances known as *keiretsu*. There are two main forms: horizontal *keiretsu* (alliances across different industries), and vertical *keiretsu* (alliances between specific industrial concerns, their suppliers, and their distributors) (Argy and Stein, 1997: 107). Horizontal *keiretsu* have been defined as:

> associations of large corporations which are clustered around a group city bank, a trust bank, a real estate agency, a life and casualty insurance firm and one or more trading companies. (Argy and Stein, 1997: 107)

The best-known examples are the 'big six': Mitsui, Mitsubishi, Sumitomo, Daiichi Kangyo, Sanwa, and Fuji. These groupings have a loose structure, and are not subject to central control. Nevertheless, members promote each others' business instincts both directly and indirectly: for example, by ordering products and services from one another. They hold shares in each other's companies, and consult regularly on strategy and collaborative endeavours. Vertical *keiretsu* are defined as 'a collection of input manufacturers and or distributors (mainly small firms) attached to a large corporation' (Argy and Stein, 1997: 108). A large concern has a group of core subcontractors; 'these in turn preside over a series of secondary and subsequent suppliers' (ibid.).

Japanese companies produce fewer of their components in-house than their western competitors. While *keiretsu* may appear to be vast and monolithic, in practice they do most of their business with non-member companies, and the amount of business done within *keiretsu* has been in decline since the early 1980s (Argy and Stein, 1997: 112). Nevertheless, the six big *keiretsu* remain very influential in certain sectors, with more than 80 per cent of market share in chemicals, construction, drugs, electrical machinery, petroleum, rubber, and shipbuilding. Newer 'vertical' *keiretsu* such as Honda, Sanyo, and Canon, have made more impact in high technology businesses like electronics.

Features of Large Business Organisations

Banks are a key element in *keiretsu*; indeed, all Japanese companies seek to establish special relations with a 'main bank' (which may even hold shares in the company). This bank plays a leading role in raising loan capital for the company as required, based on its detailed knowledge of the company's finances. Whereas many western companies recruit most of their directors from outside, internal appointees constitute the majority on the boards of all Japanese companies. Japanese companies are headed by a president, who appoints the board of directors: directors often have direct experience of production and technology, in contrast to the accountant-dominated boards of many Anglo-American concerns. Much has been written about the practices of collective decision-making said to be followed by Japanese companies. These include the system of '*ringi-sei*', or circulating consultative memos designed to achieve consensus, and suggestion systems where workers are encouraged to propose improvements, ideas which are supposedly taken on board by higher management. However, most Japanese organizations are firmly based on a top-down hierarchy, and many large companies are controlled or dominated a single key individual (Argy and Stein, 1997: 119). Small share-holding is less common in Japan than in the

West, and the majority of shares are held by institutions. Many companies purchase shares in partner firms such as customers or suppliers, not so much to obtain good share returns, as to cement business relationships and procure favours. As a result, the managers of Japanese companies are less directly accountable to their shareholders than, say, American managers.

Whereas many western companies are preoccupied with the (often short-term) goal of profit maximization, partly as a result of pressures from shareholders, Japanese companies have tended to be more concerned with the (usually long-term) goal of increasing their market share. The standing and reputation of Japanese firms is based largely on market share, rather than profitability. This may lead to highly aggressive marketing and sales policies: distribution agents for the three main daily newspaper groups (Asahi, Mainichi, and Yomiuri), for example, are notorious for their high-pressure sales tactics, which 'often makes it less trouble for consumers to subscribe to a daily newspaper than to continue to fend off salesmen' (Westney, 1996: 54). In many sectors, this kind of competition has resulted in cut-throat pricing, relying on economies of scale which drove out all but the largest players. Some analysts describe this as 'excess competition', a trend fuelled by high growth rates, and by a desire on the part of companies to lower average labour costs by expanding their operations, and bringing in cheaper, younger workers.

Traditionally, Japanese companies have concentrated on core businesses, and have been reluctant to diversify. However, there has been a growing trend towards diversification since the 1980s; the rising value of the yen meant that large companies have increasingly shifted their core production to overseas locations with lower labour costs, and have diversified their activities at home. Mergers and acquisitions have been much less common than in the West. However, creating subsidiaries (initially owned entirely by the parent company) is common practice; as core companies become too large to manage their activities efficiently, secondary aspects of the business are typically farmed out to subsidiaries. Subsidiaries, which may be located in cheaper regions of Japan, or even overseas, usually have lower labour costs than core companies. Senior staff who are underperforming may also be 'kicked upstairs' to nominally higher posts in subsidiaries, transfers which may encourage them to retire early.

Features of Small Companies

The subcontracting of production is highly institutionalized in Japan. As Francks notes, this practice may be regarded:

> either as embodying all that is exploitative in the 'dual structure' of Japanese industry or alternatively as an expression of the hierarchical but personalised long-term relationships of trust and patronage that make Japanese business culturally unique and impenetrable to foreigners. (Francks, 1999: 252)

The practice became very widespread during the interwar period, allowing large firms to hive off much of their production to smaller firms that used 'cheaper and more dispensable labour'. By the early 1980s, 82 per cent of companies with over 300 employees used subcontractors (Francks, 1999: 252). Francks compares what is often referred to as Japan's 'small and medium enterprise sector', with what development economists call the 'urban informal sector' (Francks, 1999: 183). While the existence of family-owned factories and garage-sized sweatshops producing goods for a single larger customer tends to be treated as a 'third world' phenomenon, businesses of this kind remain widespread in Japan. Almost 90 per cent of private sector Japanese workers are employed in organizations with less than 300 employees (Sugimoto, 1997: 79–80), 60 per cent of the Japanese labour force works in companies employing less than 100, and only 13 per cent in companies employing more than 1 000. In 1986, 74.4 per cent of factory workers were employed in concerns with less than 300 workers; the same applied to 96 per cent of construction workers, 76 per cent of miners, and 88 per cent of transport workers (Argy and Stein, 1997: 126). Twenty-nine per cent of all workers in the early 1980s were employed in family-only or one-person concerns, compared with 9 per cent in the USA and 8 per cent for the UK (Argy and Stein, 1997: 125).

The pressure gauges for certain machinery used in Toyota factories, for example, might all be manufactured by a single supplier (with less than a dozen employees) in an eastern suburb of Nagoya: if the orders from Toyota ever ceased, the enterprise would be instantly wiped out. Everything rests on a business relationship between the two enterprises, a relationship so unequal that it amounts to one of total dependency by the small business on the giant manufacturer. There are instances of small enterprises growing into much larger ones (Honda and Sony are among the best-known examples), but most small businesses in Japan are too preoccupied with subcontracting to develop into more entrepreneurial activities. This has led to criticism of Japan's economy as having a 'dual structure': the large 'modern' manufacturing sector is said to exploit the 'traditional' small sector. This is rejected by some analysts, who see more integration (and greater reciprocal benefits) among the two sectors than this dualistic model implies (Francks, 1999: 254, 271).

Employment and Labour

The aspect of Japanese employment that is best-known internationally is the idea of lifetime employment. According to this model, an employee is provided with job security until the age of around 55. Pay is determined largely by seniority within the organization (in other words, the older you get, the more you are paid), rather than by job performance. Associated with lifetime employment and payment by seniority is the idea of paternalistic management: the company assumes a very direct responsibility for the welfare of its employees. The opposite side of this coin is an expectation that employees will demonstrate reciprocal 'loyalty', and dedicate themselves to the higher needs of the company. This loyalty may include doing unpaid overtime, passively accepting disagreeable transfers to far-flung branches, not normally moving to work for rival companies and not using holiday entitlements. These three elements of the Japanese employment system were first discussed by James Abegglen in the classic *The Japanese Factory* (Abegglen, 1958), and have often been emphasised by culturalist scholars who see Japan's industrial relations as culturally distinctive.

Broadly speaking, most categories of workers and age groups in Japan have more limited job mobility than in other countries (though there are exceptions): in larger concerns, long-term employees are typically taken on straight from school, college, or university. Many new employees are hired on the basis of general educational level (often, an important factor in hiring decisions is which school, college or university applicants attended), and vocational training is largely the responsibility of employers. The emphasis is generally on job-specific skills within a company-specific context, rather than on transferable skills. It is still unusual for executives to change company in mid-career, and a major mid-life career change (for example, switching from working in a company laboratory to teaching science in a secondary school at the age of 44) is almost unknown. Most organizations prefer new recruits to those with previous work experience, since they like to socialise their staff into the prevailing organizational culture. Rather than specializing in particular fields, the majority of junior executives are regularly rotated to different jobs in various sections of the organization, learning about the way the company works, instead of gaining an in-depth knowledge of any one area of work.

Abegglen saw 'lifetime employment' and limited job mobility as a reflection of Japanese culture, a view that has been challenged in some of the subsequent literature (Francks, 1999: 218). To begin with, the 'lifetime employment' model is far from universal in Japan. It applies most completely to male executives in large companies: relatively few women benefit from lifetime employment, many manual workers are employed on a 'temporary' basis even by large companies (and so do not receive the same pay and conditions as their permanent counterparts), and most smaller enterprises do not offer the same long-term job security and benefits as major concerns. Blue-collar workers often change jobs in pursuit of higher wages or better conditions. In other words, the benefits package generally understood by the term 'lifetime employment' probably applies in full to less than a quarter of Japan's workforce.

Most Japanese employees receive around 40 per cent of their annual salaries in the form of twice-yearly bonuses, a system that helps promote high levels of savings. 'Lifetime' employees may receive subsidized company housing, an extremely valuable benefit given the high rent levels and exorbitant property prices in urban Japan. At the same time, company life has drawbacks: many executives put in staggeringly long hours (see Figure 3.2) (including evenings spent in compulsory, work-related drinking and social activities), and there have been numerous cases of *karoshi* (death from overwork) (Sugimoto, 1997: 94). On balance, however, there is little evidence to suggest that the Japanese work harder than, say, Americans (western Europe, with its high levels of unionization, short working hours, and month-long summer vacations, is far more 'culturally distinctive' globally in its working practices than is Japan).

Figure 3.2   Annual working hours (manufacturing industry, 1994)

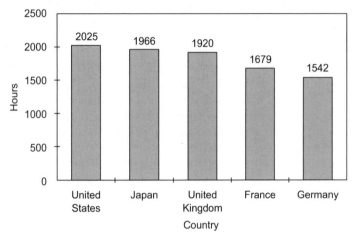

Original Source: Ministry of Labour, Japan.
Secondary Source: Kawai, Nobukazu (ed.) (1996), *Asahi Shimbun Japan Almanac 1997*, Tokyo, Asahi Shimbun Publishing Company, p. 99.

In the Japanese context, 'working' and 'being at work' are two different matters. Most Japanese organizations are overstaffed by international standards: secondary school teachers may give only 16 lessons a week, department stores are full of supernumerary sales staff, and every roadside construction site has a flag-waving safety marshal standing on the pavement. Senior bureaucrats at government ministries in Tokyo may spend most of the morning reading the newspapers, so that they will have some work left to do during their compulsory overtime in the evenings (they are obliged to be available every evening when the Diet is in session, on the off-chance that a parliamentary question might be asked about the work of their department, and an instant response has to be drafted). Most Japanese firms and organizations have long-winded consultation and decision-making processes. The Japanese 'work ethic' is not always an ethic of intensive and efficient work (though such work often does take place), but an ethic which entails spending long hours in the workplace or with work colleagues, engaging in work, quasi-work, or work-related socializing. The art of looking busy is an important one in every Japanese organization. As Miyamoto puts it:

'Don't be late' . . . means you must be at work – that is, at your desk, before anyone else; you don't actually have to be working. You could be reading the paper, or looking at a comic book, or having a cup of coffee. The important thing is to let people around you know that you arrived before starting time. (Miyamoto, 1994: 157)

To regard lifetime employment as a product of Japanese culture is rather problematic, since the practice is of recent origin and was shaped by the industrialization process (rather than the cause of rapid industrialization). Similarly, it is highly doubtful whether the Japanese are possessed of a special, culturally distinctive work ethic. Like other people, the Japanese can and do work hard when circumstances require, but they are by no means a nation of out-and-out workaholics, with an exclusive dedication to the interests of their company or organization. Indeed, surveys of Japanese employees reveal high levels of dissatisfaction. The stereotyped Japanese 'corporate soldiers' who receive a disproportionate amount of attention in much of the literature on Japan actually constitute a small minority of the workforce; many Japanese workers are sceptical about the paternalistic rhetoric of their companies, or else are excluded from the benefits of 'corporationism' on account of their inferior conditions of employment (Sugimoto, 1997: 103). For many of the footsoldiers of Japan's postwar industrialization, the corporation was less a benevolent and holistic patron, than an oppressive hierarchy demanding absolute obedience and submission (see Kamata, 1982).

Unionization

Trade unions existed in early-twentieth-century Japan, but independent trade unionism was suppressed in the late 1930s and early 1940s. In the immediate postwar period, Japanese unions were seen by the US Occupation forces as an important counterbalance to militarism, and were actively supported. During the late 1940s and the 1950s, unions staged numerous major strikes, pursuing a highly adversarial strategy in a quest for improved pay, benefits, and working conditions for their members. Notable strikes included Yomiuri Newspapers (1946), Nissan Motors (1953), and one at a Mitsui coal mine (1960).

The Nissan strike was an important turning-point: to undermine the industry-wide National Car Workers' Union, Nissan established a company-specific union and thereafter never experienced a single day of lost production due to industrial action (Argy and Stein, 1997: 148). Company unions (also known as enterprise unions) became the dominant form of unionization in the private sector; these unions largely eschew confrontation, holding ritualized 'spring offensives' in which demands for higher pay are backed by such innocuous actions as strikes held during the lunch hour. Union officials recruited from the shopfloor are given privileged treatment by management, and some even become directors of the company. Table 3.3 shows a comparison of industrial disputes in Japan, Britain, the United States and France during the 1980s through to

Table 3.3   Industrial disputes in major countries

Year	Japan		United States		Britain		France	
	Disputes	*Days lost (1000s)*	*Disputes*	*Days lost (1000s)*	*Disputes*	*Days lost (1000s)*	*Disputes*	*Days lost (1000s)*
1981	955	554	145	16 908	1 338	4 266	2 405	1 442
1982	944	538	96	9 061	1 528	5 313	3 113	2 257
1983	893	507	81	17 461	1 352	3 754	2 837	1 321
1984	596	354	62	8 499	1 206	27 135	2 537	1 318
1985	627	264	54	7 079	903	6 402	1 901	727
1986	620	253	69	11 861	1 074	1 920	1 391	568
1987	474	256	46	4 456	1 016	3 546	1 391	501
1988	498	174	40	4 364	781	3 702	2 260	113
1989	362	220	51	16 996	701	4 128	2 040	80
1990	284	145	44	5 926	598	1 890	1 529	528
1991	310	96	40	4 584	369	761	1 318	497
1992	263	231	35	3 984	253	528	1 330	359
1993	252	116	35	3 981	211	649	1 351	511
1994	230	85	45	5 022	N/A	N/A	1 671	521
1995	209	77	31	5 771	N/A	N/A	N/A	N/A

Original Source: ILO (1996) *Yearbook of Statistics*.
Secondary Source: Japan Institute of Labor (1997) *Japanese Working Life Profile 1996–7: Labor Statistics,* Tokyo, Japan Institute of Labour, p. 56.

1995. It shows that despite a significant number of industrial disputes in Japan, relatively few resulted in strike action. Some analysts argue that enterprise unions are quite assertive and effective in representing employee interests (Argy and Stein, 1997: 149), but others believe that the enterprise union model reflects a strategy for coopting and manipulating workers by company managements. One writer calls these unions 'an "auxiliary instrument" of personnel administration' (Kawanishi, 1986: 151). Enterprise unions have certainly done little to support temporary workers in their companies, emphasising building relations of trust between management and long-term employees.

Busts and Booms

The oil crisis of the 1970s was the first serious setback to Japan's postwar high-growth policies (Figure 3.3), and Japan's reliance upon imported supplies of raw materials – especially oil from the Middle East – was abundantly illustrated. The first abrupt rise in oil prices in 1974 led to 24.5 per cent rises in consumer prices; in consequence, Japan was plunged into recession. When a second hike occurred in 1979, Japan was much better able to withstand the impact. Nevertheless, the mid-1970s marked a turning point for the Japanese economy (and for most industrialized economies), as high-speed growth began to decline (Ito, 1992: 69–72). Four years of double-digit GDP growth from 1967 to 1970 were followed by much lower GDP growth rates (typically from 3 to 5 per cent) during the 1970s and 1980s.

However, despite the fact that Japan was far from the world's top-performing economy during the late 1980s and the beginning of the 1990s, land and share prices rose at exponential levels during this so-called 'bubble' period. Asset values rose five times over from 1981 to 1989 (Argy and Stein, 1997: 46). Much of Japan's new super-wealth, symbolized internationally by the Japanese purchase of the Rockefeller Center in Manhattan, and of a Van Gogh painting for a record-breaking $83.9 million, was based on excessive speculation. Part of this 'paper' Japanese wealth derived simply from the exceptionally high value of the yen, in contrast to the weakness of other major currencies, especially the US dollar. The turning point came in 'black August' of 1990 (Ito, 1992: 433–4), when the value of the Japanese stock market fell by over 16 per cent in a single month

– a development precipitated by the Iraqi invasion of Kuwait. From then on, the bubble began to burst, share and asset prices tumbled, and many newly-acquired overseas companies and assets were sold off by their Japanese owners. The overly-rapid pseudo-expansion of the economy during the bubble period produced significant pockets of bad debt, and within a few years the unthinkable began to happen, as big-name Japanese companies and financial institutions went belly-up. Downsizing and retrenchment involved the 'unravelling' of the lifetime employment system, as the first white-collar redundancies were announced (Yamamoto, 1993: 381). A 1993 survey showed that 15 per cent of Japan's top 400 companies had already shifted from seniority-based pay to individual, performance-related salaries.

One structural problem in the Japanese economy by the beginning of the 1990s concerned the high rate of personal savings and consequently low levels of consumer demand. By the late 1970s, 'excess' savings meant that lack of domestic consumption proved an obstacle to continuing economic growth. However, during the 1980s this problem was solved by a shift towards exports, which in turn generated large trade surpluses and growing international trade friction. By the 1990s, the export boom was declining in the face of competition from other economies in the region. Japan responded by reinvesting considerable amounts of capital in the form of direct foreign investment, as well as in portfolio investments in other financial assets, such as US government debt (Francks, 1998: 9). This overseas investment brought some short-term advantages, but the Japanese preference for savings over spending sapped the core strength of the domestic economy: capital was not being invested in productive new businesses. When recession began to hit Japan in the 1990s, the government could not make the classic response of cutting taxes in order to stimulate demand: Japanese people already had enough money to spend, but were choosing instead to save it. Despite the downturn of the post-bubble era, the Japanese economy continued to perform impressively on a comparative study of GDP per capita (see Figure 3.3).

As problems began to emerge, serious questions were raised about the competence (or lack thereof) with which the Finance Ministry and Bank of Japan had regulated the financial sector. A series of scandals and investigations revealed well-established practices of collusion between bank officials and the bureaucrats who were supposed to supervise them. Major companies were found to have

Figure 3.3   GDP per capita (based on purchasing power parities), 1996

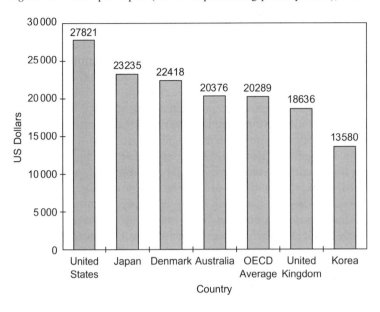

Source: OECD (1998) *National Accounts, Main Aggregates*, vol. 1, http://www/oecd.org/std/gdpperca.htm

paid large sums of money to racketeers. The Finance Ministry has never been headed by an economist, and is run largely by a self-reinforcing elite of Tokyo University law graduates who are suspicious of economics specialists. Two of Japan's leading economists have argued that the Japanese government does not employ even a single professional economist (Hartcher, 1997: 9). While a reliance on well-rounded generalists may have served Japan well during the period of postwar reconstruction and high growth, it created serious difficulties as financial markets became more complex and more globalized. The Ministry retained high levels of regulation that stifled the successful development of financial services in Japan, yet these regulations did not serve the purpose of properly safe-guarding the integrity of the banking system.

While Japan's vast and inadequately supervised banking and financial sector was left in appalling shape following the end of the bubble era, the industrial sector was also suffering. The high costs of pay and production in Japan had led to large scale shifts of production to low-wage foreign markets, such as Southeast Asia and the United Kingdom. The result was a 'hollowing out' of the Japanese economy. The corporate shells – head offices, senior management, bank accounts, deposits and debts – remained in Japan, but many core employment and revenue-generating activities had been shifted out of Japan. Nissan Motors was selling British-made Nissans (bearing Union Jack stickers) in Kobe: Japan was importing Japanese cars. One analyst suggested that 15 per cent of Japanese manufacturing would be carried out overseas by the year 2000; certainly, very few Japanese companies were increasing domestic production (Hartcher, 1997: 169). These shifts in production have weakened the domestic manufacturing base.

Meanwhile, the declining value of the Japanese yen during the late 1990s, coupled with problems in the economy, meant that for the first time Japanese companies began selling-up to foreign concerns. The economic nationalism upon which Japan's postwar industrialization had been predicated was now under threat. Ironically, the financial sector was also hollowing out: international companies were shifting their trading out of Tokyo by the early 1990s (Hartcher, 1997: 180–1), while Japanese companies were establishing trading operations in Hong Kong and elsewhere. When the Thai government effectively devalued the baht on 2 July 1997, a crisis in confidence was precipitated which led to dramatic economic crashes in Thailand, South Korea and Indonesia, with knock-on effects across the region and the globe. Much of the public and private debt owed by the affected Asian countries was to Japanese banks, by far the largest lenders in the region. This wider financial meltdown put the Japanese economy under severe pressure, leading to a decline in the value of the yen, company closures, and layoffs.

Conclusion

In the post-bubble era, it is no longer possible (if it ever was) to see Japan simply as a land of economic miracles. The rapid reconstruction and economic growth that postwar Japan experienced was based on a particular set of historical circumstances. Some analysts argue that Japan's industrial rise was primarily governed by state intervention; others see it more as a triumph of market forces. Still others emphasise the cultural aspects of Japanese business, with its distinctive patterns of industrial relations, as a central explanatory variable in accounting for the country's economic rise. However, the decline of Japanese economic strength since the end of the bubble calls all of these explanations into question. The very same structural or cultural assets which helped Japan to gain such immense economic power by the end of the Cold War seem also to have contained within them deep-rooted shortcomings. While Japan's bureaucrats and *keiretsu* bosses thrived during the hothouse conditions of high growth, they struggled to adapt to the changing international economic environment of the post-Cold War period. So long as Japan could use exports to sustain production, the problems of the economy were not insuperable. But as export markets flagged in the 1990s, those problems became acute and eventually amounted to a crisis.

The rapid shift from a world economy dominated by conventional manufacturing and trade to a 'global information society' which required the ruthlessly effective management of cutting-edge financial services, appears to have caught Japan off-guard. Some Japanese companies seem to have lacked the flexibility and independence required to compete successfully with western rivals in changing market conditions, and accordingly lost comparative advantage. Iwao argues that Japan's economic rise was based on a 'catch-up' approach that is only suitable for developing countries (Iwao, 1998: 37–9). Japanese companies placed 'excessive' emphasis on building group-learning capacity, to the detriment of fostering individual talent. Yet the current global enterprise culture requires allowing scope for individual creativity. Only by abandoning their trademark hierarchical egalitarianism can major Japanese companies perform effectively as innovative organizations. Iwao concludes: 'The Japanese economy of the 1990s is missing the massive "third industrial revolution" (or the information revolution) being led by the United States' (Iwao, 1998: 39).

The independent economist Tadashi Nakamae has suggested three possible future scenarios for Japan:

- a 'long-hollowing' (structural problems are not addressed and Japan gradually declines economically);
- 'crash and rebirth' (under which the economy virtually collapses, producing an inexorable demand for structural changes, and leading ultimately to regeneration); and

- a third scenario under which the US withdraws its military support, leaving Japan increasingly challenged as an Asian economic power by a resurgent China (*The Economist,* 21 March 1998; http://www.nier.co.jp).

'Crash and rebirth' seems the most optimistic of these scenarios: given Japan's successful track record in transforming calamities (such as the arrival of the 'black ships', and the 1945 defeat) into opportunities, a combination of domestic crisis and global 'foreign pressure' could offer the ideal catalyst for transformation. At present, however, much of Japan remains firmly in denial, assuming that economic recovery can take place without any radical overhaul.

4

Social Structure and Social Policy

How far does Japan's social structure differ from those of other societies? Mainstream scholars identify numerous points of similarity, arguing that Japan has been engaged in a process of modernization and convergence with western models. Revisionists tend to emphasise the shortcomings and the dysfunctional aspects of Japanese society, challenging the dominant view of Japan as overly rose-tinted. For culturalist analysts, Japanese social structure can only be understood through the study of distinctive patterns of order and behaviour that reflect longstanding cultural norms and mores. One view that borrows from all three perspectives is the metaphor of Japanese society as an onion, where the bulk of the population can be viewed in terms of different concentric rings. At the core of the onion are the most privileged members of Japanese society: male, permanent employees of large companies. In the outer ring are disadvantaged groups such as migrant labourers and minorities. The middle rings contain blue-collar males, women, the elderly, people hired on short-term contracts, the self-employed, and employees of small enterprises. Generalizing about the Japanese is difficult, since those at the core of society are vastly more privileged and comfortable than those on the margins.

Cultural Characteristics

Discussions of Japan's cultural characteristics can be highly contentious. 'Culturalist' approaches to understanding Japan typically emphasise certain core values and beliefs which are held to underpin society. These include: collectivism (an emphasis on the interests of the family, village, company or nation rather than those of the individual); consensus (a preference for harmony and agreement over open dissent and disputation); and hierarchy (accepting the importance of seniority and status). Much of the debate about Japanese culture centres around the question of where culture originates. If culture is seen as an inherent and largely immutable set of values passed on from one generation to the next, culture offers an explanation for the nature of society. However, if culture is seen as a construct, an artifact created by the state (especially through the education system) then culture is less an explanation for society than a manifestation of it.

Status is a core concept in Japan, where even university students have a strong sense of their position on the social ladder; second-year students refer to third-year students as their *sempai* (seniors), and to first-year students as their *kohai* (juniors). In Japan, everyone knows the age of everyone else, and many organizations produce seniority lists for internal distribution. Vertical ranking, based mainly on age, pervades virtually all Japanese institutions, determining everything from the location of each individual's desk to the order in which cups of tea are distributed (Japan National Tourist Organization, 1986). These rankings are reinforced by all kinds of linguistic constraints, since the Japanese language designates different ways of addressing one's social superiors and inferiors. In a system such as this, it is difficult for outstanding individuals to be accorded recognition, since this would upset the apple cart of hierarchy. It also makes open debate and disputation difficult; inferiors cannot easily challenge the opinions of their superiors, but often feel obliged to defer to their supposed higher wisdom.

The scholar who has done most to popularize the idea of group-based explanations of Japanese society is Chie Nakane. She argues that:

At a group meeting a member should put forward an opinion in terms that are safe and advantageous to himself, rather than state a judgement in objective terms appropriate to the point at issue. . . Freedom to speak out in a group is determined by, as it were, the processes of human relations within the group; in other words, it goes according to status in the group organisation. (Nakane, 1970: 35)

For as well as the vertical relations of seniority, horizontal relations of group solidarity are profoundly important in Japanese society. Traditionally, the Japanese place great emphasis on the importance of *wa,* or group harmony. Activities in Japanese schools, notably within particular 'home-rooms' or sports clubs, are organized around teaching students to work together collectively, to subsume their own interests to those of the group. Later, these principles are applied to the workplace, where the group might be defined by a specific department of a company.

One of the most important features of Japanese society is the persistence of patron–client relationships. In seeking to advance their own positions, Japanese people are likely to cultivate close personal relationships with certain senior individuals, such as former teachers or superiors in their company, who will use their influence to assist them. In this relationship, the superior is known as *oyabun* (parent), the inferior as *kobun* (child). The *kobun* performs certain services for the *oyabun,* in return for enjoying the benefits of his patronage, which might include help with promotion, or the arrangement of a desirable marriage. As might well be imagined, this system of patron–client relationships has important implications for the nature of Japanese politics, and particularly for the organization of Japanese political parties which are characterized by the existence of numerous factions grouped around various *oyabun* who secure the loyalty of *kobun* by dispensing political largesse (and often cash) in exchange for their support.

In general, positions of power in Japan are held by men in their fifties, sixties, and seventies, even where it might be widely recognized that a particular individual in his thirties or forties has greater talents than his bosses. Relatively few women have achieved senior positions in politics, the bureaucracy, or business. The ambitious younger person must be extremely patient, since openly to challenge a superior would cause the superior to lose face. The difference between appearance and reality is a key element in Japanese society. Whatever peoples' true feelings (*honne*) about a given situation, the façade of appearances (*tatamae*) must be kept up. To western observers critical of Japan, the idea of *honne* and *tatamae* often looks like a form of dishonesty or hypocrisy. To the Japanese, however, operating on two levels of 'reality' may seem entirely normal.

Some scholars see Japanese cultural characteristics as 'natural' phenomena that have arisen over a long historical period.

Revisionist scholars prefer to see Japanese culture as an 'artificial' construct, created and perpetuated by the state, by ruling elites, and by the needs of the capitalist order. Marxists see an emphasis on culture as a crude attempt to obscure the class relations that they believe underpin all societies. Mainstream scholars tend to emphasise convergence, arguing that Japanese culture is becoming less important in the face of modernization and social change. Some writers have even argued that certain features of Japanese culture (such as managerial methods or working practices) might profitably be exported to the West and to the developing world.

Family Structure

Traditionally, Japan had an extended family structure, and it used to be common for three generations to live together in the same household. The *ie*, or traditional Japanese household, operated according to strict social norms which clearly defined the roles of each member. However, rapid urbanization in the postwar period, combined with high land prices and poor standards of housing, mean that most Japanese people now live in much more cramped conditions than their counterparts in Europe and North America. The nuclear family, packed into a 'rabbit hutch' of an apartment or house, has become commonplace, though there are also many 'new extended families' comprising a nuclear family, plus one or more parents-in-law. Many single people, young and old, live alone in tiny flats.

The average ages of marriage for Japanese people have risen from 26.6 for men and 23.8 for women in 1955, to 28.5 for men and 26.3 for women in 1995. There are two common patterns of marriage for women: one is to marry early, soon after finishing high school or a two-year college; another is to marry later, often after working for several years on a short-term contract as an 'office lady', or temporary employee. Many private Japanese high schools are single-sex institutions, and even at mixed high schools there is considerable segregation and self-segregation of boys and girls. Similarly, in the workplace men and women typically socialize in single-sex groups, resulting in a 'quasi-homosexual' society (Miyamoto, 1994: 48, 61). Only for a relatively brief period (roughly from the ages of 18 to 25) do men and women mix together socially. It is relatively rare for husbands and wives to entertain other couples at home, or to meet them for evenings out: often men and women have separate social lives and groups of friends. There is a common Japanese saying that 'a good husband is healthy but absent'; marriage is looked upon as an economic arrangement that lends form and respectability to adult existence, but not as the central institution around which a person's inner life revolves. Even today, many marriages are arranged through formal or informal introductions by go-betweens; and social, economic and educational status are among the main criteria used in making a decision concerning marriage. Many companies in Japan assign male employees to branches and offices away from their home for months or years at a time. Partly because Japan has a very limited housing market – it is too expensive and impractical to buy and sell a home each time a new transfer comes – these men typically leave their wives and children behind in their home city, returning only at weekends (Jolivet, 1997: 70–2).

Japanese society is not renowned for its sexual morality. Pre-marital sexual activity is the norm, and indeed many Japanese men and women seek extra-marital liaisons or relationships. Numerous 'telephone clubs' exist, providing a means for men to contact available women, who may include high-school students or housewives. 'Compensated dating', where a man provides money or gifts to a woman in exchange for dates or sexual favours, is relatively common. So called 'love hotels', garish buildings renting rooms by the hour, are widespread throughout Japan, providing facilities for clandestine encounters. This kind of behaviour exists just below the surface of Japanese society, widely-known and understood, but rarely discussed in public. While social norms make it difficult to live an openly gay lifestyle, homosexuality is not uncommon, although many gays are nominally in heterosexual marriages.

Although it has risen slightly in recent decades, the divorce rate in Japan remains negligible by international standards (1.66 divorces per thousand persons in 1996), reflecting a high degree of outward social conformity. Nevertheless, these figures disguise the fact that some Japanese marriages are little more than conveniences, maintained for pragmatic reasons by couples who would separate or divorce in other societies. Sugimoto notes that the Japanese system of 'family registration' (*koseki*) makes divorce difficult (Sugimoto, 1997 136–42). Under this system, the husband is usually designated

---

Box 4.1 Key social facts about Japan

Religion	Observe both Shinto and Buddhism	84%
	Other (including Christian 0.7%)	16%
Life expectancy at birth	80.45 years	
Infant mortality rate	4 deaths/1000 live births	
Literacy	99%	
Doctors per 1000 of population	1.8	
Hospital beds per 1000 of population	16.2	
Education continuance rates	Senior High School	95.8%
	Junior College	13.1%
	University	32.1%

Source: CIA (1998), *CIA Factbook;* Japan National Statistical Office; Kawai, Nobukazu (1996) *Asahi Shimbun Japan Almanac 1997,* Tokyo, Asahi Shimbun Publishing Company; Keizai Koho Center (1997), *Japan 1998, An International Comparison,* Tokyo, Keizai Koho Center; OECD.

head of the household, children born out of wedlock are effectively 'second-class' citizens, children of divorced people may be stigmatized, all members of a family are expected to assume the same surname, and the ashes of women are usually placed in the family cremation tomb of their husband. Family registration documents are publicly available, and it is common for the families of couples who are becoming engaged to inspect these documents for evidence of irregularities. Any 'stain' on the family register can make it difficult for people to find respectable marriage partners. All in all, maintaining façade marriages is often the path of least resistance.

The Urban–Rural Divide

Patrick Smith argues that the divide between urban and rural Japan is central to understanding the country and its politics (Smith, 1997: 164–86). Japan's main cities – such as Tokyo, Yokohama, Nagoya, Kyoto, Osaka, and Kobe – are largely concentrated in *omote nihon* (the front of Japan) on the Pacific coast, in the central part of the main island of Honshu. Nearly half of Japan's population lives in these three areas: Kanto (around Tokyo), Kansai (around Osaka) and Chubu (around Nagoya). Tokyo is by far the most important of these centres: if Tokyo were a country, it would have a higher gross national product than China or South Korea, roughly equivalent to that of Canada (Sugimoto, 1997: 60). Whereas in the prewar period, Osaka was a merchant city that rivalled Tokyo, in the postwar period many Osaka-based companies moved their head offices to the capital, and Yokohama became the second largest city in Japan.

Clammer notes that cities such as Tokyo and Osaka might be considered 'world cities', in terms of their populations and their economic and cultural power. He also identifies several other categories of Japanese city (Clammer, 1997: 28–30): the 'old capitals' of Kyoto, Nara and Kamakura, with mixed economies based partly on tourism; 'traditionalized' old castle towns with a high-class character, such as Kurashiki and Kanazawa; modern industrial cities such as Toyota City (home to the car manufacturers), Kawasaki, and Kita-Kyushu; provincial cities that combine various administrative and commercial functions, and which are also educational and cultural centres, like Sapporo, Sendai, and Kagoshima; and science cities, such as Tsukuba (outside Tokyo). Clammer is sceptical about the efforts of some urban anthropologists to emphasise the political and cultural vitality of traditional urban neighbourhoods and administrative units, arguing that this vitality is being displaced by new forms of network-based consumerism (Clammer, 1997: 30–1). He argues that although neighbourhoods do still exist in urban Japan, 'except in pockets still dominated by members of the old middle class, they do not mean the kind of things that many anthropologists of Japan ascribe to them' (Clammer, 1997: 33). He prefers to see many areas as 'epitome districts', a mish-mash of residential accommodation, restaurants, cafes, entertainment outlets, convenience stores and other shops, with considerable life, but limited sociological coherence.

The Japan Sea coast, along with the other islands of Japan, is far less developed and urbanized: this is *ura nihon* (the back of Japan, hidden Japan), an outstanding example of (but not synonymous with) *inaka*, the countryside, regarded by urban dwellers as the sticks, the boondocks, the back of beyond. Whereas wealthy Europeans or North Americans frequently aspire to live in the countryside, for urban Japanese people (as for many other Asians) the countryside often represents an uncivilized place, sentimentalized but largely avoided. During the Meiji period, Tokyo exploited the countryside, turning rural people into impoverished tenant farmers lorded over by wealthy landowners. The Occupation land reforms gave rural people their own fields to till, and during the postwar period successive governments provided a range of benefits to the countryside:

> Tokyo made rural life manageable, even comfortable, with price supports, import protection against foreign farm products, subsidies, and vast public-works budgets. This was a great reversal. In effect, the countryside began to live off the capital after centuries during which it was the other way around. (Smith, 1997: 169)

Rural communities were romanticized as *furusato*, 'old home towns', the source of traditional Japanese culture and wisdom. Yet Smith sees this reversal as a hollow one: the Japanese countryside became dependent upon state beneficence, the province of pork-barrel politics and electoral gerrymandering. The 'back of Japan' missed out on the economic transformation which was taking place on the Pacific coast, becoming instead an 'internal periphery' (Smith, 1997: 171). Massive government-funded projects to 'develop' the countryside form the core of what McCormack calls 'the construction state', a political system based on large-scale structural corruption, in which major construction companies enjoy enormous power (McCormack, 1996: 25–77). By the early 1990s, over 6 million people were employed in the Japanese construction industry (more than in the entire manufacturing sector), while Japan's public works budget continued to exceed the US defence budget at the height of the Cold War (McCormack, 1996: 32–3). Smith describes Kakeya, home town of former Prime Minister Noboru Takeshita (which received at least ¥200 million a year from the Construction Ministry and other government agencies, amounting to nearly half the town's annual budget) as 'a well dressed welfare case' (Smith, 1997: 170), with problems typical of many towns in rural prefectures. Rural depopulation has been a serious problem: although Japan's population has increased by almost three-quarters since the war, some prefectures actually have a lower population today than in 1949. Rural areas of Japan are often in direct competition with low-wage Southeast Asian economies to become the location of factory investments, competitions they frequently lose.

At the political level, Japan's over-centralization means very little autonomy for prefectural governments: as former Prime Minister Hosokawa famously complained, a prefectural governor needs permission from Tokyo even to move a bus stop. Localities have been engaged in a movement towards rural revitalization, involving developing and marketing distinctive local agricultural products, stimulating rural industries, and promoting tourism (Knight, 1994: 634–46). Although there are some claims of a 'U-turn' trend of urban dwellers moving back to the countryside to enjoy a higher quality of life, these revitalization efforts have met with limited success. Knight found that many of the prime movers in village revitalization campaigns were 'return migrants' from urban areas, supported by local authorities: for all the rhetoric of self-reliance, the movement was largely reliant on external agency (Knight 1994: 645–6). There have been numerous demands for wholesale decentralization, such as former Prime Minister Hosokawa's proposal for a 'United States of Japan' (Smith, 1997: 185–6), calls echoed by globalization guru Kenichi Ohmae during his unsuccessful 1995 campaign for the Tokyo governorship (McCormack, 1996: 19–20).

Sugimoto notes that the urban–rural divide is reinforced by what he calls 'ideological centralisation': because the mass media and book publishing industries in Japan are dominated by a small number of Tokyo-based companies, it is difficult for non-Tokyo voices to be heard:

Thus the Japanese public is constantly fed views of the world and the nation that are constructed, interpreted and edited in Tokyo. Outside the capital, local situations draw attention only as sensational news stories, or as provincial items exciting the 'exotic curiosity' of the Tokyo media establishment. (Sugimoto, 1997: 64)

While this situation is certainly not unique to Japan, the degree of capital-city centralization in Japan is unusual, especially in a nation that boasts such important competing secondary cities as Osaka and Nagoya.

Women

Despite Japan's remarkable economic growth during the postwar period, very few Japanese women have obtained positions of power and authority within the country's political, bureaucratic or economic structures (see table from Sugimoto, 1997: 148). Women do perform some quite heavy manual jobs, working on building sites and driving trucks, for example, but although the labour of women workers has long been immensely important to Japan (40.6 per cent of the paid workforce were women in 1991), that labour is deeply subordinated to male power. Discrimination against female employees is thoroughly institutionalized in Japan; many women are technically part-time workers, and so are not entitled to the same benefits as male colleagues. Often women are obliged to take care of elderly relatives, especially in-laws, and have difficulty in balancing these demands with those of the workplace. For these women, unskilled part-time work is a common alternative; another is running a small business. Sugimoto argues that most women who work part-time are not frustrated would-be career women, but women who are not sufficiently well-off to become full-time housewives: their ideal is to become women of leisure. Affluent middle-class women in Japan can achieve comfortable lives, balancing family demands with hobbies and friendships: for the majority of women, however, this ideal is impossible to attain. Another alternative for women is to concentrate on voluntary work in community-based organizations, working on environmental or other issues.

Contraceptive practice in Japan lags behind both western countries and most developing countries: condoms are the most common form of birth control, and abortion is widespread. There are officially half a million abortions per annum, but the actual figure is probably two or three times greater (Jolivet, 1997: 129) (the contraceptive pill long remained effectively banned, its distribution blocked by the interests of doctors who benefited from the abortion trade, though liberalization finally took place in 1999). According to one survey, 72.9 per cent of women between 40 and 49 admitted to having had an abortion (Jolivet, 1997: 127).

Studies suggest that Japanese women hope to have well-behaved and docile children (whereas similar studies of American women suggested a desire for independent children). This preference for docility partly reflects lack of childcare support from fathers: according to some 1987 statistics, the average Japanese father spent only one hour and 32 minutes a week with his children. As Jolivet notes 'The majority of Japanese men have the extraordinary ability of living as though no one else was there' (Jolivet, 1997: 62). However, the assumption that a man should be at work makes it difficult for men to fit into family life; a retired man with no job may be seen by his family as a 'wet dead leaf, difficult to peel off the ground' (Jolivet, 1997: 68).

For many women, the pressure of living with in-laws is considerable, and in particular women are often reluctant to live with their husbands' mothers. While these difficulties are universal, the importance of seniority in Japan means that mothers-in-law have traditionally played a powerful role in the household hierarchy, a problem compounded by the prevalence of 'mother complexes' in Japanese men. Jolivet quotes one source as saying 'most of the country women who come to see me want to divorce their in-laws rather than their husbands' (Jolivet, 1997: 160). Smith argues that the position of women has improved dramatically during the post-war period, stressing that survey evidence supports the view that more than two-thirds of Japanese women are satisfied with their lot (Smith, 1987: 25). However, Lock (whose survey data Smith used) demonstrates that some of the women who claimed to be satisfied actually led dreadful lives, exploited and oppressed by husbands and in-laws: 'The kind of misery that these women have endured is simply filtered out in both survey research and ideological constructions about the homebody' (Lock, 1996: 93).

Minorities

Japan is often described as a uniquely homogeneous society, as though its relative lack of racial diversity was one of its social and economic strengths. Nevertheless, this image of Japan as homogeneous and undifferentiated has been criticized by revisionists and others as a misrepresentation (see Weiner, 1997: xii–xiv). Sugimoto (1997: 28–9) argues that Japan is actually a multicultural society, and in support of this claim he presents a table listing 14 different categories of 'Japanese' (1997: 172). There are several significant minority groups in Japan, including: *burakumin* (who are physically indistinguishable from other Japanese), Japanese-born Koreans, Ainu, and foreign residents, especially migrant workers.

The phenomenon of *burakumin* is peculiar to Japan, though there are parallels with 'untouchables' in the Hindu caste system. *Bur-*

akumin (of whom there are roughly three million, or about 1 in 40 Japanese) are descended from those 'specialists in impurity' who traditionally performed low-class occupations such as butchery, working in slaughterhouses and tanneries, grave-digging, and rubbish collection. In Tokugawa Japan, *burakumin* (who had their origins in earlier medieval times) became an outcast class. They were physically segregated from the mainstream community, lived in designated areas, and were unable to intermarry with other people (see Pharr, 1990: 76–80). It was widely believed that they were ethnically different from other Japanese. Even today, 6 000 *burakumin* neighbourhoods exist (many in the Kansai area), and it is common for the parents of prospective marriage partners to investigate their respective family backgrounds, in order to uncover any *burakumin* ancestry (see Smith, 1997: 277–83). Many companies use similar practices to screen new employees. In the postwar period, the Buraku Liberation League has campaigned against social and economic oppression, and demands special measures to improve the social status of *burakumin*. Other *buraku* organizations have different orientations and objectives (Neary, 1997; Takagi, 1991). In response to political pressures, national and local governments have provided sizeable grants and subsidies to improve *burakumin* areas. Far more *burakumin* now intermarry with non-*burakumin*. Nevertheless, the government has failed to pass legislation outlawing *burakumin* discrimination. Smith argues that the continuing existence of the minority serves the purposes of the Japanese state: 'the illusion of homogeneity is reinforced when there are islands of difference in the sea of sameness' (Smith, 1997: 283).

Japan's Korean minority numbers around 700 000; like the *burakumin*, Koreans are heavily concentrated in Honshu, especially the Kansai district. The Korean population of Japan dates from Japan's colonization of Korea in 1910, after which many Koreans were brought to Japan to provide low-cost labour (Sugimoto, 1997: 177–84). Although most Koreans are second, third, or fourth generation residents for whom Japanese is their first language, only around 200 000 have so far become Japanese nationals. The majority still retain the status of foreigners, with no voting rights and limited access to employment, promotion and pensions (except in a few municipalities, they cannot become civil servants or local government employees, and so are largely barred from many jobs, such as teaching). Until recently, all Koreans were obliged to undergo regular fingerprinting as part of official 'alien registration' procedures, and previously Koreans were forced to take Japanese names. The political situation of a Korean peninsula divided into a communist North and capitalist South has resulted in a split in the Japanese Korean community: about two-thirds carry South Korean passports, whilst the remaining third are loyal to the Pyongyang regime (on North Koreans, see Ryang, 1997). Mass organizations mobilize the two Korean communities along national lines. Korean businesses in Japan, such as Nagoya pachinko parlours, have provided substantial revenue for the North Korean economy. While some Koreans remain strongly attached to their Korean identity, 70 per cent of Koreans now marry Japanese partners, and the majority of young Koreans are integrated into wider Japanese society despite the persistence of prejudice and discrimination (see Sugimoto, 1997: 182–4; Hoffman, 1992).

Other minority groups in Japan include the Ainu, and Okinawans. There are around 24 000 people in Hokkaido who officially identify themselves as Ainu, but this figure does not include Ainu who have moved to other parts of Japan, or people who are reluctant to identify themselves as Ainu. The Ainu are an indigenous people, often compared with Native Americans and Australian aborigines: they are ethnically and culturally distinct from other Japanese. They have also faced discrimination and loss of lands at the hands of the state (see Siddle, 1996). Okinawa, an island prefecture where the majority of American military bases on Japanese soil are located, possesses a distinct culture and language; there is some dispute as to whether Okinawans are descended from 'mainland' Japanese. The residents of Okinawa have borne the brunt of the negative aspects of the US–Japan security relationship, and some scholars view this a form of systematic discrimination against a peripheral area and its people (see Taira, 1997). Tensions between Tokyo and Okinawa came to a head following the gang-rape of a Japanese schoolgirl by American soldiers in 1995, an incident which triggered strong calls for a reduction of the US military presence in Okinawa.

Labour shortages in Japan during the bubble period of the 1980s led to a rise in the use of immigrant labour from overseas. An estimated 700 000 such workers are employed in Japan, some legally, but perhaps 300 000 of them are illegal immigrants. The majority perform dirty, difficult and dangerous jobs which the Japanese are reluctant to do, such as working on construction sites, in factories, and in restaurants and bars (the 'hostess' industry). After Koreans, the second largest group of foreigners in Japan is the Chinese, who numbered over 230 000 in 1996 (JETRO, 1998: 132). Chinese immigration has a long history in Japan, and Japanese cities such as Kobe and Yokohama have 'Chinatown' areas dating back to the Meiji period. However, most of the Chinese residents of Japan are recent arrivals. Many are legitimately studying in Japan, while some Chinese arrive in Japan ostensibly to enrol in language schools, but then overstay their visas and become illegal workers. There are also well-established smuggling routes for illegal Chinese immigrants to enter Japan (Oka, 1994: 17–22).

Well-known Japanese automotive companies such as Toyota have hired large numbers of Japanese Brazilians to work in their plants (there were over 200 000 Brazilians in Japan in 1996); other sizeable companies bring in workers from Southeast Asian subsidiaries for periods of 'training'. But the great majority of foreign workers are hired by small and medium-sized enterprises. There are significant numbers of illegal immigrants from several Asian countries, including Thailand, China, South Korea, Malaysia, the Philippines, Bangladesh, Iran, and Pakistan. Foreign residents may become popularly associated with criminal activities; for example, during the mid-1990s many Iranian nationals were arrested around Yoyogi Park in Tokyo, for selling narcotic drugs and illegally-produced, cut-price telephone cards. However, the telephone cards themselves were manufactured by Japanese *yakuza* gangs that used the Iranians as a front for distribution.

This trend reflects the way in which Japanese organized crime has been modifying its tactics and operations following the passage of anti-gang legislation in 1992. Illegal foreign workers who have lost their jobs as a result of the economic recession may have many incentives to turn to crime; nevertheless, there is evidence that figures for foreign criminal activity in Japan are inflated, reflecting government attempts to blame crime on outsiders (Sugimoto, 1997: 187f; Friman, 1996: 970–1). Deportations of foreigners (mainly for overstaying) reached a peak in 1993; since then, the number of illegal immigrants has slightly declined (Immigration Bureau, 1997: 10). Some Japanese are critical of the presence of unskilled foreign workers in their society, seeing them as a threat to social order; others, however, regard such trends as an economic necessity, and an inevitable part of the much-heralded 'internationalization' process (see Oka, 1994: 39).

Religions

Unusually, Japan has two main religions: Shinto and Buddhism. These religions exist literally side by side, and most Japanese nominally ascribe to both of them (see Hendry, 1995: 115–32). However, these nominal syncretist affiliations are not typically matched by any clearly definable religious beliefs, or by any personal commitment to religious practice. While religiosity is widespread in Japan, religion in a deeper sense is much more rare: only about a tenth of Japanese people are 'actively' religious. However, token participation in some religious rituals is increasing in Japan; for example, a growing number of Japanese people pay festive visits to temples and shrines at New Year. Although this could be seen as evidence of religious revival, some scholars argue that Japanese religion is turning into a set of social customs, or simply a leisure activity, while others regard it as part of a quest for identity in an increasingly complex world (see *Religion in Japan Today*, 1992: 15). By contrast, some more inconvenient and less enjoyable religious rituals (such as the practice of visiting ancestors' graves during the August O-bon period) are declining.

Shintoism has no scriptures, and is based on the worship of mana, which Sugimoto describes as 'the supernatural or mystical power that resides not only in human beings, but also in animals, plants, rivers, and other natural things' (1997: 231). Shintoism therefore includes some animistic elements. An indigenous religion that teaches myths about the special origins and destiny of the Japanese people, Shinto was previously associated with the cult of the Emperor and with militarism (Davis, 1991: 793). One of the best-known (and most controversial) shrines in Japan is probably the Yasukuni shrine in Tokyo, where many of Japan's war dead are buried. Shinto shrines, with their distinctive *torii* (gateways, often red), are a common sight all over Japan; like many Buddhist temples, the smaller shrines are often family concerns, passed down from father to son. Japanese Buddhist temples are cultural centres, some of which house important images, manuscripts and art objects. Most Japanese people visit temples mainly for tourism or for funerals, and many Japanese priests earn most of their living from the funeral business. Despite the worldwide fame of Zen, the majority of Japanese Buddhist priests do not practice meditation; unlike their more ascetic, celibate Theravada counterparts in

Southeast Asia, Japanese Mahayana priests are free to marry, and most now lead consumerist lives which are barely distinguishable from those of secular Japanese people.

During the postwar period, many 'new religions' have sprung up in Japan, most of which are new Buddhist sects rather than entirely new religions. The most important include Rishho Kosei-kai, and Soka Gakkai, a mass organization linked to the Komeito (Clean Government) Party. Soka Gakkai claims a membership of 12 to 17 million. The movement has a primary appeal to those socially marginalized and economically disadvantaged during Japan's rapid postwar urbanization and growth. Davis describes Soka Gakkai as 'perhaps opportunistic rather than fundamentalistic' (Davis, 1991: 804). Nevertheless, the power and influence of some new religions made the Japanese authorities reluctant to interfere with questionable practices by religious sects. This became a major issue with the rise of the apocalyptic terrorist group Aum Shinrikyo, which exploited its religious status for the purpose of protection, whilst building up a large arsenal of chemical and other weaponry (Kaplan and Marshall, 1996). Despite substantial evidence linking the cult to the deaths of seven people in a gas attack in Matsumoto in June 1994, it was not until the group released deadly sarin nerve gas into the Tokyo subway system in March 1995 – killing another 12 people – that police finally took action against the movement. The preoccupation of the group with illegal activities has led some commentators to describe Aum as a 'criminal religion', rather than a new religion as such (Metraux, 1995).

Health and Demography

Japanese people enjoy exceptional longevity (in 1994, life expectancy was 83 years for women and 77 for men, the highest in the world), largely because of their excellent low-fat diet. Japan has a good health care system, supported by a national health insurance scheme that allows low-cost access to medical services. Casual observation readily reveals, however, that standards of dental treatment in Japan are poor compared with other developed (and many developing) countries. Despite the long life expectancy currently enjoyed by Japanese people, future trends are more difficult to predict: changes in the Japanese diet (which have produced substantial increases in

Table 4.1   Share of people aged 65 and over in the total population (per cent)

	1950	1960	1970	1980	1990	2000	2010	2020
Japan	4.94	5.73	7.07	9.10	12.08	17.24	22.04	26.84
United States	8.14	9.23	9.81	11.29	12.52	12.43	12.86	16.13
Germany	9.72	11.52	13.69	15.60	14.96	16.05	19.20	20.88
France	11.38	11.64	12.87	13.97	13.98	15.73	16.18	19.68

Original Source: National Institute of Population and Social Security Research (1997), *Latest Demographic Statistics*.
Secondary Source: Secondary Source: Seike, Atsushi (1997), *New Trends in Japan's Labor Market*, Tokyo: Foreign Press Center, p.11.

the average height of young people in recent decades) may lead to much higher rates of cardiovascular disease; similarly, the recent epidemic increase in cigarette smoking by young women will undoubtedly take a heavy toll on female health in the twenty-first century.

If Japanese life expectancy and the current low birthrate (1.46 in 1993, the third lowest in the world) continue at their present levels, Japan may end the twenty-first century with only around half of its present population (Sugimoto, 1997: 75). Raising and educating children is an expensive and stressful business in Japan; as women marry later and have more scope to pursue work and other interests, enthusiasm for child-rearing has declined (Suzuki, 1995). Official injunctions to Japanese women urging them to produce more children have fallen on deaf ears. A falling number of active working people is now faced with supporting an ever-growing elderly population: Japan is an 'ageing society' (see Table 4.1). Some observers see this trend as a demographic 'time bomb', which is undermining Japan's long-term economic and political standing (see Jones, 1988). One result of this trend will be to make Japan ever more reliant on female labour, and on that of immigrant workers (legal or illegal) from abroad.

Welfare

Japan has been touted as having a model welfare system, which provides 'security without entitlement' (Vogel, 1979: 184–203). In particular, Vogel highlights the role of volunteer welfare officers in identifying needs; these volunteers comprise the main form of direct social welfare provision for marginalized groups such as the destitute, the disabled, and single mothers. There are around 190 000 such volunteers – mainly retired people with an average age of 60 – each of whom makes around 120 household visits per year (see Goodman, 1998: 139–58). This volunteer system is clearly extremely cost-effective, but Goodman argues that these untrained, paternalistic volunteers sometimes play an intrusive, moralistic role, and have helped ensure that take-up rates of welfare benefits remain extremely low.

Unemployment benefits in Japan are limited, and depend upon age and experience: those under the age of 30, or who have less than 12 months' work experience, are only entitled to 90 days' benefit, whereas those over 55 are entitled to 300 days' benefit. Benefit levels are equivalent to 60 per cent of the recipient's previous salary, up to a certain limit (Argy and Stein, 1997: 315). However, unemployment rates in Japan remain low compared with other industrialised nations (see Table 4.2). Pension benefits vary widely, based on length of pensionable service and type of employment. A basic universal pension is provided by the National Pension System, while supplementary pensions are provided through various employee schemes, the largest of which is the Employee Pension Scheme (which includes all company pensions). Pensioners solely reliant on the National Pension System are not well provided for, though those in receipt of supplementary pensions may receive in the region of 50 per cent of their pre-retirement income. However, the rapidly

Table 4.2 Standardized unemployment rates (seasonally adjusted)

	1995	*1998**
Japan	3.1	3.9
United States	5.6	4.55
France	11.7	12.0
United Kingdom	8.7	6.4
Germany	8.2	9.9
Denmark	7.2	4.8

* First two quarters only.

Source: OECD (1998) Quarterly Labour Force Statistics.

ageing population, combined with the recent economic downturn, means that the major pension schemes may be unable to meet their current obligations in full by the second or third decade of the twenty-first century (Argy and Stein. 1997: 315–7).

Health insurance in Japan is provided by several officially recognized non-profit funds, one of which all citizens are obliged to join. Most of these cover 70 or 80 per cent of health care costs (which are based on a standardized scale of charges); the patient pays the remaining 20 or 30 per cent up to a maximum ceiling (Argy and Stein, 1997: 299–301).

Class and Inequality

Most Japanese people appear to reject a class-based analysis of their society, as seen in the fact that more than 75 per cent regularly identify themselves as middle class (National Survey, 1996: 60). Some sociologists argue that this self-assessment offers neither a credible nor an accurate view of Japanese society, and that such results simply reflect a weak class consciousness on the part of the Japanese. Some have argued that Japan is a largely 'classless' merit-based society, characterized by high levels of social mobility among the 'new middle mass'. Such an analysis is very attractive to conservatives who wish to downplay the importance of social class, but is strongly rejected by Marxist scholars. A major study by Ishida found that social mobility in Japan is actually very similar to that of Britain and the USA (Ishida, 1993: 256–7). Ishida rejects the idea of a 'new middle mass' in Japan, arguing that social class is the strongest determinant of income inequality and home ownership (Ishida, 1993: 260), and a far more important determinant than education. In short, Ishida argues that social class largely determines the distribution of rewards in Japan.

Conclusion

Mainstream scholars emphasise what they see as the positive features of Japanese society: low divorce rates, exceptional longevity, cost-effective health care and welfare systems, a high degree of popular satisfaction, widespread self-identification as middle class, an increasing recognition of women's roles in the workforce, considerable social homogeneity, improving conditions for minority groups, growing internationalization and evidence of religious revivalism and rural revitalization. Culturalist scholars see many of these achievements as reflections of a highly distinctive culture and history, especially core Japanese values such as harmony, consensus and hierarchy. Revisionists stress the oppressive nature of many Japanese families, the dysfunctional character of male–female relationships, the ageing society and falling birthrate, the persistence of discrimination against women, minorities and foreigners, the questionable nature of some new religions, the imbalance between urban and rural areas, and limited scope for social mobility.

Clammer argues that Japanese society is actually something new. 'Traditional' ways of understanding Japanese society need to be revised in the light of rampant consumerism: products are being consumed primarily for their symbolic value. He poses the rhetorical question:

> What kind of social organization exists here: does the consumer society in Japan constitute a definable social structure, or do we need to reconceptualize it in fresh terms? (Clammer, 1997: 47)

In a similarly provocative fashion, Sugimoto argues that Japan is a different kind of society. He makes the case for a new understanding of Japan as a 'multicultural' society characterized by widespread internal variations which are obscured or concealed by dominant patterns of 'friendly authoritarianism' (1997: 245–58). Another alternative analysis is to view the Japanese social order as an 'onion', centred on a Tokyo-based elite of white-collar males, but made up of numerous different concentric layers. These multiple layers give Japan far more richness and diversity than conventional explanations (which stress the relative homogeneity of the society) would suggest.

5

Governing Structures

Under the 1947 Constitution, sovereignty rests with the people rather than with the Emperor. The Emperor serves as the 'symbol of state': technically speaking, Japan has no 'head of state', a legacy of postwar attempts to strip the throne of all power. The Diet contains two houses: the Upper House (House of Councillors), and Lower House (House of Representatives). However, the lower house is much the more important of the two. Both houses are filled by elected members. In many respects, the formal structures of the Japanese parliamentary system reflect the British model, with executive power concentrated in the hands of the Cabinet and the prime minister. At least 50 per cent of ministers must be members of the Diet. There is an independent judiciary, and local governments at the prefectural and municipal level enjoy autonomy. Civil and social rights, including freedom of speech and assembly, are incorporated into the constitution. Citizens are equal before the law; public officials are accountable to the people, who have the right to choose and dismiss them. Despite some criticism of the 1947 Constitution as a 'foreign' import imposed on Japan by the Occupation forces, no formal motion to amend it has yet been put before the Diet.

Electoral System

Under the postwar system, the House of Representatives had 512 members, chosen from 130 electoral districts for four-year terms (the number of seats and constituencies was revised five times). Electoral districts were therefore multi-member constituencies, with between two and six Diet members representing each district. Voters had a single non-transferable vote; in other words, despite the fact that constituencies elected more than one Diet member, individual voters had only one vote. In practice, governments usually called elections before their four-year terms were up, taking advantage of favourable political conditions.

The 252 members of the House of Councillors are elected for six-year terms by two different methods. 152 are elected by districts corresponding to the 47 prefectures of Japan (each prefecture electing from two to eight members, based on size), while another 100 members are chosen in general national elections. Upper-house elections take place on fixed dates, and half of the membership of the chamber is replaced every three years. Theoretically, members of the upper house represent broader constituencies than those of the lower house, and they are therefore somewhat 'above the fray' of day-to-day politicking. In practice, however, the composition of the upper house closely reflects that of the lower house (Bingham, 1989: 5). The Diet is in session for much of the year, and as in Britain, makes use of full parliamentary debates; as in the USA, an important role is given to a set of standing committees.

The multi-member district system of the lower house was often criticized for promoting factionalism, since often much of the electoral contestation would take place between rival LDP candidates rather than rival parties. In 1991, attempts to reform the electoral system were scuppered by opposition from within the LDP, but following the collapse of LDP rule in 1993 the pressure to reform the system became irresistible. In 1994, the short-lived Hosokawa government was able to push through an electoral reform package very similar to the 1991 proposals (Foreign Press Center, 1995, 1997). Under the new system (which has not affected the upper house), the lower house has 500 seats, 300 of them assigned to single-member constituencies, and 200 (divided into 11 blocs) are allocated by proportional representation. Voters cast two ballots in the election. Constituency seats may be contested by independents, but only candidates backed by a party may compete for the proportional representation seats. Dual candidacies are also allowed: parties may include candidates for single seat constituencies on their lists of candidates for election by proportional representation. For candidates from large parties this can easily serve as a fall-back plan: unsuccessful candidates from the consituency elections may stand a good chance of entering the lower house via the proportional representation route. In the 1996 lower-house elections (the first held under the new rules), 84 of those elected under the proportional representation system were defeated candidates from the constituencies, an outcome which many voters found very unsatisfactory. On balance, the new system produced very similar results to the old one.

Box 5.1 Japanese prime ministers in the postwar period

	From	*Party*
Prince Higashikuni	August 1945	
Kijuro Shidehara	October 1945	
Shigeru Yoshida	May 1946	JLP
Tetsu Katayama	May 1947	JSP
Hitoshi Ashida	March 1948	DP
Shigeru Yoshida	October 1948	DLP/LP
Ichiro Hatoyama	December 1954	JDP/LDP
Tanzan Ishibashi	December 1956	LDP
Nobusuke Kishi	February 1957	LDP
Hayato Ikeda	July 1960	LDP
Eisaku Sato	November 1964	LDP
Kakuei Tanaka	July 1972	LDP
Takeo Miki	December 1974	LDP
Takeo Fukuda	December 1976	LDP
Masayoshi Ohira	December 1978	LDP
Zenko Suzuki	July 1980	LDP
Yasuhiro Nakasone	November 1982	LDP
Noboru Takeshita	November 1987	LDP
Sosuke Uno	June 1989	LDP
Toshiki Kaifu	August 1989	LDP
Kiichi Miyazawa	November 1991	LDP
Morihiro Hosokawa	August 1993	JNP
Tsutomu Hata	April 1994	JRP
Tomiichi Murayama	June 1994	SDPJ
Ryutaro Hashimoto	January 1996	LDP
Keizo Obuchi	July 1998	LDP

Parties: JLP, Japan Liberal Party; JSP, Japan Socialist Party; DP, Democratic Party; DLP, Democratic Liberal Party; LP, Liberal Party; JDP, Japan Democratic Party; LDP, Liberal Democratic Party; JNP, Japan New Party; JRP, Japan Renewal Party; SDPJ, Social Democratic Party of Japan.

Electoral campaigning in Japan operates under various restrictions: in particular, door-to-door canvassing is banned, since in the past candidates used to offer 'gifts' or payments to voters during canvassing. Under the 1994 reforms, requirements for the financial disclosure of campaign contributions have been tightened up, and public funds to the tune of around ¥30 billion per election have been allocated to underwrite the cost of party campaigns (Stockwin, 1999: 126–7).

The Cabinet

One important function of the Diet is to designate the prime minister (who then appoints the Cabinet). The Cabinet is held to be accountable to the Diet. Although the Diet is usually dissolved by the prime minister, the government can also be brought down in a no-confidence vote, which then precipitates a general election. A Cabinet contains no more than 20 ministers of state, and on average lasts only around nine months as frequent reshuffles are common – though in many cases the reshuffle will be only a partial one, and so this does not mean that all ministers are moved on average every nine months. However, 57 per cent of ministers last less than a year, and 77 per cent less than two (Bingham, 1989: 18). In theory, Japanese prime ministers are very powerful individuals: with a tiny number of short-lived exceptions, since 1955 they have been the leaders of the LDP, as well as being designated by the Diet and holding a range of executive powers.

Yet in practice most Japanese premiers have found themselves heavily dominated and influenced by the political, business and bureaucratic interests which provide their support. Factors producing weak prime ministerial leadership include suspicion of 'aggressive' leadership styles, a tradition of 'consensus articulation' by prime ministers, the relative strength of the bureaucracy *vis-à-vis* the executive, and the importance of interfactional negotiating skills (rather than clear policy stances) as a qualification in obtaining the post (Angel, 1989: 583). However, notable exceptions to the usual style of premiership include consummate machine politician Kakuei Tanaka, and the high-profile conservative ideologue Yasuhiro Nakasone. Nakasone succeeded in reorganizing the Cabinet Secretariat and Security Council in 1986, thereby greatly enhancing the potential for executive control, especially in crisis situations (Angel, 1989:

601). Nevertheless, subsequent prime ministers have generally been much more in the traditional, low-profile mode than Nakasone.

A typical Cabinet of 20 consists of 12 heads of ministries (Justice, Foreign Affairs, Finance, International Trade and Industry, Labour, Education, Health and Welfare, Agriculture, Forestry and Fisheries, Posts and Telecommunications, Construction, and Home Affairs), along with eight other members, including the Chief Secretary of the Cabinet, and the heads of various prime ministerial agencies (including the Defense Agency, Environment Agency, Economic Planning Agency, and Management and Coordination Agency). It is not necessary to hold a Cabinet position to exert enormous influence in Japan, since parties such as the LDP are dominated by faction bosses and power-brokers. Ministerial posts are rotated among these power-brokers and their proteges.

The lower house has the upper hand in the legislative process: a bill rejected by the upper house can still become law if it is approved by the lower house for a second time with a two-thirds majority. However, most legislation (especially important legislation) originates with the bureaucracy rather than with the legislature itself (Bingham, 1989: 11–12). Even major bills such as the annual budget bill are generally rubber-stamped by the Cabinet and the Diet; for example, from 1955 to 1977, the Diet made only one substantive revision of the budget (Bingham, 1989: 15).

If the power and effectiveness of the Cabinet and the Diet has often been questioned, there is one Japanese institution which is universally seen as extremely important: the Ministry of Finance. The vast range of powers it wields (in effect, wielded mostly by its senior bureaucrats) makes the Ministry of Finance a virtual 'super-ministry', with an extraordinary degree of control over the financial sector, and over public sector revenues and expenditure. Through its *de facto* control of the budget, the Finance Ministry has been able to exert considerable influence over the policies and priorities of other ministries, as well as over those of prefectures and municipalities which receive substantial funding from central government. The Ministry designs and operates the national tax system (though the actual collection of taxes is carried out by a separate agency), plans and operates the national financial system, regulates the banking system (including supervising the Bank of Japan), regulates securities trading, sets and collects customs and shipping duties, plays a strategic role in international economic trade, and plans and implements the national government budget system, including preparing the budget bill for Cabinet and Diet approval. For understandable reasons, the post of Finance Minister is highly coveted, yet few politicians are really able fully to comprehend, let alone direct, the Ministry's vast range of activities and operations.

Local Government

Whereas prior to the Second World War Japan had a highly-centralized political order, the Occupation reforms sought to introduce a system of local government which would check the overweening dominance of the central state, instituting a system of prefectural and municipal governments. Nevertheless, national legislation always takes precedence over local legislation, and in practice Tokyo bureaucrats often exercise considerable control over the activities of local government. Bingham notes that while the Local Autonomy Act of 1947 makes governors and mayors responsible for a wide range of public services, these elected local officials often have little power over the services they are legally obliged to deliver (Bingham, 1989: 53–4). Detailed policy and budget programmes prepared by local governments have to be approved by Tokyo. Ministers actually have the power to remove elected governors and mayors who fail to comply with their orders. The very title of the Local Autonomy Act calls attention to a core problem in Japanese politics: the degree to which real local autonomy can be said to exist in local government. To a large extent, local administration is dominated by the central Japanese state. At the same time, local governments are continually seeking to carve out greater autonomy from Tokyo, leading to considerable creative tensions in their relations with national level politicians and bureaucrats.

Japan has 47 prefectures; four of these are not prefectures in the regular sense, but three cities (Tokyo, Osaka, and Kyoto) and one region (Hokkaido) which have been given legal status equivalent to prefectures. Each prefecture has a prefectural assembly with an elected membership. Governors, who are elected, are the chief executives of prefectures, and have a wide range of powers. They preside over a considerable number of public programmes, notably: public law and order (including local courts and police, health and welfare (including hospitals, social services and environmental protection), infrastructure (including roads, transport, land development, utilities and parks), and education and culture (including

schools, libraries and art galleries). Because many of these programmes come under the jurisdiction of national ministries, governors are obliged to work closely with the relevant bureaucracies in
all manner of budgetary and regulatory matters. Around 60 per cent
of local government revenues derive from central government funds
of one sort or another (Abe *et al.*, 1994: 66). Many prefectures and
large cities maintain sizeable offices in Tokyo; rather like foreign
embassies, these offices have the task of maintaining close contact
with the relevant national level officials, and monitoring the latest
developments concerning budgetary or policy issues (Steiner, 1965:
321–3).

Municipalities in Japan have various different forms: large cities
(with a population over 500 000), cities, towns, villages, and 23
'special wards' in Tokyo. Mayors are elected; like prefectural
governors, they have strong executive powers and are nominally
accountable to weak assemblies. Nevertheless, the 1960s and 1970s
saw an increasing trend towards more open and effective local
government, as community groups and citizens' movements moved
into the political arena and sought to break the dominance of cosy
old-boy networks which had previously characterized prefectural
and municipal politics.

Positive evaluations of Japanese local government tend to stress
the successes of prefectures and municipalities in initiating policies
and carving out greater autonomy. Local governments have played
a significant role in areas such as welfare and environmental policy.
Negative evaluations of Japanese local government emphasise the
subordination of local politics to national control. Reed cautions
that local autonomy and centralization are value-laden terms; social
scientists should be wary of idealizing the local and deprecating the
central (Reed, 1986: 3–4). He points out that both central and local
government have plural, multiple identities rather than unitary
connotations. Based on a very detailed study of relations between
central and prefectural governments in Japan, Reed concludes that
although the intergovernmental system is not very good in Japan, it
is generally good enough to be reasonably effective. At the same
time, he observes that despite the low quality of most local politics in
Japan:

> Mayoral and gubernatorial elections are a major source of flex-
> ibility and responsiveness in the Japanese political system even
> under these seemingly adverse circumstances. (Reed 1986: 170)

Despite its generally lacklustre performance, local government in Japan does contain the potential to act decisively and to great effect, as was the case when pollution problems threatened Japan's economic miracle in the 1970s.

The Judiciary

The constitution states that the judiciary must be independent, and in theory it could play an important role in shaping the interpretation of legislation, and make decisive interventions over controversial matters. Nevertheless, the Supreme Court has generally played a very low-profile role in Japan. Some important judicial decisions have influenced government policy; for example, decisions by courts in the 1960s that found major companies guilty of causing hazardous pollution helped precipitate new legislation, and the setting up of an environment agency. But Upham argues that following important judgements, the bureaucracy steps in to take control of the situation, refusing to recognize an institutional role for the judiciary in shaping social change (Upham, 1987: 27). The lengthy, drawn-out nature of Japan's legal procedures limits the capacity of the judiciary to act swiftly and effectively. In criminal cases, virtually all those brought to trial are convicted.

The Bureaucracy

Although extremely powerful and prestigious, the Japanese bureaucracy is relatively small and inexpensive. While there were 1 156 290 national government officials in 1997 (Japan Almanac, 1999: 68), this figure includes people such as university lecturers and air traffic controllers. The core of the 'civil service' as commonly understood is Administrative Service I, which includes the managerial and clerical staff of the ministries and most agencies, and numbered 227 725 in 1987 (Koh, 1987: 71). Many Japanese government offices are cramped and rather seedy: the corridors of power are often stacked with cardboard boxes containing old documents. Fast-stream bureaucrats (who are drawn largely from top universities such as Tokyo University and Kyoto University) are traditionally highly-respected; they are seen as an extremely dedicated and competent elite, and as far more trustworthy than the majority of elected politicians. At the same time, these bureaucrats are also regarded as somewhat arrogant, rule-bound, and inflexible.

Japan's central bureaucratic institutions have three main forms: the 12 ministries (listed above, and see Figure 5.1), 13 agencies under the Office of the Prime Minister (the Management and Coordination Agency, Hokkaido Development Agency, Defence Agency, Economic Planning Agency, Science and Technology Agency, Environment Agency, Okinawa Development Agency, National Land Agency, National Public Safety Commission, Fair Trade Commission, Imperial Household Agency, and the Financial Supervisory Agency), and 16 other agencies (such as the National Tax Administration and the National Police Agency) that report either to one of the ministries, or one of the prime ministerial agencies. As McVeigh (1998: 73) notes, the agencies under the prime minister's office are staffed by bureaucrats who are 'on loan' from ministries, a system which tends to consolidate the power of the ministries, and to promote a similar bureaucratic mindset within agencies. Nevertheless, rivalry between different bureaux, ministries and agencies does undermine the efficiency of the Japanese civil service, which is often unduly preoccupied with the fighting of pointless turf battles.

In recent years there have been moves to rationalize the structure of the Japanese bureaucracy, in order to 'slim down' the civil service and eliminate the widespread overlaps between ministerial and agency functions. During 1998, enabling legislation was passed to allow for a reduction in the number of ministries and major agencies from 21 to 11, by 2001. Some analysts are quite sceptical about the likely effectiveness of such changes, which could actually serve the interests of the bureaucrats by consolidating their power in new, vast, and almost impregnable super-ministries. Nevertheless, significant changes now look inevitable.

The Bureaucratic Dominance Debate

A central question is: who holds power in Japan? Where does the power reside? In short – Who runs Japan? In general, most people might assume that power rests in the hands of the government of the day. But in the Japanese case, many scholars have disputed the extent to which politicians are really in effective control of the country.

Figure 5.1   Japanese government organization

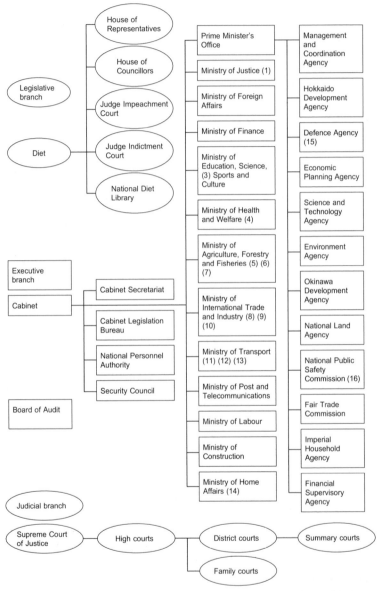

(1) Public Security Investigation Bureau (2) National Tax Administration Agency (3) Cultural Affairs Agency (4) Social Insurance Agency (5) Food Agency (6) Forestry Agency (7) Fisheries Agency (8) Natural Resources and Energy (9) Patent Office (10) Small and Medium-scale Enterprise Agencies (11) Maritime Safety Agency (12) Marine Accidents Inquiry Agency (13) Meteorological Agency (14) Fire Defense Agency (15) Defense Facilities Administration (16) National Police Agency

Source: *Japan Almanac*, reproduced with permission.

According to van Wolferen:

> The Japanese prime minister is not expected to show much leadership; labour unions organise strikes to be held during lunch breaks; the legislature does not in fact legislate; stockholders never demand dividends; consumer interest groups advocate protectionism; laws are enforced only if they don't conflict too much with the interests of the powerful; and the ruling Liberal Democratic Party is, if anything, conservative and authoritarian, is not really a party, and does not in fact rule. (Wolferen, 1989: 25)

He goes on to argue that most outsiders have been deceived by appearances: although Japan has the outward trappings of a liberal democratic state, sovereignty does not rest with the people (whatever the 1947 constitution may say). Power in Japan belongs to a political, bureaucratic and corporate elite, but the precise location of the power is difficult to establish: power is somewhat diffuse in what van Wolferen terms 'the elusive state'.

There is, naturally, an alternative perspective. Albrecht Rothacher has argued that while power is not so clearly focused in Japan as in countries with presidential systems (USA, France), or other countries where the government is commonly formed by a single party (Britain), Japan is quite comparable with countries which have complex coalition arrangements, and where five or six key individuals are the principal power-brokers – countries like Italy, Belgium, the Netherlands, Italy and Israel (1993: xi). Essentially, Rothacher regards leaders of the LDP's various factions as the equivalent of party leaders in other systems.

He views the Japanese power structure as a pyramid (Rothacher, 1993: 2–4), with the LDP's faction leaders at the top, then the LDP's parliamentary party below, along with the senior bureaucrats of the main ministries, and the heads of the *keiretsu* conglomerates. Together they comprise around 350 people. Below them is a third tier which he calls the 'elite at large', comprising around 1 600 people. This includes around 250 who cannot be readily classified in terms of bureaucracy, business or politics – people such as journalists, prominent yakuza, academics and representatives of different interest groups. The fourth tier consists of around 10 000 'elite aspirants', up-and-coming managers from the business sector, provincial politicians, and middle-ranking civil servants.

Rothacher's central argument is that a distinct Japanese power elite does exist and can be identified: power is not so diffuse as van

Wolferen claims. However, Rothacher does not concentrate much on the decision-making process itself: he is concerned with who holds power, rather than who exercises it. Most legislation is drafted, not by politicians, but by bureaucrats. LDP cabinet ministers rotated their jobs on average about once a year; they were rarely in post long enough to stamp their ideas on a particular ministry, even if they were minded to do so. Van Wolferen points out that Cabinet meetings in Japan last only 10–15 minutes, and almost invariably rubber-stamp the decisions already made by the top civil servants in the various ministries (Wolferen, 1989: 32). In other words, even if we accept the composition of Rothacher's pyramid, LDP faction bosses are only nominally at the top. Real power is not wielded by elected politicians accountable to parliament, whatever the external structure may suggest.

At the core of the problem is the simple fact that, although Japan has a multi-party parliamentary system, a single party held the reins of power from 1955 to 1993, and again formed the core of the government from mid-1994. The Liberal Democratic Party was produced by a merger between two conservative parties. Apart from a brief period of socialist rule (1947–8), the Japanese government was in the hands of the conservatives from the time the 1947 constitution was enacted, until 1993. For academics sympathetic to Japan, this political stability tends to be cited as evidence of a smooth-running, relatively conflict-free political order, and to the national genius for cooperation. It is often argued that Japan's phenomenal success in economic reconstruction could never have been achieved without the political continuity provided by the LDP and its forebears.

One problem in approaching this issue is that the education and background of many LDP politicians closely resembles that of many Japanese civil servants. Around 25 per cent of LDP Diet members are ex-bureaucrats, and around half the postwar prime ministers of Japan have come through this route. Senior civil servants commonly receive plum retirement jobs when they leave ministerial service (usually early), either in business, politics, or with other public sector agencies – a process known as *amakudari,* or descent from heaven. Some commentators have suggested that 'ascent to heaven' might be more appropriate as a description, since these superannuated bureaucrats typically receive salaries and benefits well in excess of their former civil service renumeration. Civil servants are hired annually straight from university, and therefore belong to a cohort based on year of graduation. When one of their cohort becomes vice-minister (the highest position within a ministry), the remainder promptly retire to allow him to assume unchallenged seniority within the organization. The new vice-minister is obliged to help his colleagues find re-employment outside the ministry (Johnson, 1995: 149–50).

The upper echelons of the civil service are dominated by graduates of Tokyo and Kyoto Universites, along with a few other elite national and private universities. Senior Japanese bureaucrats invariably had strong personal ties with LDP politicians, with whom they worked closely on the drafting of policies and legislation. Around 60 per cent of these civil servants are law graduates, and a large proportion are graduates of the Tokyo University Law Faculty. These elite bureaucrats, many of whom attended a small group of 'high-level' feeder high schools in Tokyo, constitute a self-reproducing group drawn mainly from the middle class. The LDP has 17 'policy research council divisions' which work closely with one or more ministries in the preparation of legislation. The process by which drafts are developed is a complex one, which is open to contrasting interpretations.

Critics of the system argue that it is characterized by 'bureaucratic dominance'; the civil servants are in effective control of the process. During the American Occupation, it was decided to govern Japan through the existing civil service; in consequence much of the prewar bureaucratic power was retained. The distrust felt by many Japanese people towards their politicians – and the lack of legitimacy enjoyed by those politicians – led them to give more esteem to 'neutral' bureaucrats. Even recently, 80 per cent of all legislation passed was originally drawn up by bureaucrats rather than politicians. Furthermore, legislation gives extensive powers to the bureaucracy to pass official ordinances which are effectively new laws; these ordinances outnumber actual laws by around 9:1. The bureaucracy therefore has quasi-legislative powers in its own right. Chalmers Johnson argues bluntly: 'Who governs is Japan's elite state bureaucracy' (1995: 13; for a full account, see 115–40). Johnson argues that bureaucratic influence is not confined to initiating legislation, but also includes direct meddling in the Diet's deliberative process (Johnson, 1995: 124).

An alternative view, however, is that of party-dominance, the argument that the LDP has the upper hand in the power relationship. This view has gained currency since the late 1970s. It is partly borne out by figures which show that Japanese senior bureaucrats themselves believe – by a narrow margin – that ministers have more power than they do. Overall, however, the general picture is of two groups that are quite finely balanced, rather than a clear-cut superiority of one over the other. Koh notes that according to Chalmers Johnson, the recent period has seen an increase in bureaucratic 'sectionalism' and 'infighting' – the bureaucrats, in other words, have experienced similar problems to those traditionally experienced by the politicians.

Koh offers a third alternative: he regards the LDP and the bureaucrats as two finely-balanced competing forces, with neither able to dominate the other: despite an apparent shift towards the party politicians, there is no overall dominant group. Keehn similarly argues that there is a 'symbiotic relationship' between the two sides: 'for the most part, a powerful bureaucracy has served LDP interests' (1990: 1037). Haley claims that the image of a 'ruling triumvirate' of politicians, bureaucrats and business leaders is a 'false model' which obscures the limited capacity of the Japanese government to control the private sector (Haley 1987: 357). He characterizes the Japanese policy process as one of 'governance by negotiation'.

Van Wolferen has emphasised the key role played by bureaucrats in the Japanese order (Wolferen, 1989: 145). In the end, however, he does not argue for a straightforward 'bureaucratic dominance' interpretation. Van Wolferen takes on board much of Koh's argument, but comes to a far less sober and more disturbing conclusion. He believes that the administrators of what he calls the Japanese 'System' are all themselves its victims. He claims that:

> They are victims of a self-deceit . . . the pretence that they do not exercise power, together with the concomitant denial of any need for universally accepted rules to regulate that power, and hence the problem they have in accepting unambiguous leadership. . . They protect themselves by means of an elaborate rationale denying the forces that actually govern the System and explaining everything as a natural result of Japanese 'culture' . . . Some of them whom I know personally are horrified by the realisation that the System is not, in fact, under control. (Wolferen, 1989: 430)

In other words, what Koh regards as a pretty satisfactory balance of power (which bears comparison with various western democracies) is viewed by van Wolferen as a system out of control.

The Policy Process

A weakness of all the analyses cited above is that they neglect the role of the business sector – especially that of major companies – in Japan's high-level decision-making. Some scholars argue that Japan is actually ruled by an 'iron triangle' of politicians, bureaucrats and businessmen. According to Krauss and Muramatsu (1988: 208–10), Japan operates a system of 'patterned pluralism'. Patterned pluralism has the following features:

- a strong government and bureaucracy;
- blurred boundaries between state and society;
- the integration of social groups into government;
- political parties which mediate between government and interest groups;
- government which has been thoroughly penetrated by mediating organizations such as political parties; and
- interest groups which form alliances with political parties and bureaucratic agencies.

In short, the main feature of governance in Japan is the remarkable degree to which the functions and goals of government, the ruling party, the bureaucracy, and interest groups have been merged together. This was a style of governance that reflected the long tenure of the LDP from 1955 to 1993. Importantly, the Japanese elite is rather homogeneous. Most of its members are graduates of small number of well-known universities, such as Tokyo, Kyoto, Waseda and Keio. Certain faculties of these universities, especially the Tokyo University Law Faculty, have produced a remarkable proportion of the country's leaders. In 1986, for example, there were 22 administrative vice-ministers (the top-ranking civil service post) in Japan: 16 were alumni of the Tokyo University Law Faculty, three had attended other Tokyo University faculties, two were Kyoto University graduates, and only one had attended neither university (Koh, 1989: 141).

How does the process of policy formulation work? Nakano (1997) views the Japanese policy-making process as very complicated; terms such as 'bureaucratic dominance' and 'party dominance' serve to obfuscate what are very elaborate interactions between different players. According to the circumstances of each case, a variety of decision-making processes are employed, reflecting attempts by the various components of the dominant order to accommodate their respective interests. Nakano argues that 'policies cause politics' (1997: 14–16). By this he means that where a policy agenda initiated by bureaucrats will require legislation, this has the effect of activating a range of interest groups from both the government and non-governmental sector. Each stage of the legislative process causes further ripples, as consultation takes place with different government departments. Meetings are held between politicians and parties, and with consultative councils and commissions of inquiry. Proceedings in the Diet begin with a committee stage, and negotiations concerning possible amendments are held with opposition parties. Later, the legislation is approved by the full Diet.

Nakano criticises the assumption that participants in the policy-making process always give priority to the interests of their immediate group (it has been argued that bureaucrats give priority to their own bureau's interests rather than to those of their ministry, and that LDP Diet members put the interests of their *zoku,* or policy tribe of interest group lobbyists, before those of the government as a whole). He found numerous examples where personal ties between different participants from competing interests led to unexpected forms of bargaining and deal-making. The need to agree on a core agenda leads to the creation of various 'by-products', in order to compensate or to appease those who have lost out on the deal. Because of the imperatives of keeping all sides happy, the progress of new legislation is unpredictable, and can produce 'accelerations and leaps, stagnations and reverses that sometimes defy logical explanation' (Nakano, 1997: 16).

Parliamentary legislation does not lie at the heart of all policy-making. Important decisions often involve business leaders in addition to bureaucrats and politicians. Nakano sees two main modes of governance here: elite accommodation politics, in which big business is a key player, and client-oriented politics, where small businesses and other interest groups share in the allocation of benefits (Nakano, 1997: 65).

Elite Accommodation Politics

This form of policy-making brings together the three elements of the so-called 'iron triangle': prominent government politicians, the leaders of the *Keidanren* (Federation of Economic Organizations), and senior officials of the economic ministries and agencies. The

Keidenran principally represented the core industries which bene-fitted from state-led initiatives to rebuild Japan's economy after the war: iron, steel, banking, and electricity. Following the 1960 Secur-ity Treaty riots which gave rise to a political crisis in Japan, industry leaders joined forces with bureaucrats and politicians to present a united front in facing down the leftist challenges to the capitalist order (Nakano, 1997: 90). Just as Prime Minister Ikeda set out to buy off public dissent through the 'income doubling plan', so Japan's big companies backed the strategy of rapid economic growth, which led to strong ties with the ruling political and bureaucratic elites. Corporations accepted increased regulation in exchange for more involvement in policy formation. The strategy of rapid economic growth was effectively an elite pact, formed in the interests of mutual preservation. Thus the present-day form of patterned pluralism emerged over time, as a result of shared political and economic imperatives.

There are multiple connections between the three elements of the triple alliance. Politicians from the LDP influence bureaucrats via their control of appointments, and by recruiting former bureaucrats to become LDP Diet members. Bureaucrats can influence business through their powers of 'administrative guidance', and their author-ity to devise secondary legislation of a regulatory nature. In return, business provides most of the funding on which the LDP's political machine relies. However, the economic downturn of the 1970s helped produce more flexible, less monolithic relationships between the three components. The *Keidenran's* influence declined signifi-cantly, leaving individual industries and companies more freedom to create direct bilateral ties with politicians via campaign contribu-tions and the emergence of *zoku* (see below p. 101). Nakano (1997: 91) argues that the iron triangle has now become much less iron and rather more angular than before, with a less pervasive influence on politics and policy-making.

Client-Oriented Politics

A second form of policy-making identified by Nakano is the system of client-oriented politics, which allows for the maximization of private interests through various political mechanisms. Most of Japan's interest groups have become clients of this system (Nakano, 1997: 93), which effectively offers a non-ideological alternative to the earlier politics of ideological confrontation. Among the leading clients are the farmers' organization Nokyo, the Japan Medical Association, and a range of industrial lobbies. The close relations which these clients enjoyed with the ruling elite led to many policies directly contrary to the public interest, such as the banning of the contraceptive pill to protect doctors' income from abortions, and campaigns by consumer organizations to maintain high food prices by blocking imports (Wolferen 1989: 53). Below the national level was a parallel pattern of interest groups, including provincial public corporations and members of regional assemblies, which formed part of a complex web of vested interests which were the beneficiaries of government-related contracts.

The patterns of governance described by Nakano typically exclude or limit popular participation in the decision-making process. Closed circles of politicians, administrators and interest groups are often the sole parties to important decisions, and there is little reference to considerations of public interest. The LDP has an impressive track-record in converting opposition groups (such as environmental protestors) into loyal supporters, by offering them benefits in exchange for their cooperation. In a similar fashion, Calder (1993: 246) describes the interrelationship of the Japanese industrial sector and the bureaucracy as based upon 'circles of compensation', circles including both the regulators and the regulated. Supported by state-provided benefits, members of these circles offered various kinds of support to the bureaucracy in return. For both newcomers and outsiders, penetrating these charmed circles is difficult. Japanese elite governance is, paradoxically, both inclusionary and exclusionary. While efforts are made to include as many voices as possible in the policy-making process, this strategy has the effect of excluding dissident interest and minority views, as well as downplaying considerations of public interest.

Conclusion

In terms of formal structures, Japan's political order closely resembles those of western liberal democracies. The academic debate is concerned less with the formal order, than with how power is held and exercised in practice. For mainstream scholars, the Diet has become increasingly powerful during the postwar period, and party politicians are in a dominant position *vis-à-vis* bureaucrats. For revisionist scholars, Japan is a 'façade democracy', in which elected politicians are largely the captives of bureaucratic and business interests. For scholars using culturalist approaches, Japan has its own distinctive form of political institutions and processes; these should be understood as indigenous adaptations of western models, which cannot readily be understood using conventional social science categories and criteria.

6

Political Society: Parties and Opposition

Few aspects of contemporary Japan inspire as much controversy as its party political order. For mainstream scholars, Japan is a working liberal democracy similar to those of western Europe or the United States. For revisionists, Japanese electoral politics are a travesty that has little to do with popular representation, and everything to do with structural corruption and special interests. For culturalist scholars, Japan's politics reflect the distinctive nature of the country's history and culture, and attempts to draw comparisons with other nations are therefore often inappropriate.

The Nature of the LDP

The Liberal Democratic Party (LDP) is based upon a factional structure, and, for better or worse, factions (known in Japanese as *habatsu*) played a central role in keeping the LDP in power for 38 years. In recent decades, the LDP has usually had about five factions, each led by a faction boss who provided financial patronage (amounting to the equivalent of millions of pounds) to his parliamentary associates, in exchange for their support during the post-election horse-trading sessions which determined the allocation of ministerial portfolios. Jobs were assigned in the proverbial smoke-filled rooms. As Tomita, Nakamura and Hrebenar explain, the faction system means that 'the abilities of individuals, no matter how capable they may be, have little if any influence over whether they will receive key political positions' (Tomita *et al.*, 1992: 252). This means that faction leaders attain high political office, including the post of prime minister, more or less regardless of aptitude. In 1991, for example, popular premier Toshiki Kaifu was ousted in favour of Kiichi Miyazawa, simply because Miyazawa then led one of the richest and most powerful factions. Faction leaders were in competition with one another for money and power; very often, LDP candidates in multi-member constituencies faced their strongest competition from candidates put up by rival LDP factions, rather than candidates from opposition parties. How are we to analyse and evaluate the faction system? Four broad views may be identified: mainstream, revisionist, culturalist, and political economy.

• The first explanation is one that has been favoured by many mainstream scholars who see Japan as an admirable political system. They regard factions as *de facto* political parties, such as the 'Takeshita LDP', or the 'Abe LDP'. Tomita, Nakamura and Hrebenar declare:

> These parties, by serving as mutually restraining forces and because of their constantly changing alliances, help to advance politics. Through this pluralistic process, it has been argued, the factions contribute significantly to the dynamism of Japanese politics. (Tomita *et al.*, 1992: 270)

Uchida goes even further, arguing that 'the LDP's factions could be more appropriately called "parties", and the opposition parties "quasi-parties"' (quoted in Hayes, 1995: 78).

Arguments of this kind support the view that the Japanese political system does have many democratic characteristics. According to this view, the LDP's factional system does respond to public demands; having rival factions within the LDP raises the level of the policy debate. Factions are sometimes referred to as 'study groups', and often employ specialist advisors who work on particular aspects of public policy. Other commentators also use negative arguments to rationalise the pervasiveness of factions in the LDP. Hayes, for example, wrote that 'voters apparently have not been dissatisfied with this practice, however, since they have not as yet turned against it' (Hayes, 1992: 80). Did failure to vote out the LDP imply tacit approval for the faction system? An alternative and more critical view is that voters voted for the LDP in spite of its factitiousness and other shortcomings; electoral support for the LDP did not give a thumbs up to the faction system.

- A second, more revisionist interpretation of the LDP's factions sees them as the greatest obstacle to the 'modernization' of the LDP, and arguably of the Japanese party system generally. Because so much power is concentrated in the hands of the faction leaders and their financial backers, there is little scope for rank-and-file members to have an input into policy formation; there is no direct equivalent of the local constituency associations and annual conferences which characterize political parties in many European countries. All major decisions are taken by the faction leaders, behind closed doors. Political scientists who derive their notions of the party from western models tend to see the faction system as impeding the emergence of mass-membership, popular parties in modern Japan. The LDP lacks a genuine mass base; although it claimed to have 5.8 million members in 1988, most of these were signed up through the support networks of individual Diet members, and were loyal to a specific individual rather than to the party as a whole. Thus the idea of allowing individual party members to elect the party president would make little sense; party members who have been recruited by individual Diet members would be likely to vote en bloc, rather than according to personal preference.
- A third view sees factions in terms of Japanese culture. Culturalist interpretations stress the extent to which *habatsu* reflect the Japanese emphasis on patron–client relations, 'quasi-familial relationships, Confucian ideas of obligation, and group loyalty' (Woodall, 1996: 105–7). Baerwald claims that criticisms of the faction system reflect a kind of political cutural imperialism, attempts by non-Japanese to privilege their own concepts of the political party (Baerwald, 1986: 16–18), and assumptions that Japan needs to 'catch up' with the West by developing an Anglo-American-style two-party system. Baerwald even expresses personal support for the continuation of the faction system as a source of pluralism. A problem with Baerwald's argument is that pressure to reform the faction system has always come from inside Japan: both the media, and the *zaikai* (business groups which fund the LDP) have long expressed disgust at the workings of party factions (Masumi, 1995: 211–18).
- By contrast, Woodall argues that Japanese culture cannot explain the faction system in the LDP, which he sees as the outcome of substantial incentives for factional affiliation and support by Diet members (Woodall, 1996: 107). In other words, political economy

explanations are crucial. This fourth argument stresses the importance of factions in endorsing prospective LDP candidates, in providing political funds, and allocating political posts. Factional connections could also help create what Woodall calls 'constituency service networks': for example, local developers and construction contractors could be mobilized to support selected candidates by national-level faction bosses (Woodall, 1996: 111–12). The importance of factional politics was especially apparent during elections for party president (since the LDP party president always became prime minister during the 1955–93 period); during some of these elections, 'wads of bills and empty promissory notes for posts were tossed about in particularly large quantities' (Masumi, 1995: 207–8). In distributing ministerial posts, an important principle was the maintenance of a balance of power among factions: spoils had to be equitably shared and allocated.

In addition to the faction system, LDP Diet members are also members of *zoku*, or 'policy tribes'. First formed in the 1970s, these groupings of parliamentarians focus on particular policy areas, such as construction, defence, education, telecommunications, tobacco, and transport. They build up close working relationships with counterparts in industry, the bureaucracy and in research institutions. In theory, the aim of the *zoku* is to allow politicians to gain sufficient specialist knowledge to set the political agenda for a particular policy area (thereby undermining bureaucratic dominance). In practice, there is considerable evidence that *zoku* have often behaved in a self-serving manner, promoting a dangerously close relationship between sectoral interests and elected representatives.

Accounting for LDP Dominance

The pre-eminent position of the LDP during the 1955–93 period partly derived from the Public Offices Elections Law. The multi-member constituency system, used until electoral reform was implemented in 1995, tended broadly to favour the LDP (see Table 6.1) which alone had the financial resources to put up several candidates in a single constituency. This resulted in low levels of electoral competition, since around 80 per cent of seats were regarded as

Table 6.1 House of Representatives election results in seats, 1993–96

	1993		1996 (National)		1996 (Prefectural)	
LDP	223	(36.6)	70	(32.8)	169	(38.3)
SDP(J)	70	(15.4)	11	(6.4)	4	(2.2)
JRP	55	(10.1)				
Komeito	51	(8.1)				
JNP	35	(8)				
JCP	15	(7.7)	24	(13.1)	2	(12.6)
DSP	15	(3.5)				
Sakigake	13	(2.6)	0	(0)	2	(1.3)
NFP			60	(28)	96	(28)
DP	35	(16.1)	35	(16.1)	17	(10.6)
DRP			0	(0)	1	(0.3)
Minor Parties	4	(0.9)	0	(3.6)	0	(2.3)
Independents	30	(6.9)	0	(0)	9	(4.4)
TOTAL	511	(100)	200	(100)	300	(100)

Figures in parentheses indicate the percentage of the vote obtained

Original Source: Ministry of Home Affairs, Japan.
Secondary Source: Norihiko Narita (ed.) (1995), *The Diet, Elections, and Political Parties,* Tokyo, Foreign Press Center, p. 145, supplement (1997), p. 8 (see p. xi for abbreviations)

'safe'; in the 1989 lower house elections, for example, there were only 838 candidates standing for 512 seats – a ratio of 1.64 candidates per seat. In a four or five-member constituency, the main competition was often for the last seat, since the other results were virtually a foregone conclusion. The multi-member system also encouraged the participation of small parties. A party which could come fourth or fifth could win a seat, though it might never have won any single-member constituency in its own right. This had the effect of splitting the opposition; instead of two or three significant opposition parties, Japan usually had five or six. As Hrebenar notes: 'The fragmentation of the opposition into relatively impotent, small organisations has facilitated the LDP's continuance in power' (Hrebenar, 1992: 37).

Another important reason for the LDP's formidable electoral strength was the under-representation of Japan's urban population in the constituencies of the House of Representatives. To a considerable degree, pre-1995 electoral districts were based upon maps drawn up in 1947, when the country's population was still over-whelmingly rural. Over the past 45 years, socioeconomic change has led to large-scale urbanization, but this shift in the centres of population was not reflected by an adequate reallocation of seats to the cities. The result was a problem of malapportionment: the number of voters per Diet member ranged from around 106 000 to 336 000. LDP strength was concentrated in conservative rural areas, where the party assiduously cultivated Japan's small but dispropor-tionately influential farming lobby. As a result, urban voters lost out – they had to pay for the heavy rice production subsidies to Japanese farmers, and for the protectionist policies which limited foreign imports of beef, for example. The smaller opposition parties had little chance of winning seats in rural areas, and were forced into competing with each other in a limited number of urban constitu-encies, instead of challenging the LDP on a more equal footing across the country.

At the same time, some scholars (such as Curtis, 1988: 49–52) have stressed that the rural vote was not a complete explanation for LDP success: by the late 1980s, only about a quarter of LDP voters lived in villages and small towns; 46 per cent lived in cities with a population of more than 100 000. Nevertheless, the rural bias in the electoral boundaries was historically important in building up LDP strength. Despite a number of minor adjustments in the representa-tion of constituencies, the LDP was able to stall on implementing substantial reforms for more than three decades. One LDP tactic was to argue that it would be best to dispense with the multi-member constituencies altogether, replacing them with single mem-ber constituencies. Opposition parties consistently opposed this reform, on the grounds that it would lead to the demise of the smaller opposition parties and hence the increased dominance of the LDP.

Why did the LDP win votes in such large numbers? In western countries, political scientists tend to analyse voters in terms of their economic and social status. Some writers have argued that Japanese party politics are not strongly connected to sociocultural divisions in society. Whilst it is true that there is no direct equivalent of, say, the Jewish or Hispanic vote in the United States, a major study of the Japanese voter by Scott Flanagan *et al.* has argued that 'value cleavages' and 'social networks' play a vital part in determining voter choice. Flanagan found that voters with what he calls 'modern values' are much more likely to vote for opposition parties than those with 'traditional values'. Since modern values tend to be associated with young people, it follows that the LDP draws a disproportionate amount of support from older sections of the population. Perhaps more importantly, many Japanese voters use their votes to support a candidate with whom they have some direct or indirect personal connection: a business contact, a former class-mate, or more commonly someone who is felt likely to be able to bring specific benefits to their local community or to an organisation with which they are involved. As Flanagan notes:

> Community bloc voting, which is often based on the exchange of community votes for government funding of local projects and the rounding up of personally obligated votes, favors the ruling party and helps explain its uninterrupted majority control of the Diet for over thirty years. (Flanagan, 1991: 196–7)

Clearly, social networks which allow candidates to acquire votes en bloc rather than through individual choice operate far more effec-tively in rural areas than in, say, Tokyo, Osaka, or Nagoya. The LDP can easily do well in the countryside, but faces difficulty in large cities, which have a more complex social structure. Theoreti-cally, gradual changes in the values held by the Japanese, coupled with changes in the make-up of society, ought eventually to lead to a decline in the fortunes of the LDP. However, the party showed itself to be remarkably resilient in weathering changes in wider society until 1993.

Business and Political Funding

The High Cost of Electoral Politics

How does the LDP operate? Money is the lubricant which oils the Japanese political machine, and every LDP Diet member needs money by the suitcase-full, in order to preserve his or her (usually his) standing and ensure re-election. Members need to have at least a couple of staffed offices in their constituency, at which their *koenkai* or support groups are based. Since for the majority of LDP MPs from 1955–93 the main political rival was a fellow member of the same party who was another MP in the same constituency, facilities of this kind were not shared with his colleagues. LDP Diet members operate first and foremost as individuals, then as members of a particular faction (*habatsu*), and only thirdly as members of the party as a whole.

Younger Diet members joined factions (*habatsu*) within the LDP; factions were led by prominent politicians who were able to attract more funding, which they then disseminated to their protégés and supporters. For a young Diet member deciding whether to join a faction, there were sticks as well as carrots. As one of Kakuei Tanaka's lieutenants, Ichiro Ozawa, is said to have told prospective new faction members: 'If you join the Tanaka faction, you will receive funding and organizational backup. If you don't join, our faction will back a strong opponent in the district' (Schlesinger, 1997: 182). An important duty of LDP MPs is to attend social events such as weddings and funerals, which invariably means giving a financial donation (typically ¥10 000 for funerals, and ¥20 000 for weddings). One group of junior LDP Diet members published details of their finances, showing that in 1987 they spent an average of ¥116 million, and received an income of ¥126 million. Their formal salaries and allowances amounted to 15 per cent of this sum, while political donations (mainly from constituency *koenkai*) amounted to 43 per cent, fund-raising parties 16 per cent, and 8 per cent from party HQ and faction bosses (Rothacher 1993: 55). They employed an average of 3.7 secretaries at the Diet, and another 12.5 in their constituencies.

These figures show that direct financial support from factions to junior Diet members was actually declining by the 1980s, in response to public criticism of money politics (Woodall, 1996: 109). However, it is important to distinguish between funds channelled directly through faction leaders, and funds channelled through local sources, partly at the instigation of national faction bosses: a good faction boss could pull numerous strings to help mobilize local support for a candidate, creating what Woodall calls 'constituency service networks'. More senior Diet members could receive direct donations from large corporations, greatly increasing their incomes – as well as numerous other fringe benefits such as company-supplied cars, and offices at nominal rents. The decentralization of campaign funding by the bubble period of the 1980s meant that prominent politicians had greater scope than before to enrich themselves.

Although on paper political contributions by Japanese companies are subject to stringent legal restrictions, in practice these rules can easily be circumvented. For example, a politician can sell 'tickets' to a fund-raising event at an exorbitant price; and companies frequently buy up blocs of these tickets using their 'entertainment' budgets. The annual budget of the LDP was estimated at ¥10 billion in the mid-1980s – more in election years. Although some authors argue that there is nothing inherently corrupt about these practices, others disagree. There is little doubt that most Japanese politicians are wealthy individuals, often having few obvious sources of substantial legitimate income. Rothacher gives a number of examples of fund-raising tactics used by LDP politicians, tactics which could easily lead them into illegal activities: sale of 'party tickets' (which raised ¥9.5 billion in 1987); stock speculation, especially in so-called 'political stocks' (where the politician has a stake in or close links with the company); land speculation; rewards for services rendered; goodwill contributions; and silent partnerships in business (Rothacher, 1993: 54–60)

In response to concerns about political fundraising, legislation passed in 1994 introduced a system of subsidies for political parties, which was intended to obviate the need for improper relationships between politicians and business. The subsidies involved are extremely generous, but there are serious concerns about how these funds are used, especially since corporate donations were not outlawed when the subsidy system was established (Foreign Press Center, 1995: 86–8).

Allegations of corruption at the heart of the Japanese system represent one of the most serious indictments of the LDP and its factions. Some scholars have argued that the LDP's factionalism is directly responsible for the political corruption that plagued Japan in the 1970s, 1980s, and 1990s. According to this analysis, the different factions are not just raising money to compete in elections with other parties: they need funds to compete with one another for power and influence. In the past 20 years, there have been three outstanding examples of corruption at the highest levels of Japan's government: the Lockheed scandal which engulfed premier Kakuei Tanaka in 1976; the Recruit Cosmos scandal which brought down Prime Minister Noboru Takeshita in 1989; and the Sagawa Kyubin scandal, which contributed to the end of LDP dominance in 1993. Each successive decade saw a major scandal, with the political fallout progressively increasing. An examination of these scandals does much to reveal the dark side of the Liberal Democratic Party and its factional system.

Nicknamed the 'computerized bulldozer' on account of his formidable grasp of detail and ruthless determination to have his own

---

Box 6.1   Kakuei Tanaka (1918–93)

Tanaka was a colourful character, a self-made politician who never finished secondary school. Briefly jailed in the late 1940s, he rose rapidly through the ranks of the LDP, becoming a Cabinet minister at age 39. Tanaka channelled large amounts of public money to his home prefecture of Niigata, enriching himself in the process. By 1983 (the height of his powers) his local support organization 'Etsuzankai', boasted 98 000 members in Niigata, including 26 mayors and 13 prefectural assemblymen. At the national level, he had a vast network of connections. Tanaka became prime minister in 1972, but resigned over corruption allegations in 1974. In 1976 he was arrested and subsequently tried on bribery charges involving Lockheed; he was convicted on several counts in 1983, but remained an important political kingmaker almost until his death.

---

way, Kakuei Tanaka (Box 6.1) never deferred to the views of his bureaucrats. The good of the country, however, was far from his sole concern: Tanaka diverted vast sums of public money to his own prefecture of Niigata, all the while enriching himself through a network of companies which specialized in buying up large areas of land in areas designated for development by the government. In 1983, his faction comprised 66 lower house members, and 53 in the upper house. Chalmers Johnson credits Tanaka with the main responsibility for institutionalizing money politics in the postwar Japanese political system.

Tanaka became a victim of his own success in 1974, when a magazine published articles exposing his corrupt practices and he was obliged to resign, supposedly on grounds of ill-health. The worst, however, was yet to come – in 1976, evidence emerged that the American aircraft manufacturer Lockheed had paid Tanaka (and a number of other prominent LDP figures) substantial bribes to award the company a contract to supply All Nippon Airways with a number of Tri-star planes (see chart in Hunziker and Kammura, 1996: 135). Tanaka was subsequently tried for corruption and in 1983 he was found guilty on a number of charges. However, Tanaka's influence did not end when he was ousted as prime minister, or convicted of corruption: he remained a political kingmaker almost until the end of his life (Schlesinger, 1997: 93–5). Far from destroying him, the Lockheed scandal helped to make Tanaka what he was. Tanaka always claimed that what he had done was nothing out of the ordinary; to use Johnson's phrase, his deeds simply reflected the 'structural corruption' in the Japanese political system. According to Johnson, the public long tolerated abuse of power by politicians, so long as the bureaucrats remained uncorrupted:

> People like Tanaka actually performed a vital function for the system, redistributing income from the rich sectors to the poor ones and ensuring that high-speed growth did not benefit one group to the exclusion of others. (Johnson, 1986: 20)

For Johnson, Tanaka performed a valuable function in extending the power of elected politicians at the expense of the entrenched influence of the bureaucrats – indeed, in this sense Tanaka is said by Johnson to have begun the process of democratizing the Japanese order. Although Johnson does say that Tanaka went too far, his article betrays a considerable admiration for the former premier's achievements as a local boy made good.

MacDougall is less positive, arguing that although some of Tanaka's achievements may have been impressive, his belief in his own innocence testifies to a fundamental gap between Japanese politicians and the voting public (MacDougall, 1988: 224). In other words, public cynicism about politicians led to a breakdown of real contact between the two, leaving the politicians in a moral and intellectual vacuum. Constant exposure to the seedy machinations of LDP factional politics behind the proverbial *kuromaku* (black curtain – a theatrical term) had created an alternative reality in the minds of Tanaka and his associates. When he published a revised version of his earlier article on Tanaka in 1995, Johnson argued that despite the importance of Tanaka's role in challenging bureaucratic dominance, the *zoku* system he developed was corrupted by companies, and in turn corrupted the bureaucracy itself:

> The result was a system so corrupt that it seemed beyond reform, and that disillusioned many citizens with the promise of parliamentary democracy itself. Whatever else Tanaka may have achieved, he did not make Japanese politics accountable to the people. (Johnson, 1995: 211)

Tanaka's fall from grace was followed by promises of reform by the LDP, and factions were technically abolished, for example. But the failure of these measures was vividly illustrated 13 years later when another major scandal brought about the downfall of a

Japanese premier. The Recruit-Cosmos scandal differed from the Lockheed scandal in that the company involved was not a foreign concern, but a Japanese one (see Rothacher, 1993: 108–18, Taro, 1990). The company distributed free shares to a large number of prominent politicians, mainly from the LDP, but also from opposition parties. Politicians later sold the shares, making large sums of money. Five LDP cabinet ministers, including Prime Minister Takeshita, were obliged to resign when the public learned of this high level 'insider trading'. Takeshita at first admitted to having received shares and contributions worth $1.6 million; later on, he 'remembered' another $400 000's worth. In total, the company had made donations of $10 million to various politicians.

Although the scandal had an immediate impact on the 1989 upper-house elections, where the LDP lost its majority, the LDP's encouraging results in the February 1990 elections for the House of Representatives suggested that the gap between structural corruption and scandalous behaviour was not always clearly reflected in electoral outcomes. Once so-called 'independents' had joined the LDP, the party held 285 seats, as opposed to 295 prior to the election. The LDP's share of the popular vote declined from 49.4 per cent (1986) to 46.1 per cent, which was slightly above that of 1983. Although scholars sympathetic towards Japan protest that what westerners would term corruption is considered acceptable behaviour in Japan, this explanation needs to be regarded with some caution. The argument that the benefits of longstanding rule by the LDP greatly outweigh any drawbacks became increasingly difficult to sustain after the Recruit-Cosmos scandal. The LDP survived the immediate scandal, but had sustained serious wounds which led eventually to the collapse of the government. When the party was hit by the Sagawa Kyubin scandal in 1992 (the first arrests took place in February), it was ill-equipped to recover. Perhaps the forces of democratization which Tanaka had helped along finally rebounded on the very same 'money politics' with which they were earlier associated: the public was finally beginning to question Japan's elite-dominated political order.

The Politics of Construction

As Schlesinger argues, a book published by Tanaka in 1972 entitled *Building a new Japan* 'was at heart a contractor's fantasy' (1997:

144). With an estimated 6 million employees, the construction business became a powerful force in the land; connections between politicians, construction companies and Ministry of Construction bureaucrats are so pervasive that McCormack calls Japan 'the construction state'. Tanaka built his political machine out of the construction business, and the triumvirate of Takeshita, Ozawa and Kanemaru which inherited Tanaka's political mantle in the late 1980s was similarly up to its knees in wet concrete. Their dominance of the Japanese political order coincided with the 'bubble' years of Japan's economic boom, a boom based largely on public works and private building sprees, a veritable explosion of rampant construction (Schlesinger, 1997: 216–21). Among the most high-profile projects were a staggeringly expensive highway across Tokyo Bay, and the new Kansai International Airport, built on a vast man-made island.

According to Schlesinger (1997: 221), Kanemaru, the principle political 'fixer' during this period was estimated to have received as much as a billion yen annually in kickbacks from construction companies, and other leading politicians were alleged to have received sizeable amounts. Woodall demonstrates the importance of the LDP's contruction *zoku*, or 'policy tribes' in systematically colluding with the distortion of public policy for sectional interests (Woodall, 1996: 112–22). His study is a detailed indictment of the *zoku* system, illustrating the extent to which LDP Diet members serving as construction 'tribesmen' became stooges of the very industry they were supposed to monitor and regulate. Woodall relates that Kanemaru himself came to a sticky end when investigations into the Sagawa Kyubin parcel delivery firm revealed more than $50 million (much of it in cash and gold bullion) in Kanemaru's office mostly received as gifts and bribes from construction companies and the *yakuza* (Woodall, 1996: 12–13). Kanemaru was forced to resign from his post as LDP vice-president in August 1992, and was later indicted on charges of tax evasion. The Sagawa Kyubin case had greater ramifications for the LDP than either the Tanaka or Recruit-Cosmos scandals, since the fall of Kanemaru was a crucial factor in the defection of self-styled reformists Ozawa and Hata from the LDP.

Nevertheless, Woodall's study shows that the politics of construction is not as simple as the classic example of Tanaka would suggest: he identifies an 'enigma of Japanese pork'. Although exceptionally powerful figures such as Tanaka and Kanemaru did succeed in diverting a disproportionate amount of public works funding to their own constituencies, Woodall argues that in general 'construction tribalists' (politicians with a special interest in construction issues; to put it less politely, the parliamentary stooges of the construction industry) channel funding to the firms which pay them substantial contributions, irrespective of the location of the project itself (Woodall, 1996: 117–19). It could therefore be argued that Japanese politicians are not so much guilty of distorting the national budget for their own local interests, as distorting the national budget for particularist, sectional interests: the behaviour of the construction tribalists is not simply a questionable but somewhat defensible support of constituency interests, but rather a matter of out-and-out corruption.

Opposition Parties: Fragmentation and the Quest for Credibility

It is tempting to look upon Japanese party politics under the 1955 system as essentially stagnant, lacking a real adversarial dimension. But to do so would be to oversimplify grossly. During the LDP period, 1955–93, Japan had a one-party dominant political system (Figure 6.1); yet the dominance of the LDP did not always derive from an overwhelming electoral mandate. Indeed, the LDP last won over 50 per cent of the vote in lower-house elections in 1963, though it came very close on several later occasions. In the 1990 lower-house election, the LDP won 46.1 per cent of the votes, and 53.7 per cent of the seats, or 275 out of the 512. Yet the LDP was then joined by 11 of the 21 independents, which meant that the party did command just over 50 per cent of the vote, as well as a majority of the seats. Despite these reservations, however, it must be recognized that over 50 per cent of Japanese voters were voting for non-LDP parliamentary candidates in lower-house elections from 1967 onwards. There was far more support for opposition parties than has often been realized, and the reasons for that support need to be examined, as well as the reasons why opponents of the LDP failed to oust them long before 1993.

Under the 1955 system, there were four main opposition parties in Japan: the Japan Socialist Party (SDPJ) (which later changed its name to the Social Democratic Party of Japan, hence the abbreviation), the Clean Government Party (Komeito), the Japan Communist Party (JCP), and the Democratic Socialist Party (DSP). The

Figure 6.1   House of Representatives election results for LDP and SDPJ, 1958–93

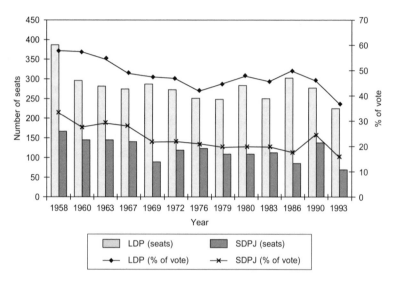

Source: *Japan Almanac*, reproduced with permission.

most important was the Japan Socialist Party, which was by far the largest opposition party. Dating back to 1945, it took part in the socialist-led coalitions that ruled Japan from June 1947 to October 1948. In much of the literature on Japanese politics it is noticeable that opposition parties in general, and perhaps the SDPJ in particular, are given rather short shrift. In large measure this is a function of the fact that American Japan specialists tend to display an overt lack of sympathy for left-wing parties; there is a pronounced failure to grasp what they are all about. A common criticism of the SDPJ was that it lacked ideological coherence, containing shades of opinion ranging from unreconstructed Marxists to pragmatic social democrats. However, this observation could be made about socialist parties in numerous other countries, many of them far more successful in electoral terms than the SDPJ.

In some respects, the SDPJ was just as factionalized as the LDP. And whereas the need to retain power imposed a degree of discipline upon LDP factions, the fact that real political power consistently eluded the SDPJ allowed the party to evade confronting the shortcomings of its factional system. As Stockwin put it, SDPJ factions 'resemble the factions in the LDP, except that their contests are sideshows whereas those in the LDP occupy center-stage' (Stockwin, 1992: 102). However, SDPJ factions tended to be based to a far greater extent on ideological issues, rather than mere patron-client networks. Stockwin identified around 10 different factions in the SDPJ in the late 1980s and 1990 (not bad for 136 MPs), classifying them broadly into left-wing, right-wing, and centrist categories. Nevertheless, he noted that these factions were more 'amorphous' and 'shadowy' than LDP factions; different Diet members gave him different lists of members. Nevertheless, it could be argued that the SDPJ was more similar in structure to the LDP than to other opposition parties such as the JCP and Komeito. Quite apart from the factions, there were parallels between the close relationship the LDP enjoys with the bureaucracy and public sector, and the relationship between the SDPJ and the public sector unions.

The SDPJ faced a troubled history following the advent of rule by conservative parties in 1948. The party suffered splits in 1951 and again in 1960, when moderate and radical wings parted company; on both occasions, a key issue was the party's attitude towards the Mutual Security Pact with the United States. The more radical elements within the SDPJ always opposed the pact; 1960 saw massive street demonstrations in protest at its renewal. The DSP was born around this time, when moderates set up a party of their own. Despite its moderate policies, the DSP achieved little electoral success, and undermined the strength of the much larger SDPJ. Ironically, despite accusations of extremism often levelled at the SDPJ, public opinion has often been closer to SDPJ policies on defence issues than to policies of the ruling LDP.

All too often, however, the SDPJ was associated with dated symbolic causes, whilst the main political agenda was determined almost entirely by the LDP. By the 1970s this situation had changed significantly at local level, where many cities and urban prefectures were run by SDPJ mayors, who introduced innovative and popular new social programmes. But the 1973 'oil shock' led to a tightening of municipal budgets, and the LDP began working hard to regain the political initiative, which often included stealing the SDPJ's best ideas and offering to accommodate the opposition. By the 1980s, many former SDPJ-run local authorities had fallen to the LDP; and, as in Britain and the United States, much of the decade was characterized by a climate of conservatism. This shift in popular opinion forced the SDPJ to engage in a process of self-criticism.

Box 6.2   Takako Doi (born 1928)

Japan's most prominent woman politician, Doi was leader of the Japan Socialist Party from 1986 to 1991. She presided over a period of party reform and modernization, supporting a more open style of politics that had a strong appeal to women voters. Doi raised the JSP to new heights of electoral success in 1989 – only to see these gains slip away by the end of her leadership. In 1993, she became speaker of the Diet.

In 1986, the SDPJ completed a thorough-going policy review, replacing references to 'Marxism Leninism' with the phrase 'scientific socialism', and talking of 'workers' power' instead of 'the dictatorship of the proletariat'. After the election of Takako Doi (the first woman leader of a Japanese party – see Box 6.2) to head the SDPJ that same year, the party saw a revival in its political fortunes, a revival which culminated in a spectacular performance in the 1989 upper house elections (Stockwin, 1992). In these elections, Doi was very successful in capitalizing upon public dissatisfaction at the misbehaviour of LDP politicians during the Recruit scandal, and in the subsequent sexual scandal surrounding the short-lived Prime Minister Sosuke Uno (the scandal was not that Uno had a mistress, but that he was paying her well below the going rate). The SDPJ achieved more than 30 per cent of the vote, and the LDP was reduced to a minority position in the upper house for the first time. This impressive performance was not, however, repeated in the lower house elections of 1990, and in 1991 Doi resigned the leadership of the SDPJ. Whilst Stockwin argued that the 1990s saw the SDPJ in resurgence after long decline, this view rested upon an overly optimistic reading of the 1989 and 1990 election results. The party's performance in the 1992 upper-house elections was distinctly disappointing, marking the beginning of a terminal decline for the SDPJ. When the end of LDP rule finally came in 1993, the SDPJ was the largest party in the seven-party coalition that formed the new government. But the party was also a major loser in that election, gaining a mere 70 lower-house seats – just over half of the 136 it won in 1990.

The plot thickened in July 1994, when the demise of two successive anti-LDP coalitions led to a bizarre and once unthinkable coalition between the Socialists and the LDP, with SDPJ leader Tomiichi Murayama as prime minister. The 1955 system had now truly collapsed: instead of an ideological stand-off between the two main parties, Japan was ruled by an alliance of the old adversaries. Murayama proceeded to tear up all the principal policy axioms of the SDPJ, including the party's longstanding opposition to the existence of the Self-Defense Forces. In January 1996, Murayama handed over the premiership to LDP president Ryutaro Hashimoto, but the two parties remained in a formal alliance until mid-1998. Lower-house elections in October 1996 saw the party reduced to only 15 seats, and the downward trend continued in the July 1998 upper-house elections.

In retrospect, the alliance between the LDP and the Socialists poses questions about the real nature of the 1955 system. Fukatsu (who claims to have coined the term '1955 system' in 1976) argues that the LDP–Socialist alliance was actually 'the emergence of the system's ultimate form' (Fukatsu, 1995: 168–9). For many years, the public rivalry between the two parties had been a sham; behind the scenes they had made private deals which brought monetary benefits to the opposition. Stockwin similarly argues that the coalition 'may not be quite the unnatural hybrid that many portray it as', since the parliamentary SDPJ was already quite conservative on most policy matters, and inter-party competition had long been 'perfunctory' (Stockwin, 1996: 270–4). Outside ritual disagreements on defence issues, there was little divergence of views between the parties, and considerable sharing of the benefits of Japan's economic success.

Smaller Parties

The Japan Communist Party has offered a longstanding alternative to the mainstream parties. Although it has never joined any government coalition, the JCP has more active members, more 'front' activities, a bigger budget and more publication subscribers than any other party (its newspaper claimed about 3 million subscribers during the 1980s). What it lacks in political power it attempts to make up in terms of organization, showing the way forward for more professional parties to emerge in Japan. Nevertheless, personal ties still play a part in securing votes even for the purist JCP. As the Socialists have abandoned many long-held ideological positions and Japanese political parties have become increasingly interchangeable and indistinguishable in the eyes of the electorate, the Communist Party has gained credibility through its continuing adherence to a

well-established identity, and improved its performance in the 1996
lower-house elections – from 15 seats to 26 seats – on the basis of
around 13 per cent of the popular vote. Nevertheless, increased JCP
support appears more to reflect voter dissatisfaction with other
parties than a genuine surge of support for Marxist–Leninist
ideology in late twentieth-century Japan. Following the 1998
upper-house elections, the Japan Communist Party became the
third-largest party in the House of Councillors.

In 1967, the SDPJ began to face competition in the lower house
from another new party seeking the middle ground in Japanese
politics, Komeito, or the 'clean government' party. Closely aligned
with a Buddhist sect called Soka Gakkai, renowned for its prosely-
tizing zeal, Komeito set up a highly-organized network of neighbourhood advice centres in the cities, and set to work building up a
grassroots base of support by responding to the needs of urban
dwellers whose problems and concerns had not been taken seriously
by either the money-bound LDP, or the ideologically dogmatic
Socialists. Komeito and Soka Gakkai underwent a formal separa-
tion in 1970, but this was merely a cosmetic change: 'it is no secret
that nearly all support for the party still comes from the religious
parent' (Davis, 1991: 801). Komeito's attempts to create a solid base
of support at constituency level suffered from the classic weakness of
political strategies adopted by centre parties: local support was not
translated into substantial numbers of seats at a national level,
because the party was based upon constituency activism rather than
a broad appeal. Komeito had the effect of further dividing the
opposition.

Like the DSP, Komeito did succeed in attracting many voters
from less-affluent sections of the work force, particularly those from
small and medium-sized firms who were not incorporated into the
big unions which formed part of the national labour organization.
But a weakness of these parties by the late 1980s was that they were
widely perceived as having made accommodations with the LDP, to
the extent that they held policies which were virtually indistinguishable from those of the ruling party. Members of both parties were
implicated in the Recruit-Cosmos scandal. Both the DSP and
Komeito were clearly hoping to form a coalition with the LDP at
some point in the future: ironically, in 1993 they ended up in
coalition, not with the LDP, but with the SDPJ. Komeito developed
a close alliance with the New Frontier Party and its leader, Ichiro
Ozawa, an alliance which did little to enhance the standing of either

party (see Johnson, 1995: 225). Ultimately, Komeito could not really transcend its solid but narrow Soka Gakkai support base, a base which made the party mistrusted by potential allies and prospective voters alike. The party's original aim of securing a majority in the Diet (Helton, 1966: 231) remained a pipe-dream, more than 30 years after Komeito's foundation.

The Labour Movement

Despite the weakness of most Japanese unions, there is a close relationship between union membership and voting preference. In fact, union membership is a more useful variable than the white collar/blue collar distinction: union members are far more likely to support left-wing parties than their non-unionized counterparts (Watanuki, 1991: 70). The Americans built up the power of unions during the Occupation period in order to create a wider range of political forces in the country, though later they outlawed a pro-posed general strike, and banned public servants from striking. There were numerous serious labour disputes in post war Japan: Toyota was almost brought to its knees at one point in the 1950s, and Japan National Railways was infamous for its regular and crippling strikes. But like the opposition parties, trade unions in Japan have a history of division and failure to mount an effective challenge to the dominant conservative order. About 24 per cent of workers were unionized in 1995 (Japan Institute of Labour, 1997: 48), a decline from 35 per cent in 1970, and 31 per cent in 1980. Whereas previously different union federations were affiliated with different parties (the DSP with Domei, which was dominated by private-sector unions, and the SDPJ with Sohyo, dominated by public-sector unions), in 1989 the majority of unions joined a single national federation called Shin Rengo, which had 7.7 million members in 1995. The creation of this federation weakened the traditional support base of the SDPJ, which had already been undermined by the privatization of public sector enterprises which had traditionally formed the backbone of Sohyo.

About 94 per cent of labour organizations are so-called 'enterprise unions', which are specific to a particular company, rather than representing occupational categories across a range of employers. This tends to lead to a cosy relationship between union leaders and company management, producing smooth labour relations characterized by such phenomena as strikes held during lunch hours. These unions have been widely praised by economists and management consultant types, who have seen them as one of the secrets of Japan's postwar success; they are held to have encouraged innovation and reform and to have helped Japanese workers achieve high wage levels. They are also sometimes seen as promoting a greater say for workers concerning their jobs and conditions. Critical analyses view most of these unions as mere fronts for employer interests.

Much more radical than the enterprise unions were public sector unions such as that of the old Japan National Railways (until privatization in 1987), and the Japan Teachers' Union. These unions had well-established records of opposing the LDP, but their particular grievances made their tradition of support for the SDPJ a mixed blessing: the close association between the Socialists and public-sector unions limited the popular appeal of the SDPJ. But unions provided SDPJ candidates with considerable support at election times, and have also provided financial support to the party. In addition, many SDPJ Diet members (at times up to half) have been ex-union officials. With the decline of many progressive public-sector unions, as a result of falling membership and the privatizations of the 1980s, one of the main sources of traditional support for left-wing parties was eroded; this decline was one factor in the electoral weakening of the SDPJ during the early 1990s.

The End of LDP Rule in 1993

The LDP, continuously in office for 38 years since 1955, was ousted from power in the general election of July 1993. Had the old order collapsed, or had it metamorphosed itself into some new form? To understand the end of LDP dominance in 1993 requires looking further back, first to the series of scandals which dogged the LDP through the late 1980s and early 1990s, and then to May 1992. In that month Morihoro Hosokawa, a former LDP MP and prefectural governor from a distinguished aristocratic family, established the Japan New Party, which had a rather vague platform of political reform. Hosokawa explicitly set out to bring about a realignment in the existing political order, breaking the LDP's long stranglehold on power. When Prime Minister Kiichi Miyazawa lost a crucial no-confidence vote moved by members of his own party on 18 June

1993, more than 50 MPs deserted the LDP. Two new parties were formed by the deserters, parties emerging out of political groupings which had been some months in the making: the Japan Renewal Party, and the New Harbinger Party. The Japan Renewal Party (which began with 36 MPs) was the more important of these, since its two key figures Tsutomo Hata and Ichiro Ozawa (Box 6.3) had been prominent leaders of the LDP's younger generation, forming their own faction the previous year. The New Harbinger Party consisted of younger LDP MPs of only 1–2 terms standing. Like the JNP, these parties trumpeted support for reform, and claimed to favour cleaning up politics, ridding it of its systemic corruption.

A general election was called on 18 July 1993, and the three new parties together won over 100 seats in the 512-seat lower house. Although the LDP remained by far the largest party with over 220 seats, the new parties were able to block the formation of an LDP minority government by joining forces with four of the old opposition parties (including the Socialists and Komeito), creating a seven-party coalition. A number of features of the new political order were striking. The first is that the LDP was very little weakened by the election results themselves. The party had been weakened primarily by the defections to new conservative parties, rather than by the actual outcome of the election. Since LDP Diet members had their

---

Box 6.3 Ichiro Ozawa (born 1942)

Ozawa is from Iwate prefecture; his father was an LDP politician and minister. He attended Keio University and studied unsuccessfully for the bar before inheriting his father's Diet seat in 1969. Long a key member of the Tanaka faction, Ozawa became secretary-general of the LDP in 1989. In 1993 he broke away from the LDP, forming the Japan Renewal Party, and so precipitated the end of 38 years of LDP rule. He was the key figure behind the Hosokawa and Hata administrations, and for a while the darling of the American media. In his bestselling 1993 book *Blueprint for a New Japan,* he advocated a more assertive international role for Japan. But Ozawa's unpopularity and his controversial reputation contributed to the collapse of the anti-LDP coalition in 1994. The JRP subsequently merged into the New Frontier Party, which was then renamed the Liberal Party. Ozawa became leader of the Liberal Party, and a prominent opposition politician. However, at the end of 1998 Ozawa agreed to form a coalition with the LDP.

own private *koenkai,* or constituency organizations, the defectors were able to take the great bulk of their support with them when they joined new parties. The old Japan Socialist Party, by contrast, lost heavily in the elections, dropping from 134 seats to 70. It seemed that many voters who wished to express their dissatisfaction with the LDP were very happy to do by switching their allegiance to new conservative parties. In some ways, the fact that these new parties contained many seasoned ex-LDP politicians actually made it easier for voters to shift their support, secure in the knowledge that they were choosing people with extensive experience in government who could continue to run the country in the time-honoured postwar fashion.

Ironically, the SDPJ was making overtures towards the Japan Renewal Party from early on, whereas even after the results were announced Hosokawa was claiming that his party would not do a deal with the JRP, since the JRP was still too close to the LDP to be ready to instigate real reform. Nevertheless, it could well be argued that the biggest loser of the 1993 elections was the SDPJ, rather than the LDP.

Masumi (writing originally in 1985) argued that despite its short-comings, the LDP faction system survived simply because: 'A split would mean the collapse of LDP governance and the loss of the means to secure posts and nurture support bases' (Masumi, 1995: 208). This is precisely what happened in 1993. Why, then, were the electoral prospects of the LDP sabotaged by key figures within the party who decided to break away? Although dissatisfaction over the corruption issue was one aspect of the conflict, the disagreements went deeper. Hata and Ozawa were particularly unhappy about the pattern of bureaucratic dominance that had been established in the Japanese political order, in which much of the real decision-making was in the hands of civil servants rather than politicians. They recognized that some individual premiers had been successful in increasing the power of politicians at the expense of bureaucrats – Tanaka, and to a lesser extent Nakasone but felt that on the whole this did not amount to a lasting shift in the balance of power. They were frustrated by the inertia and inflexibility of senior LDP politicians such as Takeshita and Miyazawa, and felt that it was time to go on the offensive against bureaucratic power. Hosokawa, who became prime minister in the new coalition government shared this view.

A further feature of the new generation of conservative politicians which emerged in the 1993 election was their desire for Japan to assume a more prominent political role in the international. community, and be more outspoken in its foreign policy objectives. In other words, whilst the new parties might have seemed less conservative than the LDP in their desire to weed out corruption, the realignment was actually part of a neo-conservative project to revitalize and reinvigorate a Japan that would then be able to play a more assertive global role, placing Japan and the USA on much more equal terms than had previously been the case.

The International Dimension

One reading of the transition from LDP to coalition rule emphasises the importance of international factors. The old-style *modus operandi* of the LDP worked well when the Cold War was in full freeze and the Japan could get away with sheltering under the US security umbrella, all the while professing an omnidirectional foreign policy. But the new world disorder demanded, in that phrase beloved of modern military strategists, a capacity for 'flexible response' which the dinosaur LDP and their friends in the ministries simply did not possess. This accounts partly for the coup d'etat staged by the party's Young Turks. Ozawa often stated that one of the main reasons for his disillusionment with the old order was his dismay at the LDP's inept handling of the crisis resulting from Iraq's 1990 invasion of Kuwait. However, Kohno argues that such an interpretation is 'merely impressionistic': the Cold War ended in 1989, so why did the LDP retain power until 1993? (Kohno, 1997: 143–4).

Elite Ambition

A second reading sees the main motivating factor for the Hata/ Ozawa breakaway as personal ambition, or – as Kohno more grandiosely terms it – 'the basic incentives of individual political actors and their strategic behavior under the given institutional constraints' (Kohno, 1997: 155). Hata and Ozawa had previously been under the patronage of key LDP power-broker Shin Kanemaru. But Kanemaru was ousted from the LDP in 1992 following some nasty infighting, his departure expedited by the Sagawa

Kyubin corruption scandal. This left the two men high and dry, and meant that their best chance of seeking their fortunes was to desert the LDP. This was especially true of Ichiro Ozawa, a controversial figure who was the brains behind the JRP breakaway. Ozawa was distrusted by many Japanese voters and many of his fellow politicians as a Machiavellian operator, who disguised his ambitions with a thin veneer of reformism. Van Wolferen, an admirer of Ozawa, claimed that many of Ozawa's ideas resembled the views expressed in his own book, *The Enigma of Japanese Power* (1989). Van Wolferen wrote a glowing tribute for the cover of the 1994 English edition of Ozawa's book, *Blueprint for a New Japan* (first published in Japanese the previous year), calling it: 'An unprecedented manifesto that goes to the heart of Japan's problems with itself and the world.'

The irony of Ozawa's position as a self-proclaimed 'reformist' was his own background as a protege of Tanaka, and a sidekick of notorious kingmaker Shin Kanemaru: Ozawa himself epitomized the kind of politics which needed to be reformed. As Schlesinger put it: 'Ozawa was widely considered to be part of the problem of politics, not a solution' (Schlesinger, 1997: 267). Ozawa attempted to distance himself from dirty dealing – claiming, for example, that he had been merely emptying ashtrays and fixing drinks during one dubious meeting between Kanemaru, Takeshita and a Sagawa Kyubin executive. Ozawa's widely-read book *Blueprint for a New Japan* had almost nothing to say about corrupt or improper relationships between politics and business, concentrating instead on strengthening the power of politicians over bureaucrats, and on developing a more independent foreign and defence policy (see Williams, 1996: 290–5). Indeed, one chapter of the book was particularly reminiscent of Tanaka's similarly-titled 1973 bestseller *Building a New Japan,* calling for a huge investment programme to shift economic development out of Tokyo, involving the construction of eight new international airports, and thousands of miles of new Shinkansen lines and expressways (Ozawa, 1994: 159–70). Ozawa explictly advocated expanding the 'construction state', not bringing it to heel.

For Woodall, the split in the LDP orchestrated by Ozawa actually had structural causes: the fall of Kanemaru and the end of LDP dominance was precipitated by the 'political thrichinosis' brought on uncontrollable factional demands for ready cash, 'the spiraling ante and the ever more costly by-products of systematized political clientelism' (Woodall, 1996: 145). This endemic problem – factionalism beginning to collapse of its own internal contradictions – (combined with their personal ambition) prompted Ozawa and Hata to flee the LDP for greener, more secure pastures. However, Kanemaru himself hinted that one reason for his amassing such sizeable ill-gotten gains was precisely in order to bankroll 'a future political realignment' (Schlesinger, 1997: 267), implying that Woodall's pattern of cause and effect should be questioned. Perhaps Ozawa and Hata were already plotting the creation of a new party, when Kanemaru stumbled before he could raise them all the necessary funds: the LDP then fell victim to a bungled assassination attempt, which left the party wounded, but very much alive.

Voter Rejection of the Old Order

These perspectives, focusing on the 1993 events as an elite struggle, tend to relegate the electorate to a subordinate role: the voting public appears to be amenable to manipulation from above. However, a re-reading of the final chapter of the Flanagan *et al.*'s book *The Japanese Voter* (1991), offers a rather different picture of the proceedings: a third view. Although this book was published in 1991, and so goes no further chronologically than the 1990 lower-house elections, it contains some interesting information and analysis about long-term voting trends in Japan. The most important is that Flanagan identifies a long-term decline in the hard-core LDP vote, the small farmers and the self-employed. He also notes changing social values: the rise of so-called 'modern values' which tend to be associated with support for opposition parties. The Japanese electorate emerges as increasingly volatile, able to be swayed by short-term 'valence' issues such as political scandals. In other words, there seems to be a long-term trend towards voting for short-term reasons. According to Flanagan, the Japanese voter: 'is unhappy with the ruling party but unwilling to see the opposition gain power. This dilemma transforms Japanese elections into an "empty choice" ' (Flanagan, 1991: 466). By implication, the electorate was ready and waiting for parties such as the JNP and JRP: there was considerable potential support for new Japanese parties, especially parties without the negative connotations of the LDP, but with reassuringly conservative credentials.

Stephen Johnson points out that the standard view of the elections – the LDP losing power as a result of a wave of popular discontentment with them – simply does not square with the facts. He writes:

> this election provides yet another example of the electoral resilience of the LDP, which would almost certainly have stayed firmly in place as the ruling party, had the Hata/Ozawa group not defected from its ranks *before* the election. (Johnson 1994: 9)

He also points out that the JNP had already received a similar share of the vote in the July 1992 upper-house elections, so Hosokawa could hardly claim to have made a dramatic electoral debut, or to have 'broken the mould' of Japanese politics. In other words, then, the demise of the LDP was a direct result of manoeuvring at the elite level, rather than the outcome of popular electoral politics. Another important factor was the record low voter turnout of just over 67 per cent, lower in urban areas, and only around 51 per cent in Tokyo. This hardly suggests an electorate on the rampage: it seems abundantly clear that the LDP lost power, not with a bang but with a whimper.

However, Johnson argued that in the Yamanashi constituency he studied, people appeared not to be voting simply on the basis of personal loyalties or networks, but actually out of a real desire to elect someone from the JNP. He claimed that this reflected less a dissatisfaction simply with the LDP, but a wider dissatisfaction with all the established political parties. In some constituencies at least, people were voting for a general shake-up in the Japanese order. Nevertheless, Kohno claims that an explanation focusing on voter behaviour fails to explain why a disgruntled electorate did no more than effect a partial breakup of the LDP (Kohno, 1997: 144).

Developments in Japanese Politics after 1993

In April 1994, Hosokawa was forced out of the premiership; partly as a result of an old corruption scandal, partly because his position had become virtually untenable as he struggled to deliver on a political reform package which he had trouble selling to many of his coalition partners, and partly as a result of pressure on him from hostile bureaucrats in the Finance Ministry. Following Hosokawa's resignation, Hata took over as premier, but the SDPJ deserted him, leaving the ruling coalition with a minority of the parliamentary seats. At the end of June 1994, the SDPJ formed an extraordinary new coalition government with the LDP and the small Sakigake Party, a coalition led by Tomiichi Murayama, the first socialist premier since the 1940s. Murayama proceeded to renounce most of the key tenets of SDPJ belief, including opposition to the existence of the self-defense forces and to the Japanese flag. Murayama proved rather a popular prime minister on a personal level, but thereafter his party was unable to make any credible electoral showing.

At the end of 1994, the Japan New Party, the JRP and the DSP merged to form the New Frontier Party, later renamed the Liberal Party. The LDP regained the premiership at the beginning of 1996, though the party remained reliant on support from the SDPJ and Sakigake. For a while it seemed that a new order was emerging, comprising the LDP and a vaguely reformist conservative party: in effect, a two-party system of identical twins. The LDP was able to consolidate its position in the October 1996 lower-house elections, coming close to regaining an overall majority. But the limited electoral appeal of the NFP, especially under the leadership of the increasingly unpopular Ozawa, helped open the way for the rise of another reform party, the Democratic Party, which won impressive gains in the 1998 upper-house elections. Democratic Party leader Naoto Kan (previously of Sakigake) was a former health minister, who became a public hero when he was forced to resign after he exposed the complicity of the ministry in allowing the use of HIV-contaminated blood. Meanwhile the Socialists were in terminal decline, Komeito retained a degree of support, and the communists flourished.

By the end of 1998, developments had turned full circle: Ozawa's Liberal Party joined a coalition with the LDP, which was now led by the lacklustre machine politician Keizo Obuchi. The old guard and the 'reformers' were back together again, confirming what many had long suspected: there were no substantive differences between the LDP and its supposed opponents. All the hopes and promises of 1993 had ended in failure. As Stockwin notes, post-1993 developments abundantly demonstrated that 'the natural condition of Japanese party politics is fragmentation' (Stockwin, 1996: 274–5). Japanese political parties, like the Japanese public, have rather lost the plot. In this fluid situation, no certainties remain: though the

LDP can no longer rely on assuming a dominant position, new forces have failed to topple the old hegemony.

By sabotaging the grand old party of Japanese politics, the new generation of conservatives may have weakened the relative position of politicians *vis-à-vis* bureaucrats, as bureaucrats are more able to play off bickering coalition partners against one another. Van Wolferen speculated:

> It is conceivable that future coalitions composed of the existing splitters of the LDP, new splitters, what is left of the LDP and the older, minor parties could become indistinguishable from what the LDP has been – a passive and secondary player in Japan's government. (van Wolferen, 1993: 60)

In other words, given the resilience of 'the System' and its capacity to neutralise challenges (whether from within or without), the ambition and even hubris of the ex-LDP rebels could actually undermine the very reformist causes which they profess to espouse. Developments by 1998 have ten ded to support revisionist views that the 1993 upheavals were much less far-reaching than they appeared.

Conclusion

For mainstream analysts, the developments in Japanese politics since 1993 vindicate their central arguments. Japan does have a pluralist system, power can change hands, and factions do resemble mini-parties. Revisionists are much more sceptical, seeing the fragmentation of recent years as evidence of chaos and collapse in the Japanese order, rather than pluralism. Those who view Japanese party politics from a political-economy perspective often see the entire political order as fatally vitiated by structural corruption, and hopelessly distorted by special interests such as the construction industry. Culturalist analyses view Japanese politics as highly distinctive, failing to conform to the tenets of western political science, but nonetheless functioning successfully according to a logic of its own.

7

Socialization and Civil Society

How are Japanese people socialized into the prevailing political order? To what extent do different elements of Japanese society act as checks and balances on the power of the state, and the ruling elite? This chapter examines two aspects of Japanese society: sources of socialization (such as education and policing), and the nature of civil society, as manifested in the media, community organisations, and protest movements. Most mainstream scholars would argue that Japanese institutions are highly successful in producing good citizens, and that the majority of Japanese people play a constructive role in the political and civic order. Revisionists are generally more sceptical, believing that the Japanese state in some way compels or coerces its citizens into compliance and outward conformity. Those analysts who use culturalist approaches view Japanese society as primarily shaped by cultural norms and traditions, rather than by state-led social forces and institutions.

Sources of Socialization and Social Control

The Education System

The history of Japanese education is a complex subject of study. The most important episodes in this history are the Meiji period, and the postwar Occupation. During the Meiji period, in the second half of the nineteenth century, Japan was preoccupied with the task of 'catching up' with the West by engaging in an extremely rapid process of industrialization and modernization. Part of that modernization

127

was the establishment of a system of education, a system inspired by French, German, British and American models. It was a highly-centralized system based around tightly-disciplined state-run schools, and a few elite public universities (see Goodman, 1989: 32–3). By 1905, 95 per cent of children were receiving primary education. The school system was designed to inculcate nationalist principles, principles that were incorporated into the Imperial Rescript on Education of 1890 (see Passin, 1982: 151–2). This official statement stressed the nationalistic aims of Japanese education, emphasising filial piety and loyalty to the Emperor, including a militaristic injunction to bear arms for the state in times of emergency.

During the American Occupation, the prewar education system was seen as one of the main factors that had led to the rise of militarism in Japan. The Occupation authorities undertook a purge of teachers and education officials, had 'militaristic' textbooks rewritten, and imposed limits on central government control over schools. Schools and teachers were given power to decide their curriculum and textbooks, and elected local school boards were established based on the American model. The 1947 Fundamental Law on Education had parallels with the constitution, and placed an emphasis on equal opportunities. It reflected ideals of egalitarianism and democratization, and contained a provision that 'Education shall not be subject to improper control, but it shall be directly responsible to the whole people' (Schoppa, 1991: 32–4). Since the war, two alternative visions of what education is all about have been in strong competition with one another: a vision of education as a centralized system directed by the state for national objectives, and as a decentralised system run on democratic lines.

After the end of the Occupation, conservatives sought to make changes in the education system, especially with regard to the powers of the Ministry of Education over textbooks and the curriculum. Despite the strong resistance of the Japan Teachers' Union, there were several key conservative successes in the immediate post-Occupation period. In 1956, the elected local school boards were abolished; in 1958, the Ministry of Education curriculum was made compulsory; and, in 1963, it was decided that local authorities rather than teachers were to select textbooks. By the 1970s, the uniformity being fostered by system based on entrance exams for academic generalists was increasingly seen as a problem, and there was growing pressure for diversification of the system (Schoppa, 1991: 34–48).

The Education System Today

Japan's schools are widely praised for their successes in teaching core skills, and Japanese pupils almost invariably top international league tables for their levels of literacy, numeracy, and scientific knowledge. These impressive skill levels reflect a highly demanding school system, which is organized around the preparation for entrance examinations. There are entrance examinations even for some kindergartens and elementary schools, as well as for middle schools, but the most important are usually those for senior high schools and universities. Many – though not all – entrance examinations use a standardized format of multiple choice questions; they typically test rote learning and powers of memorization, rather than creativity or critical thinking.

Since passing or failing entrance examinations really does largely determine a child's future (many companies and other organizations recruit more or less directly from particular vocational schools, colleges and universities, and there is little concept of 'lifelong learning' and little scope for 'late developers' in Japan), the pressure to succeed in them is enormous. The tyranny of entrance examinations leads to highly structured and often extremely boring lessons, in which a teacher works through an approved textbook mechanically (usually covering one page per class hour). The contents of textbooks are a matter of intense controversy, since the Ministry of Education compels teachers to use approved textbooks, and the approval process is intensely political, especially for subjects such as history and social studies. Critical academics and teachers have accused the Ministry of censoring textbooks, especially by playing down Japanese aggression before and during the Second World War (see Herzog, 1993: 196–217).

Pressure to succeed in the education system comes primarily from parents. Like many other Asian societies, Japan is characterized by a special breed of mothers facetiously known as 'education mothers' (*kyoiku mama*), mothers who will stop at nothing to advance their children educationally. 'Education mothers' typically visit their childrens' schools regularly, join the PTA (parent–teachers association), and ingratiate themselves with the principal and other teachers, as well as seeking out the best *juku* schools (private cram schools) for their children to attend during evenings and at weekends. *Juku* are a huge industry, and are considered enormously important for examination preparation; a common complaint of high-school teachers is that students are too tired to study properly, because they spend long hours attending *juku* after the end of the school day.

Whereas secondary school students in many countries typically move from classroom to classroom between lessons, in Japan pupils have virtually all their classes (apart from science lab classes and sports classes) in their own 'homerooms', staying in the same group throughout the day. They are rarely divided into different sets or streams for different subjects. Student participation in classes is often limited to copying from the board and answering occasional questions based on homework exercises. A typical 'homeroom' class might have 48 or 50 pupils. Secondary school teachers use various techniques (such as calling on pupils by their class numbers, or row by row) to make sure that all students take turns in answering questions, since older children and teenagers rarely volunteer information in class. Each class has its own homeroom teacher who carries a considerable degree of responsibility for the welfare of its members, even outside school hours. In the event of a pupil having any particular problem, the homeroom teacher will often visit the family at home. Despite the pressures of homework and cram schools, many pupils devote considerable time and energy to club activities, particularly sports activities ranging from traditional Japanese sports such as *kendo*, to baseball, swimming, and volley-ball. Some clubs meet at 7 am to spend an hour and a half practising each morning before the beginning of classes, then stay on for a further two hours after lessons end.

Discipline is strictly observed in most Japanese schools. Pupils stand up when the teacher enters the room, and bow on an order from the class captain before sitting down. A similar ritual takes place at the end of each class. Pupils are responsible for cleaning the board after each lesson. They wear uniforms (in most local authority schools, the boys' uniforms are modelled, bizarrely, on nineteenth century Prussian uniforms) and they are closely monitored for infringement of uniform rules. Cleaning the school (including the public areas) is the responsibility of the pupils, and is done after lessons have finished. While many Japanese schools are immaculate, in schools with a more liberal discipline regime, cleaning is less meticulous: the cleaner the school, the stricter the school discipline.

During the early post-Occupation period, the Japan Teachers' Union (Nikkyoso) was a powerful force, with a huge membership, and a successful track record of campaigning for improved pay and conditions for teachers (Thurston, 1973: 40–79). Nikkyoso was closely connected with the Japan Socialist Party; in effect, the Cold War bipolar national politics in Japan was mirrored in schools across the country, as unionized leftist teachers struggled for power with conservative school principals and boards of education. However, as Schoppa notes, this ideological standoff became increasingly empty, and less and less related to real problems in the education system: 'Conditioned by years of hard fought ideological combat, these actors show few signs of noticing the shift in subject matter' (Schoppa, 1991: 22). While in theory, unionized teachers favoured a more open education system with a more liberal disciplinary regime, and the freedom to use non-authorized textbooks, in reality they were major beneficiaries of orderly school regimes and mechanical teaching methods. Despite long working hours and excessive paperwork, teaching in most Japanese schools is a relatively straightforward business; negligible class preparation is needed, the same textbooks can be assigned year after year, pupils rarely ask questions, and teachers receive good salaries and long vacations. In effect, leftist teachers and rightist education authorities established a cosy and collusive understanding, a practical *modus operandi.* Neither side had any real interest in introducing reforms, certainly not reforms which would lead to more challenging teaching methods, more student-centred learning, or more critical thinking by pupils.

Despite this shared vested interest in the educational status quo, there was a growing awareness that the school system was failing to produce more creativity. Prime Minister Nakasone (1982–7) was vocal in his advocacy of educational reform, arguing that violence and bullying in schools meant the need for better teaching, more internationalization of education, and reform of the entrance examination system (Schoppa, 1991: 211–50). Similar arguments have been made by successive governments. As Japan embarked on the painful transition from an industrial to a post-industrial society, the workforce was ill-prepared to adapt to the new global information economy. Japan might be able to produce hardware – such as computers – but the software was increasingly coming from the West, from more flexible societies such as the United States and Europe. Neither the over-centralized educational bureaucracy, nor teachers with a declining union movement (see Thurston, 1989: 186–205) who had little incentive to increase their own workloads or improve their own skills, proved remotely capable of responding to the challenge. In the abstract, bureaucrats, teachers and parents all favour far-reaching educational reforms, but in reality all are locked into the existing system focused on examination cramming. As Goodman explains:

> Parents want a more liberal system but are afraid of how their own children's chances might be affected; employers want more creativity in production, but do not want to lose the conformity, instilled by education, that goes into that production; politicians publicly support the liberalisation of the system in their search for votes, but often tacitly approve of a system that seems to have led directly to the Japanese 'economic miracle'; bureaucrats are only 'servants of the people', and yet the Ministry of Education will fight to prevent even the slightest loss of its centralised power.
> (Goodman, 1989: 34)

The higher-education sector is in rather worse condition than the school sector. University and college students typically regard their years in higher education as a reward for hard work at high school, and a period of rest and recuperation before entering the workplace. University students commonly sleep in lectures, examinations are not taken seriously, and almost everyone graduates. McVeigh argues that little education actually takes place in Japanese higher-educational institutions: 'students perform student roles in a sort of ritualized rhetorical reality which lacks educational substance' (McVeigh, 1997: 219). McVeigh's very critical view of Japanese higher education is contested by many other scholars, who argue that the tertiary sector in Japan performs relatively well, and is indeed improving. McVeigh argues that his perspective reflects his own experiences of teaching in 'typical' private colleges and universities, rather than the elite national universities that have attracted greater scholarly attention. McVeigh's arguments apply with greater force to social sciences and humanities, than to natural and applied sciences.

In Japan there is a fiercely hierarchical league table of universities and colleges, and many university students have a 'complex' about their failure to gain admission to better institutions. While there are several highly-regarded private universities (such as Waseda and Keio), students at second or third-tier private universities typically wish they had gained admission to more prestigious public universities. Even students at leading national universities such as Nagoya University or Osaka University are often bitter that they failed to enter the more prestigious Tokyo University. The Japanese higher-education system is so pervaded by a sense of hierarchy that many university graduates consider themselves to be failures. Since there have been no substantive attempts to reform Japanese higher education, it could be assumed that the prevailing emphasis on socialization rather than education in colleges and universities is a deliberate policy, supported by elite policy-makers in both the public and private sectors (McVeigh, 1997: 219).

Education and Politics

In theory, the Japanese education system is highly meritocratic. Those who succeed in passing the right entrance examinations can be admitted to the best elementary schools, junior high schools, senior high schools, and then to top colleges or universities. Most of the best schools are public rather than private, and so are easily affordable for the great majority of families. Yet, in practice, the degree of social mobility in Japan is very similar to that of Britain and the United States (see Ishida, 1993). Prestigious universities such as Tokyo University receive most of their students from a small number of 'feeder' high schools, the majority of which are in the Kanto (greater Tokyo) area. These schools in turn have close relationships with a few junior high schools that supply most of their students; and these junior high schools tend to draw most of their students from a limited pool of elementary schools. Indeed, even some kindergartens have entrance examinations. Many of the successful entrants to Tokyo University will have attended the same well-known *juku*, where they crammed together for the entrance examination. Some families move house, or even send children to stay with relatives, in order to enter the right school catchment area. Access to the best schools and universities therefore remains largely the prerogative of the middle classes, and especially of upper-echelon families whose parents (usually fathers) command high salaries.

Rohlen argues that Japan's high schools:

> . . . are best understood as shaping generations of disciplined workers for a technomeritocratic system that requires highly socialized individuals capable of performing reliably in a rigorous, hierarchical, and finely tuned organizational environment. (Rohlen, 1983: 209)

From a political perspective, this view of education has potentially disturbing implications. McVeigh argues that Japan's education system is designed to serve the interests of the ruling elite, placing emphasis on the need to create a docile workforce in the interests of economic growth and social order (McVeigh, 1998). In other words, the education system is supposed to help suppress dissent and limit the parameters of political participation, 'maintaining an orderly, predictable and controlled environment that is conducive to elite goals and economic pursuits' (McVeigh, 1998: 179). According to McVeigh, the Japanese education system does not teach values of democracy, individual rights and grassroots initiative as commonly understood in western countries: Japanese education is not 'converging' with an Anglo-American model, but derives from a completely different set of assumptions about the relationship between state, society, and the individual. The education system provides the Japanese establishment with an ideology of meritocracy by means of which power and privilege can be legitimated and ordinary citizens disempowered.

Policing and the Criminal Justice System

This book has discussed alternative interpretations of Japanese society, including one which views Japan as based upon the group, and ruled by principles of harmony and consensus, and another which views Japan as based upon principles of social control, the state imposing order upon the population through a range of mechanisms. How far does the nature of Japanese society, with its characteristic emphasis on the group, produce Japanese politics? Or how far is the Japanese political order itself producing a high degree of conformity to group norms? The whole problem can be examined from two alternative perspectives.

One important factor in shaping Japanese society is the mechanisms of social control which exist in Japan. In particular, how can we explain the very low rates of crime and other 'deviant behaviour' in Japan? As with the impressive literacy rates and high standards of numeracy achieved in Japanese education, statistical evidence seems to suggest a model system. Is this testimony to the Japanese national character, or does it reflect an oppressive set of government policies which have the effect of limiting personal freedom?

Mouer and Sugimoto (1989: 234–71) suggest that the issue may be considered in the light of what they call two 'illustrative analogies', cormorant fishing and falconry. In the Japanese art of cormorant fishing, the cormorants are kept on long leashes and trained to respond to instructions, even handing over everything they catch to their master. In the western art of falconry, the falcon is free to fly around in search of prey, but is also trained to return to the hand of its keeper. They compare this with two alternative images of Japanese society: the organized society, with its tight discipline imposed from above, and the associative society, characterized by more fluid structures which nevertheless preserve a general cohesion. Whilst these are metaphors rather than exact descriptions, Mouer and Sugimoto argue that the former corresponds broadly with Japanese society, and the latter with western society. However, it could be argued that both images imply that individual Japanese citizens (the birds) are subject to the overarching guidance and control of a master, in the form of the state. The group model would deny the existence of such an authority, seeing the coordination of collective activity as an inherent, almost an instinctive, phenomenon.

Whatever the nature of the control mechanisms which underpin Japanese society, the results in terms of crime statistics are impressive. David Bayley, a Los Angeles police officer who has studied the Japanese police at first hand, entitles the first chapter of his book 'Heaven for a Cop' (Bayley, 1991: 1–10). For example, he notes that in 1987 there were 6.5 times as many murders per person in the US as in Japan. Levels of less serious offences are also proportionally lower. Guns are tightly controlled in Japan, and play a very small part in the crime picture. How are these low levels of crime achieved? Explanations focus on two areas: policing practices, and wider social behaviour. In practice the distinction is not hard-and-fast, since the kind of policing practices adopted in Japan would not be readily acceptable in western societies.

These practices include the use of small 'police boxes' (*koban*) in every neighbourhood, which entails keeping the police very close to the goings-on of the community (a practice which has been successfully emulated by the Singaporean police); and, rather more insidiously, the 'residential survey', when police officers visit every Japanese home twice a year. They ask a long list of questions, including who lives at the property, how they are related, how old they are, whether they work and if so where, and what motor vehicles they own (see Bayley, 1991: 79–82). All this material is recorded on special forms, along with lists of valuable items owned by the household, and more general information about what is going on in the neighbourhood, whether there are any suspicious people around, and similar questions. They also visit commercial premises and collect similar sorts of information. The average patrol officer in Tokyo makes about 450 of these visits each year. The information gathered does not go onto a central computer or even a central filing system, but remains in the police box for use by the local officers. The data is not used by other government bodies, though it may be used by detectives, or by members of special police agencies concerned with monitoring political dissidents.

Often middle-aged police officers with considerable experience and well-developed social skills carry out these visits, rather than younger officers. Not everyone cooperates, though most do. A list of good topics of local conversation is posted up in each police box and frequently updated; the police use these topics to strike up rapport with people and persuade them to fill in the forms. Some leftists refuse, and it is harder to elicit interest in community matters from apartment dwellers than from house dwellers. For this reason, many forces have put extra resources and assigned more experienced officers to conduct residential surveys in apartment buildings, which are seen as more likely to house criminals and subversives. Not all local police forces are able to gather sufficient in-depth information about their neighbourhoods, however, especially in large cities, and there is some evidence that the *koban* system is becoming less effective. In rural areas, police use *chuzaisho*, or residential police boxes, where officers actually live full-time (see Ames, 1981: 17–33). These small police stations cover a wider area than the urban *koban*.

One striking feature of the Japanese system is that crime prevention is a core activity, accorded a status (and resources) comparable with that of crime investigation. All Japanese neighbourhoods have crime prevention associations (Ames, 1981: 41–6), and volunteers may go around wearing special armbands. Until recently they used to confiscate cigarettes from the under-20s, and admonish youths for unseemly behaviour, though changing social mores make these kind of interventions more difficult than before (Bayley, 1991: 87). More conservative elements in the community, especially local businesses such as shops, often provide the core of support for these associations, since they stand to gain most from low crime rates

(Parker, 1984: 68). Special patrols may be established when serious crimes have been committed, such as those organized by parent groups in Kobe following a brutal child murder case in 1997.

Apart from the practices of the police themselves, socioeconomic factors may play some part in the low crime rates; given that unemployment is relatively low, there are few ethnic tensions and few slums or ghettoes (though all three of these points are somewhat contentious). Punishment for convicted criminals in Japan is fairly lenient – there is limited capital punishment, and the prison population is only 20 per cent of that of the United States. However, the social stigma and attendant consequences associated with punishment are strong deterrents in themselves; for example, a Japanese schoolteacher convicted of drunken driving would almost certainly lose her or his job, being considered a person unfit to take responsibility for teaching children. More difficult to correlate with the low incidence of violent crime is the fact that violence pervades popular culture in Japanese – especially the *manga,* or comic book. These comic books, widely available and often read by children, contain many horrific scenes and frequently feature violence against women, such as the gang rape of schoolgirls. Does this fictional violence actually offer a release for dangerous emotions which would otherwise manifest themselves in disturbed behaviour?

According to Bayley, there are three key factors which account for the control of 'deviant behaviour': propriety, presumption, and pride. By propriety, he means the innumerable rules about what is proper behaviour, which so characterize all forms of life in Japan. Bayley makes the provocative contention that 'Japanese orderliness in large matters, such as crime, seems to be related to orderliness in small things' (1991: 177). This is an argument on the general principle that if you take care of the pennies, the pounds will take care of themselves: if you train people not to drop litter and to tie their dressing gowns the proper way, then they won't do anything criminal.

By presumption, he means the informal group pressures which govern Japanese behaviour. Bayley argues that Japanese society is communitarian rather than individualistic – a clear sign that he subscribes to a 'group model' view of Japanese society. By pride, he means that because people take great pride in performing their personal, social and professional duties properly, they are unlikely to commit transgressions which would undermine their sense of self-worth. It is rather interesting that Bayley, himself a police officer, comes so readily to the conclusion that the police (or even the state as a broad entity) is not primarily responsible for the low crime rate. A very different view, unsurprisingly, is expressed by revisionist scholars. Gavan McCormack is extremely critical of the use of confessions by the criminal justice system in Japan, pointing out that 86 per cent of criminal convictions in Japan today are handed down on the basis of confessions, and that defendants are convicted in 99.9 per cent of cases sent to trial (McCormack, 1986: 187). The latter statistic is especially disturbing. Although Japanese prosecutors and Justice Ministry officials argue that this high conviction rate reflects the fact that doubtful cases are not brought to court (Parker 1984: 107), this argument is hardly persuasive. Public prosecutors have considerable powers which give them the upper hand in criminal trials. McCormack points out that before the Second World War, political deviance was regarded as criminal, and that the criminal justice system has frequently been used to defeat or to neutralize political protest. He also cites political cases in which suspects have been held on remand for very lengthy periods without trial – as long as ten years, in one case – in violation of basic principles laid down by the United Nations. The system of so-called 'substitute imprisonment' (limited to 28 days in total) is described by McCormack as 'a relic of Japan's authoritarian past' (1986: 193). He explicitly questions Bayley's favourable appraisal of the standards of behaviour maintained by the Japanese police. As Parker quotes one Japanese police officer as saying when asked why suspects confess so readily: 'It is no use to protest against power' (1984: 110).

While Bayley argues that substitute prison is used rarely, he notes that in recent years 90–100 000 people have been held in this way annually. In 1985, 62.5 per cent were held for less than 10 days, which means that 37.5 per cent (or somewhere around 37 500 people) were held without charge for more than 10 days. Those held in this form of detention have no automatic access to lawyers and are not eligible for bail, which means that (in Bayley's words) 'confession becomes in effect a condition for bail' (1991: 145). They are also not held in regular prison buildings, but in so-called 'police jail', although these jails have now come under the aegis of the Ministry of Justice. Bayley does point out, however, that even leading figures implicated in the 1989 Recruit Scandal were held in this form of custody for 23 days: he implies that there is a fundamental equality before the law in operation here. Bayley is sceptical about reports that Japanese police officers have physically abused prisoners, arguing that evidence is limited. He also notes:

> Precharge detention is an opportunity for moral suasion to be applied to erring individuals. Pressure to confess is only partly to obtain convictions. More important, it is applied to teach, to humble, to extract contrition and repentance. Arrest is tantamount to conviction. . . The primary purpose of Japanese criminal justice, unlike American, is not to exact punishment. Its actions are symbolic, indicating social exclusion. . . An analogue of what the Japanese police want the offender to feel is the tearful relief of a child when confession of wrongdoing to parents results in an understanding laugh and a warm hug. (1991: 149)

Yoshio Sugimoto sees matters rather differently, claiming with regard to the 'residential survey' that:

> In this situation, ideological control – in Gramsci's term, hegemony – is in full swing. The agencies of social control promote a worldview supportive of the established order in every area of life until it becomes part of the 'world-taken-for-granted'. With successful implementation of this process, self-policing becomes a daily reality. (1986: 70)

In other words, the appearance of popular consensus is in fact simply a manifestation of 'self-policing', the outcome of direct and indirect forms of state-imposed social control.

Crime and Deviant Behaviour

The generally positive image of law and order in Japan is severely tarnished by the ubiquitous presence of organized crime, in the form of *yakuza*, or gangsters. These gangsters, conspicuously dressed in tasteless suits and white shoes, and often driving huge American cars, control illegal businesses such as drugs and prostitution, and appear to operate with virtual impunity. They enjoy cordial, even jocular relations with local police (Ames, 1984: 105–29), who act against them only when they transgress certain implicit rules (such as by murdering innocent bystanders). Many *yakuza* bosses enjoy close relations with prominent conservative politicians, and are effectively immune from prosecution.

Sokaiya are a form of gangsters who engage in extorting money from companies by threatening to disrupt shareholders' meetings. Their parasitic activities were widespread during the 1980s and 1990s, seriously harming the economy, and as many as one-third of all Japanese companies were estimated to have paid off these extortionists. The existence of *yakuza* gangs, with an estimated national membership of 86 000 in 1992 (Hanes, 1996: 138), is a serious indictment of the effectiveness of the Japanese police. Yet Ames notes that there are many parallels between the police and the *yakuza*, from political perspectives to sartorial preferences (Ames 1984: 120–4).

Another problem area is that of juvenile delinquency, especially in the field of auto crime. As with the *yakuza,* criminal activity of this kind is collective and group-oriented. Teenagers form gangs known as *bosozoku* (reckless driving tribes) (Ames, 1984: 84–5). In fact, much of their driving is not so much reckless as infuriating: they typically ride flotillas of large and extremely noisy motorcycles at slow speeds through urban and residential areas, in the evening, or at night. Later on, they move up to racing around in cars. Sometimes rival *bosozoku* engage in fighting and their members may become involved in other more serious criminal activities such as theft. Despite their superficially anti-social, quasi anarchistic pose, the behaviour of gang members is in fact highly ritualized, there is a strict group hierarchy and tight internal discipline, and most 'graduate' or 'settle down' when they become legal adults at the age of 20 (see Sato, 1991, especially 72–104). Sato concludes that '*Bosozoku* was a symbolic rebellion which was born and nurtured partly by the mass media and producers of consumer goods' (1991: 101). Like the *yakuza, bosozoku* mirror the structures and hierarchies of the mainstream Japanese society from which they appear to deviate.

It is difficult to establish the extent to which the social conformity manifested in Japan's low crime rate is related directly to the promotion of support for 'established order' in the form of votes for the LDP. Can it be argued that people who have been socialized into obeying laws are more likely to hold conservative political attitudes, and are therefore more likely to vote for conservative parties such as the LDP? This would seem on the face of it logical, but it is very difficult to prove. There is, not surprisingly, evidence that Japanese voters who support increased police powers tend to be conservative politically, but that is something rather different. What we would need to establish here is whether the Japanese were more inclined to vote for conservative parties (the LDP) than voters in other countries (such as Britain or the US) who had not been subjected to the same mechanisms of political and social control; and we would also have to establish that the conservative voting behaviour was a direct manifestation of social control rather than, say, approval of LDP economic performance. On balance, the verdict may be a Scottish one of 'not proven'.

An alternative view, which may be equally critical both of the ideal-type group model approach, and of Sugimoto's theory of Japan as a 'control state' could draw on the idea of the distinction between *honne* and *tatamae*, the difference between the external face of Japanese behaviour and the true feelings of the individual. It could be argued that whilst control mechanisms such as the rather oppressive policing techniques practised by local *koban* officers are effective for the most part in modifying outward behaviour *(tatamae)*, the *honne* may nevertheless remain non-conformist and continues to cherish subversive, rebellious or aggressive thoughts. In other words, we need to distinguish between thoughts and actions which are expressed, and those which remain unexpressed or repressed. Outward conformity with the system may hide inner rebellion, which manifests itself at election times. This explains why outwardly demure Japanese housewives and nondescript bank clerks sometimes took immense pleasure in sending anonymous donations to anti-Narita Airport protestors, or casting their votes for the Japan Communist Party. Many Japanese people have a well-developed capacity for working on two levels of reality, and this extends beyond the niceties of daily life and into the political sphere. For all the socialization processes, individual life is still going on beneath the façade. Japanese people may often appear to think and behave very conventionally, but appearances are deceptive, and do not begin to tell the whole story.

Forms of Social Organization and Participation

The Role of the Mass Media

Given the relative weakness of oppositional forces such as unions and consumer groups in Japan, those who argue that Japan is a true liberal democracy have often claimed that the Japanese mass media functions in a fashion similar to that of the media in the United

States or Europe. Such scholars emphasise the role of the Japanese media as a 'watchdog', monitoring and criticizing the actions of government. Revisionist scholars, by contrast, have argued that Japan is not a functioning democracy in the western sense. The Japanese media are portrayed by revisionists such as Karel van Wolferen as the 'lapdogs' of the political establishment (van Wolferen 1989: 93–100).

A small number of organizations are responsible for most of the national-level news output in Japan. NHK is a semi-governmental broadcasting agency modelled on the BBC, whilst each major newspaper group has close commerical links with a private television station: the *Yomiuri Shimbun* (circulation 14.5 million) runs NTV; the *Asahi Shimbun* (12.9 million) operates TV Asahi; the *Mainichi Shimbun* (6.3 million) is involved with TBS, the specialist financial paper *Nihon Keizai Shimbun* (*Nikkei* for short) (4.5 million) with TV Tokyo; and the *Sankei Shimbun* (3.2 million) with Fuji TV (circulation figures from Foreign Press Centre, 1994: 19). Whereas in the 1960s the three major newspapers followed a similar 'oppositional' editorial line, led by the *Asahi*, during the 1970s the *Yomiuri* won the circulation war and adopted a more conservative, pro-LDP stance. The *Asahi,* however, has continued to espouse left-wing editorial positions on key issues such as Japan's 'peace constitution'. The *Mainichi* has suffered from financial and circulation problems, and is seen as having somewhat lost its way over the past 20 years. Both the *Nikkei* and the *Sankei* are conservative-oriented business newspapers that model themselves on the *Wall Street Journal* and the *Financial Times*. Although the mass-circulation dailies are the most prestigious print media outlets, there is also a thriving weekly and monthly magazine sector, which tends to be the place where vigorous critical reporting – ranging from the extremes of muck-raking journalism to serious political debate – takes place. As Table 7.1 shows, newspapers in Japan are more widely read and circulated than in any other country in the world.

On the face of it, Japan has a free press (freedom of speech is guaranteed under the constitution). Yet in practice several threats exist to that freedom. The most conspicuous of these is the threat of cooptation. Successive LDP administrations gave special privileges to the large media groups, allowing them (for example) to purchase prime office sites in central Tokyo at prices well below market value. More controversial is the system of *kisha* (reporters) clubs that operates in Japanese government circles (Feldman, 1993: 63–79).

Table 7.1   Newspaper circulation and diffusion rates

Country	Circulation (millions)	Diffusion rate*
Japan	53	425
Republic of Korea	18	412
Russia	57.4	387
United Kingdom	22.1	383
Germany	25.9	323
United States	60	236
France	11.7	205
Poland	5.7	148
Mexico	10.2	116
China	50.5	43
India	27.5	31

*Diffusion rates are in copies per 1000 population.

Original Source: UNESCO (1995), *Statistical Yearbook*
Secondary Sources: Kawai, Nobukazu (ed.) (1996) *Asahi Shimbun Japan Almanac 1997,* Tokyo, Asahi Shimbun Publishing Company, p. 257; Haruhara, Akihiko (1997), *Japan's Mass Media,* Tokyo, Foreign Press Center, p.19.

Around 15 reporters from the major news groups have privileged access to press clubs at the prime minister's office, at party offices and the offices of party factions. Club members are provided with extensive facilities at the expense of the relevant government agency, party, or faction: these may include meals and sleeping quarters as well as telephone and fax lines. The system has the effect of turning the reporters concerned into 'insiders', in contrast to other journalists (such as those working for local newspapers, weekly or monthly publications, and foreign correspondents) who are excluded from the special access to information available to club members.

Nor are those journalists on the inside limited to contacting politicians at their offices: *kisha* club members conduct regular 'night attacks' on the homes of the figures to whom they are assigned, sometimes playing mah jong with them into the small hours. 'Night attacks' are followed up by morning visits, and leading Japanese politicians such as the cabinet secretary can fully expect to be tailed by reporters throughout their waking hours. Understandably, such an intense relationship between politicians and the small team of reporters assigned to cover them has led to a falling off of journalistic objectivity and standards. In each of the major scandals that have beset LDP politicians over the past 20 years, reporters were well aware of what was going on long before the stories broke. There was, in effect, systematic collusion between press and politicians to conceal shady goings-on. *Kisha* clubs maintained an internal discipline that prevented members from obtaining 'scoops': a common line was agreed upon by reporters, and anyone 'going it alone' faced being ostracized by the club. Politicians expected club members to produce favourable coverage of their activities, whilst club members jealously defended their news sources from the prying eyes of rivals outside the charmed circle.

When scandals did break, it was generally because outsiders had managed to expose sleaze concealed by the clubs: Prime Minister Kakuei Tanaka, for example, fell from grace in the 1970s following exposure of his corrupt practices in a weekly magazine, followed up by pressure from foreign correspondents and later an investigation by the US Senate. As Maggie Farley shows, the Recruit-Cosmos scandal was exposed by *Asahi Shimbun* reporters – but reporters in the Yokohama bureau, not those on the Tokyo parliamentary beats (Farley, 1996: 148–9). In other words, the *kisha* club system itself merely reflects the internal structures of Japanese news organizations: the clubs are not the actual root of the problem, but a cartel set up by rigidly hierarchical media groups which do not regard the critical quest for information as a fundamental institutional goal.

Since the mid-1980s, the main initiative for change in the Japanese media has come neither from the dinosaur-like flagship newspapers, nor from worthy-but-dull NHK, but from private television stations seeking to steal a march on their competitors. The conventional interviewing style of Japanese television journalists was until recently extremely non-confrontational. They addressed politicians in polite, respectful language, following a predictable line of questioning – indeed, politicians were often supplied with the questions in advance. But during the mid-1980s, commercial television stations began to produce a different style of news programme which featured more rigorous interview formats. The prime mover behind these changes was TV Asahi. Two programmes led the way: *News Station,* screened every weeknight at 10 pm for over an hour, and *Sunday Project,* a weekly interview slot. Aggressive campaigning by programmes such as these helped arouse public interest in corruption scandals during 1992–3, and may have contributed marginally to the end of LDP rule in July 1993 (McCargo, 1996).

According to one Japanese television journalist: 'The defeat of the LDP in 1993 was an opportunity for the media to change our traditional role. We failed' (interview, 31 August 1994). The collapse of the LDP's monolithic power provided an opportunity for the media groups to revamp their own structures, but this has not been done. In March 1994, veteran Nikkei journalist Yasuhiro Tase published a book in Japanese entitled *Crime and Punishment of Political Journalism* (Seiji Janarizumu no Tsumi to Batsu), which highlighted the low ethical standards of reporters. Although the book attracted considerable interest and attention, its impact was very limited.

Whilst the relationship between the media and politicians changed somewhat following the political upsets of 1993, there was no decisive break with the old convivialities of the *kisha* club system. Japanese journalists share with other citizens a sense of perplexity about political developments since the 1993 election, especially after the rise to power of a once unthinkable hybrid LDP-Social Democratic Party coalition. The Japanese media, like the Japanese public, somewhat lost its political bearings. But the continuing close proximity between reporters and politicians, coupled with the conservative perspective of the big corporations controlling the main newspapers, means that Japan's media functions only as a rather weak counterbalance to the power of the state.

Voluntary and Professional Associations

Japan is rich in associational life, possessing a great abundance of social capital in the form of neighbourhood associations (*chonaikai*), public safety committees, police support groups, voluntary organizations, volunteer social workers and probation officers, parent-teacher associations, and interest groups of all kinds. An impressive range of collective activities exists in Japan: on a typical Sunday morning in a Japanese residential district, teams of residents can be seen weeding paths, clearing gulleys, and gathering up rubbish. Community networks of this kind can be very effective in helping Japanese politicians to create support groups, and to mobilize community bloc voting (Flanagan, 1991: 196–7). Curtis explained how neighbourhood associations were a key element in one successful LDP candidate's campaign organization and strategy (Curtis,

1971: 87–125). While there is an ever-present tendency for Japanese social capital to be enlisted in the service of politicians, this rich community organization can also give rise to independent political life, when circumstances so require.

The prominent role played by women in many community groups partly reflects the limited career choices available to Japanese women. Sugimoto suggests (1997: 153–4) that becoming a 'networker' is considered by many Japanese women a reasonable alternative to paid employment or full-time home-making. Networkers engage in a wide range of activities, from running workers' collectives or recycling shops to engaging in protest movements concerning environmental or other issues.

Citizens' Movements and Radical Protests

Movements that appear to have a 'grassroots' basis, especially movements that seek to undermine the hegemony of traditional political elites, are of great importance as indicators of the character and quality of a country's politics. Good examples of such movements are popular uprisings or protests, often organized around single issues such as environmental destruction. The emergence of such movements is often hailed as a sign that a country possesses a 'civil society' that challenges the state's monopoly of political power. In the case of Japan, the rise of citizens' movements (CMs) in the 1960s and 1970s is one of the clearest indicators of the potential power of Japanese civil society. Yet these *ad hoc* movements – that flourished in the face of the serious pollution problems which gripped Japan during this period – do not appear to have been consolidated thereafter into more lasting vehicles for political participation.

To understand the conditions that gave rise to the citizens' movements, it is necessary to realise that Japanese economic development was proceeding at a quite phenomenal pace during the period in question. Between 1960 and 1968, there was a 270 per cent increase in mining and manufacturing, and heavy oil consumption increased by 450 per cent – whilst the number of private cars quadrupled (Hayes, 1995: 137). Although pollution control laws already existed in many prefectures, enforcement was extremely patchy. Local authorities were keen to attract investment to their areas, and so often turned a blind eye to potential pollution hazards.

In many cases, there were close personal ties between the politicians and the companies involved.

One of the most notorious cases of pollution occurred in Minamata, on the southern island of Kyushu. Between 1953 and 1960, 46 people died and 75 became seriously ill as a result of concentrations of organic (methyl) mercury (Ui 1992: 103–32). The mercury had the effect of destroying human brain cells, and could cause neurological damage leading to symptoms such as loss of coordination, lack of sensation, loss of speech and tremors and convulsions. In severe cases, the mercury could cause death within weeks, although it could also have a much more gradual effect. Where pregnant women were exposed to mercury, children were born with what became known as congenital Minamata disease.

From 1956–60, a number of different research teams worked on trying to identify the source of mercury. One team which concluded that the likely source was a factory owned by a major chemical firm called Chisso Corporation was disbanded under pressure from the Ministry of International Trade and Industry (MITI). However, local fishermen had long since come to the conclusion that the company was to blame, and they began a campaign for compensation. When they attempted to storm the factory in frustration, riot police and townspeople joined in, as did the regional trade-union association – all on the side of the company. In August 1959, the company agreed to pay compensation albeit on a rather minimal scale.

But in 1965 there was a second outbreak of mercury poisoning, this time in Niigata prefecture. Following a successful lawsuit by the victims, the company responsible was forced to pay substantial compensation. Unlike in Minamata, local people in Niigata had backed the pollution victims rather than the company. Their success led to a renewed fight for compensation by the Minamata victims, which achieved considerable success in 1973. The Niigata case demonstrated that concerted action by local people, combined with the use or threat of court action, could produce concessions and compensation from even the most uncompromising companies. Cases such as these greatly increased public awareness of the issues involved, and the methods used by campaigners in these cities were imitated all over Japan.

Where did the phenomenon of the citizens' movements (CMs) come from? Protest movements existed in Japan during the 1950s, mainly organized around labour disputes in mines, factories and schools. The citizens' movements, though often highly localized, brought in a broader range of participants than had these disputes. Arguably, the original model for the movements derived from the large-scale protests organized in 1960 by those who opposed the revisions made to the Mutual Security Treaty with the United States, protests which at their height involved hundreds of thousands of people.

Three main types of CM emerged in the years that followed: environmental movements, antiwar groups, and civil rights groups. In 1973, there were estimated to be more than 3000 citizens' movements active in Japan. According to one survey done in 1973, more than 60 per cent of the movements were focused on environmental issues. Most of these aimed either at bringing to an end existing industrial pollution and compensating its victims, or else preventing an industrial development in a particular locality where that development was likely to have an adverse impact on the environment. Originally, at least, these movements were referred to as *shimin undo*. Krauss and Simcock describe the ideal of the *shimin undo* as:

That average citizens were spontaneously creating new forms of democratic organisations in the best traditions of grassroots egalitarian democracy to gain control over their own destinies and work for the 'public good'. (1980: 212)

Such public-spirited idealism greatly appealed to academics who saw these movements as signalling the emergence of 'real' democracy in Japan. Yet in large measure the ethos of the movements reflected deep dissatisfaction with the nature of the prevailing political order. Not only did those joining the movements distrust the ruling LDP – committed to a policy of economic development, and so seen as in cahoots with big business – they were also unhappy with the stance adopted by opposition parties such as the JSP, which did not have a strong local network, and in any case was primarily focused upon national issues.

In practice, however, few of the citizens' movements lived up to the ideals of unselfish civic action. More commonly, the movements were organized around specific local grievances. As Krauss and Simcock put it 'many local movements' size and goals has less an aura of public service than of private complaint' (1980: 198).

Whatever their precise motivation, the citizens' movements were an extremely important phenomenon. Margaret McKean notes that most active members of the movements regarded 'ideology' as a dangerous thing which might threaten the unity of the campaigners. The movements derived their strength from being 'a broad coalition of many kinds of people, built around a particular social problem' (1981: 147). Conservatives within the groups were anxious to ensure that they were not participating in a 'red' left-wing movement. Even more progressive members of the movements would tend to support the JSP or JCP because they saw those parties as potentially more responsive to popular demands than the LDP, rather than out of any real sympathy for their leftist ideologies. Where members of the movements did see themselves as communists or socialists, they did not want these personal beliefs to become part of the anti-pollution movement, since this might alienate some potential supporters. Student participation was not welcomed for similar reasons: 55 per cent of the activists interviewed by McKean said that offers of help from students should be rejected.

A number of different tactics were used by the movements to achieve their goals. These included: pollution-prevention contracts (agreements usually made between the local government and companies, sometimes with the involvement of a CM, or including a CM); the single-share movement (where members of CMs bought shares in companies, thereby gaining the right to attend shareholders' meetings and raise questions; electoral politics, backing candidates with anti-pollution views; petitions; lobbying, and direct action (such as sit-ins) (see McKean 1981: 149–62). On the whole, there was a preference for relatively safe and conventional campaign tactics, rather than those which were violent, or disruptive.

Nevertheless, there is no doubt that the citizens' movements were effective in forcing the Japanese government to act. Provoked both by the environmental protests, and by the lawsuits which the CMs initiated and won, the government passed an anti-pollution law in 1967, revising and strengthening it in 1970. The following year, an Environment Agency was established to direct and monitor policy in this area, headed by a director-general of cabinet rank. Gradually, the level of protest declined; by the 1980s, the citizens' movements had all but disappeared.

Although it has been argued that the movements did increase popular political awareness, laying the foundations for the progressive local authorities which were prevalent in the 1970s, it now seems clear that they did not signal a radical shift in Japanese political culture. Rather, they demonstrated that Japanese citizens could be mobilized to resist the forces of the state where a particular tangible issue had a direct (and adverse) effect upon their daily lives. Margaret McKean has argued that the disillusionment and scepticism which the citizens movements produced concerning the nature of the Japanese political process was a healthy development:

> Theoretically speaking, the possibility of misgovernment at best, tyranny at worst, is the suspicion on which democracy is justified. Disillusionment is the catalyst that makes it possible for budding citizens to make sense out of democratic principles. (McKean, 1980: 272)

McKean believed that the movements had both socialized citizens into becoming more effective political actors, and legitimized political conflict itself. In many cases, individual citizens realized for the first time that they had rights, had been treated unjustly, and were entitled to recompense. The movements also had the effect of pushing political parties into taking the idea of responding to grassroots pressures far more seriously than had hitherto been the case. The fact that these movements were home-grown suggested that Japanese political culture was not merely conformist, conservative and submissive: ordinary people showed their capacity for protest against the prevailing order. Reed (1981) argues that the emergence of vigorous environmental protest groups in Japan, and the consequent creation of a 'strong' environmental policy by the Japanese government, undermined many previous assumptions about Japanese politics.

Yet unfortunately, even if McKean was right in the short term, the lasting consequences were limited. By the 1980s the LDP had acted to make accommodations with many citizens' movements by adjusting its policies. In doing so it was able to prevent the opposition parties from monopolizing environmental issues for their own benefit. Van Wolferen notes that by the mid-1980s citizens' movements were comparing themselves to 'wind-chimes in winter', tinkling sounds which had become irritating and irrelevant: token measures and a change of LDP rhetoric had snuffed them out (Wolferen 1989: 56).

At the same time, new and flourishing grassroots organizations emerged in certain locales, especially where locals were opposed to the presence or proposed expansion of US military facilities, as was the case in Zushi and Okinawa (Jain, 1991; Ruoff, 1993; Egami,

1994). Where serious issues remained unresolved, such movements continued to be salient political actors. In the city of Zushi, environmental protestors were able to win the office of mayor and have introduced a form of 'Green democracy' based on freedom of information and widespread public consultation (Ruoff, 1993). The 1995 Great Hanshin earthquake also helped stimulate the voluntary sector: volunteers who sought to assist earthquake victims established new non-profit organizations in Kobe to manage the emerging 'volunteer work boom'. While the phenomenon of the 'citizens' movements' as understood in the 1970s did not endure, new manifestations of similar political tendencies have contined to emerge.

Beverley Smith argues that rather than demonstrating the emergence of incipient popular democracy in Japan, the citizens' movements operated within narrow constraints:

> While the citizens' movements made advances in defining citizen rights and the legitimacy of opposition, the nature of the organisations and the issues they addressed set limits on the scope of discussion, especially in exploring the relationship between citizen and state. (Smith, 1986: 172)

She also notes that by the 1980s environmental campaigners were becoming less effective at monitoring the activities of the industrial sector, that references to Minamata disease were being deleted from school textbooks, and that new secrecy legislation made it more difficult to gain access to company documents. All this would seem to suggest that these movements – which at one time were heralded as taking over from conventional parties as the key organizations providing popular input into the political process – had little substantive impact. It could even be suggested that the parochial concerns of the movements dissipated people's political energies and distracted them from mobilizing full-scale opposition to the LDP, though this view tends to assume that those involved in the movements could readily have been drafted into more conventional party political campaigning.

Despite all this, the strength of the citizens' movements does illustrate that there is considerable latent opposition within the Japanese order, which can be mobilized under the right conditions. The citizens' movements may well be less significant for what they did or did not accomplish, than for what their emergence revealed about the nature of Japanese society and politics.

Radical Protest

So far, this book has examined two different aspects of political opposition in Japan: opposition to LDP rule from other parties, particularly the Japan Socialist Party; and opposition in the form of citizens' movements, particularly those mobilized around environmental issues. It could be argued that neither of these forms of opposition really challenged Japan's group-based consensus society: the opposition was concerned with reforming the system, rather than attacking it. Yet Japan has also seen more extreme forms of opposition that are less easy to interpret from a conservative vantage point: the radical protests of the 1960s and 1970s, and especially the conflict over the construction of Tokyo's Narita airport. It could be argued that the very recourse to protest demonstrates the protestors' relative impotence, rather than their capacity to effect change: are protests evidence that popular participation is possible, or examples of the limits of popular participation?

A key inspiration for opposition groups was the *Anpo* protest. The heyday of the Japanese New Left, this protest mobilized several million people against the US–Japan Mutual Security Treaty Revision, bringing together large numbers of students (both radical and non-radical), intellectuals, university professors, housewives, actresses and trade unionists, as well as groups dedicated to armed struggle. Despite its huge support, *Anpo* failed to block the treaty from being approved, leaving the Japanese progressive movement feeling frustrated. Yet for all the electoral and political failures of the Japanese left, Marxist ideas were highly influential in Japan's postwar politics. Over the following decade, a variety of new forms emerged for radical protest. Some groups, such as the infamous Japanese Red Army, resorted to acts of terrorist violence in order to promote their left-wing agenda. More interesting for a detailed discussion here is the Sanrizuka protest movement, based around resistance to the construction of a new airport outside Tokyo (for a very detailed account, see Apter and Sawa, 1984).

The government first announced its intention to construct a new Tokyo airport in 1962. When the decision to go ahead at Narita – in a fertile farming area outside Tokyo known as Sanrizuka – was formally confirmed in 1966, residents formed the *Hantai Domei* Opposition League dedicated to preventing the construction of the airport by every available means, including petitioning and court action. Most of the site had originally been imperial lands, and a hard core of local farmers had longstanding connections with the area. This first phase of the campaign resembled many of the citizens' movements discussed above. Where the farmers differed from most citizens' movements was in their deep emotional attachment to the land, and their determination not to be ousted from it.

When officials arrived to survey the land in October 1967 they had to be protected by 2 000 riot police, and the following month students from Tokyo joined in the campaign to prevent the survey being carried out. Groups of students and radical activists took up residence in the area, forming small communities devoted permanently to the anti-Narita cause. After a bitter struggle, one of the runways was finished in 1973. But the Opposition League managed to build two metal towers, one 62 metres high, on the runway, and these were guarded round-the-clock by campaigners. Eventually, in 1977, riot police stormed the towers and destroyed them. The Opposition League responded by building a 20-metre-high ferro-concrete fortress, but this proved short-lived. In March 1978 the campaigners attacked the control tower and smashed it up, but the authorities responded by rebuilding it; and in May 1978 Narita Airport, guarded by 14 000 riot police, was opened. There had been six deaths, 7 000 wounded and 3 000 arrested over the previous 12 years.

What is so interesting about the Narita protest was its combination of conservatism and radicalism. The farmers had, for the most part, been supporters of the LDP prior to the announcement of the airport project. Indeed, many cherished patriotic memories of the imperial system, and saw themselves as deeply loyal Japanese citizens. They may appear to have been subversive in their actions against state authorities, but their protest was rooted in a desire to defend their history and identity; it was the action of struggle itself that radicalized them. This was in sharp contrast with the militant students and political activists who joined them, who were essentially rebels in search of a cause. For the most part, the militants became involved at Sanrizuka because they saw the airport issue as an ideal vehicle to promote the revolutionary values they held dear. They hoped that:

> if the public could be polarised and the trade unions radicalised, then each confrontation would reveal more fundamental antagonisms. The scope of the conflict was broadened by shifting from universities, which in the last analysis remained only universities,

to Sanrizuka, where the militants brought into play a dynamic of class, power, state and society. (Apter and Sawa, 1984: 81)

The Sanrizuka protest is a difficult phenomenon to categorize or to quantify: perhaps the best description is 'a struggle over land and over principles'. Yet the precise nature of the principles is not entirely clear; certainly, the farmers and the militants would offer different explanations as to the nature of those principles. The all-consuming nature of the protest, its highly-organized and single-minded character, were distinctively Japanese: energies which other Japanese have channelled into successful economic activity were here channelled into rebellion against the state. Karel van Wolferen notes that many ordinary Japanese people felt a sneaking sympathy for the radicals, 'and privately cheered them on' (Wolferen, 1989: 337). He cites example of riots in the 1960s where ordinary salary-men joined in with radical students, helping them set fire to cars and stone the police.

According to Krauss (1988: 112–3), later studies (including his own) bore out the close connection among young Japanese people between 'libertarian values' such as self-indulgence, permissiveness, cynicism and individualism, and a tendency to support political protest. He claims that the student movement of the 1960s was closely related to the emergence of a particular 'post-industrial' generation at this point in Japanese history. If we accept Krauss's view, the rise of radical politics in Japan during the 1960s may have very little to do with political ideas or issues *per se*. He sees traditional Japanese society as being challenged not by political subversion, but by a tide of post-industrial individualism (1988: 113–15). Radicalism was essentially a lifestyle choice for bored post-industrial youth.

Smith, however, sees democracy as having been 'derailed' by the failure of citizens' movements and radical protests to have a more lasting impact upon Japan's political landscape (Smith, 1986). She regards the Sanrizuka movement as clear evidence that it was possible for Japanese people to look beyond the essentially con-servative values associated with economism, and laments the fact that the heightened political awareness produced by the Narita issue did not have a wider effect. Steinhoff takes a more positive view of the 1960s protest culture, arguing that the citizens and radical movements had the effect of institutionalizing civil liberties, and 'establishing very generous limits of political expression, well beyond what the average citizen can conceive of utilizing' (Steinhoff, 1989: 193). She does note, however, that the Japanese government has been able to 'tolerate and ignore a very high level of political protest' (1989: 194), which shows that democracy is still relatively new to the Japanese.

Contrasting Perspectives on Japanese Civil Society

For mainstream scholars, there are innumerable parallels between Japanese civil society and the civil societies of western democracies. For all its shortcomings, the Japanese education system is seen as highly effective in producing a literate and numerate population. The Japanese police and criminal justice system offer an outstanding model of crime prevention which other countries should study. The media provides Japanese people with detailed information about politics and current events, and alerts them to scandals and abuses of power when necessary. At the same time, the rich community structures of Japanese cities, towns and villages make for a high degree of associational life, and these structures can form the basis for various forms of social and political participation, ranging from electoral mobilization to environmental protests.

For revisionist scholars, the picture is much more bleak. The Japanese education system strives to produce unthinking citizens who will dedicate themselves to diligent consumerism, and will be deeply reluctant to challenge the prevailing order. This conformity is reinforced by an anodyne and largely uncritical media that constantly fails in its duties as a watchdog, and by a quietly repressive police and justice system. Although community groups can form the basis of protest movements and grassroots resistance, the establishment is highly skilled in co-opting them, neutralizing their dissent, and turning them into support organisations for conservative politicians.

For those scholars who emphasise culturalist perspectives, the education system is an important source of socialization into values – such as harmony and hierarchy – which are central to Japanese society. These values are reinforced by other social institutions such as the media and the police. Japanese communities reflect a group model of organization which is quite distinctive, and although groups may sometimes adopt collective stances which challenge the interests of political power-holders (as in protest movements), both sides then typically seek to find ways of solving their differences, through compromise and the sharing of benefits.

8

Japan's External Relations

As one of the world's largest economies, Japan might be expected to play a major role on the international stage. However, two main factors have militated against a global role for Japan, both of them legacies of the Second World War. The first is a lingering distrust of Japan, felt especially by China, Korea, and other victims of Japanese aggression. The second factor is a reluctance on the part of Japan to assert itself internationally, a reluctance which reflects the formal 'self-disarmament' implied in the 1947 constitution. By permanently renouncing the right to wage war, Japan effectively retreated to the back-benches of the international community. As such, Japan has been described as an 'incomplete superpower', combining a giant economy with much smaller global clout. At the same time, Japan's lack of natural resources means that the country remains heavily reliant on imports of oil (especially from the Middle East) and raw materials (especially from Asia). In other words, Japan has a huge stake in the maintenance of international order, yet lacks conventional mechanisms for helping preserve or establish such order.

One obvious symbol of this relative impotence is the composition of the UN Security Council: Japan has a much stronger economy than the UK (or China, France and Russia), yet does not have a permanent seat on the Council. To some extent, this paradox reflects the determination of the Second World War allies to retain their seats at the world's top table: but it also derives from domestic opposition to Japan claiming an international status commensurate with its economic standing. Japan has long enjoyed a senior status among the world's industrialized nations (as evidenced by membership of G7), but this is not matched by a clear role as a regional leader in Asia. Revisionist perspectives on Japan have emphasised the contradictions inherent in Japan's relations with the rest of the

Map 2   Japan in Pacific Asia

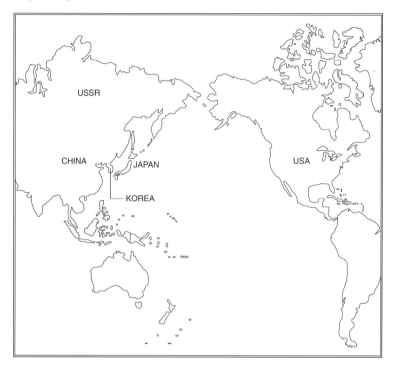

world, whereas mainstream accounts offer a more sympathetic view, and culturalist perspectives emphasise the distinctive historical nature of Japan's international position.

Japan's Self-defence Forces and the US–Japan Alliance

Since the 1947 Constitution banned the Japanese from re-arming, at the onset of the Cold War the Americans were obliged to take on the main burden of defending both Japan and the wider Asia-Pacific region from the threat of attack by either the Soviet Union or China. Whilst these commitments have been scaled down over time, notably with the US withdrawal from Vietnam in 1975, at their height they included huge military forces in the Philippines and Okinawa, as well as in Korea and mainland Japan.

The Japanese position on defence is unique, not only because of the special nature of the Japanese constitution, but also because of the political and psychological sensitivity of the issue within Japan. The humiliating defeat of the country at the end of the Pacific War left a whole generation of Japanese people deeply uneasy about the pursuit of militarism, and highly suspicious both of their own political leaders and of American interests and intentions. It is not enough to see clause 9 of the Constitution simply as a proscription imposed upon Japan from outside; it also struck a chord with many of the Japanese people, particularly those with left-wing or liberal views.

At the same time, right-wingers have always been uncomfortable with a constitutional stipulation which seemed to them to violate the sovereignty of Japan. On numerous occasions, conservatives (many of them senior politicians in the ruling LDP) have sought in various ways to expand Japan's military role. Unlike in many countries, where foreign policy issues are often perceived as separate from the normal domestic political agenda, the question of Japan's defence posture has always been of the utmost political importance. And Japan's self-defence forces (SDF) enjoy a curiously ambiguous status; they are 'exclusively defence-oriented', which means that they:

1. can only act if attacked,
2. must take only minimum actions required for defence; and
3. the size of their capability must be limited to the minimum necessary for defence: that is, there should be no offensive or strategic weapons.

In international law, 'self-defence' covers both individual and collective defence, but clause 9 is usually viewed as meaning that only acts of individual defence are permissible. It is not clear how this definition would hold up in the event of a military crisis. The self-defence forces are also under civilian control, answerable to the prime minister and the cabinet, members of which must all be civilians according to the Constitution. Conscription is banned, and so is overseas despatch of the self-defence forces. This last stipulation was not a legal ban, though, but a resolution passed by the upper house in 1954.

In 1976, Japanese defence policy was clarified in the National Defence Programme Outline (NDPO) (see George, 1988: 239–45).

This included the principle of a gradual, progressive improvement in Japan's defence capability up to specific force levels which would allow the SDF to carry out two main tasks: full surveillance during peacetime, and capacity to deal with limited acts of aggression. To reassure the public, the NDPO was linked to a maximum ceiling on military expenditure of 1 per cent of Japan's GNP (this ceiling was officially exceeded in 1988 and 1989, and questions have been raised about the accounting procedures used in meeting the 1 per cent target). Successive annual white papers on Japan's defence policy published since 1976 have emphasised four central points:

- an 'exclusively defence-oriented policy' (in other words, force cannot be used until an attack takes place);
- a pledge never to become a military power which will threaten other countries;
- the adherence to three non-nuclear principles, which are not possessing, manufacturing or harbouring nuclear weapons; and
- a commitment that the military will remain under civilian control (Defense Agency, 1997: 103–4).

The irony of the situation has been that although the LDP (1955–93) was repeatedly re-elected on the strength of policies which promoted economic growth, the majority of the Japanese public has broadly supported the views of the opposition and media 'peace coalition' on defence questions. The LDP has therefore always been extremely cagey about defining Japanese defence policy. Areas of controversy include:

1. What is meant by 'the principle of self-defence'?
2. What is meant by 'minimum necessary defence capability'?
3. What is meant by 'limited and small-scale' military aggression?
4. What is the area to be defended under the self-defence provisions?

For this reason, Japan has always been reluctant to provide the United States with any clear commitment to take over particular defence functions, or play a specific defensive role. Rather, Japan has quietly but steadily increased the size and capability of the SDF.

The US–Japanese security relationship has been evolving since the Occupation period, as the Americans have put increasing pressure on Japan to expand their defence forces and capabilities. A wide range of views has been expressed about the nature of the relationship, ranging from former US Ambassador to Japan Mike Mansfield's claim that: 'US–Japan relations is the most important bilateral relationship – bar none' (Mansfield, 1989); to more pessimistic American views which see Japan as a potentially dangerous force to be 'contained' by foreign policy initiatives; and left-wing Japanese criticisms of the security alliance as a militaristic continuation of the Occupation.

As early as 1950, the Americans ordered the Japanese to establish a substantial police reserve of 75 000 men to replace US troops who were being moved to Korea (George, 1988: 245–6). 1951 saw the signing of the US–Japan Security Treaty, which stated that the US would maintain forces in Japan, but with the proviso that Japan would increasingly take over responsibility for its own defence provisions. The worst year for US–Japanese relations since the Pacific War was 1960, when the Mutual Security Treaty was revised. The new 'Treaty of Mutual Cooperation and Security' met with widespread opposition and was greeted by angry street demonstrations. Yet in one sense the treaty was highly favourable to Japan: although the USA promised to defend Japan, Japan made no such pledge to come to the aid of the United States. The supposedly 'mutual' treaty was entirely one-sided. But this very lack of equality left Japan in a firmly subordinate position to the United States, dependent upon continuing good relations with the Americans. As Japan gained in economic power, this relationship of political subordination to the United States became increasingly problematic.

Partly in recognition of the changing economic status of Japan, the American 'Nixon Doctrine' of 1969 called upon US allies in Asia to assume more of the financial burden for their defence. The Vietnam debacle was reducing American enthusiasm for military entanglements in the Asia-Pacific region; and, increasingly, Japan was expected to pay a larger share of the American defence costs. By the mid-1980s the Japanese were paying around $21 000 a year for each American serviceperson on their shores, and in 1990 the Japanese government agreed to pay 50 per cent of the entire cost of the American defence establishment. The USA was unhappy about the nominal 1 per cent of GNP limit on defence spending set by the Japanese, pressing them repeatedly to raise the proportion to 2 or 3 per cent. Their ever-increasing trade deficits with Japan did nothing to placate American unease.

Nor was it just money that the Americans sought. During the late 1970s and 1980s, they pressed the Japanese to assume a wider role as a strategic partner in the defence of Pacific Asia, partly as a response to build-ups of Soviet air and naval power in the north-west Pacific at a time when the United States had become increasingly concerned about the threat of conflict in the Middle East in the wake of the 1979 Iranian Revolution. The Americans began to believe that their own capacity to respond to potential military threats was severely stretched, and that Japan needed to assume greater responsibility for regional security around its immediate territorial waters and air-space.

Japan's first response to American pressure was directed at rebutting the charge that Japan was enjoying a 'free ride' in defence terms. The Japanese government emphasised what it called its 'Comprehensive Security' policy, which involved counting development aid and efforts to ensure supplies of food and energy as part of an overall security strategy (George, 1988: 257–9). In other words, though the Japanese might not be making a substantial direct military contribution, they were supporting international political and economic stability in innumerable different ways. This argument did little to impress the Americans, but the phrase has continued to have currency as part of the arguments of those who favour only moderate, incremental increases in defence spending and activities.

During Yasuhiro Nakasone's term as prime minister (1982–7) there was a distinct change in the direction of Japanese foreign policy. Whereas most previous Japanese prime ministers had been machine politicians reluctant to impose a clear policy direction on the country, Nakasone was famous for having filled a number of notebooks with lists of things to do when he became premier. Nakasone took a hawkish line on defence matters. He referred to Japan on a visit to the USA as a 'giant aircraft carrier', and quickly agreed to commit Japan to a number of specific defensive roles which his predecessors had been loathe to embrace. In particular, he agreed that Japan would take on responsibility for defending sea-lanes within 1000 nautical miles of Japanese shores (George, 1988: 261).

Under his premiership, the Defence Agency issued a statement saying that the concept of 'self-defence' need not apply only on Japanese soil, territorial waters or airspace, but could extend beyond

Table 8.1   Defence expenditure and military power

	Defence expenditure (US$ per capita)		Numbers in armed forces (1000s)	
	1985	1997	1985	1997
United States	1537	1018	2151.6	1447.6
United Kingdom	803	611	327.1	213.8
France	843	708	464.3	380.8
Russia	n/a	435	n/a	1240
Japan	254	325	243	235.6
North Korea	290	246	838	1055
South Korea	218	320	598	672
China	27	30	3900	2840
India	12	13	1260	1145

Source: International Institute for Strategic Studies (1998), *The Military Balance 1998/1999*, London, Oxford University Press.

the immediate area of Japan itself. This was a significant change in previous interpretations of the concept of self-defence, and came much closer to satisfying American demands. Whilst it could be argued that Japan was not agreeing to anything radically new, there was a perceptible shift away from the idea of a purely defensive strategy and towards assuming a specific regional security role in its own right.

Nakasone also sought to break through the 1 per cent GNP ceiling, and made a couple of attempts to do so by appealing directly to public opinion. Although he was not decisively successful in doing so, partly because of opposition from within the LDP and bureaucracy, Nakasone did succeed in modifying popular attitudes on this controversial issue. Nevertheless, whilst more Japanese people began to be reconciled to the *fait accompli* of the SDF and the Security Treaty, this did not mean that they supported an expanded defence role for Japan such as his government advocated.

The Mid-Term Defence Programme Estimate (MTDPE) for 1986–90 envisaged a shift away from the idea of 'standard defence force' (absolute minimal response capability) to the more substantial 'necessary defence power' linked to the size of real threats. Nakasone saw Japan's status as an economic superpower widely recognized and acknowledged. Nevertheless, he had several important failures:

- Nakasone openly supported the idea of revising the 1947 Constitution to amend the 'peace clause', but he was not able to accomplish this objective. Like other LDP premiers before him, he was restrained by the strength of the forces ranged against him.
- Nakasone did not succeed in upgrading the Defense Agency to a fully-fledged ministry.
- Nakasone was not able to revise the security treaty.
- Nakasone did not preside over a big increase in defence spending: the incremental rises of previous decades continued.

How powerful are the self-defence forces today? On the one hand, Japan possesses sizeable military assets, and ranks as the number five defence spender in the world. Expenditure for fiscal year 1997 was around ¥4.9 trillion, or roughly US$38 billion. In March 1997, the strength of the forces stood at 273 751: 179 430 in the ground self-defence forces, 45 752 in the maritime self-defence forces, and 47 207 in the air self-defence forces, plus 47 900 reserve personnel (see Table 8.1 for a comparison to other countries). The SDF has 363 combat aircraft and 156 ships of various kinds (including 16 submarines and 58 destroyers) (Defense Agency, 1997). Yet, quite recently, independent analysts suggested that the Japanese forces could only hold up a serious attack for a couple of days; their defensive posture meant that they possessed only a narrow range of capabilities. According to Hanami, 'a substantial military budget does not easily translate into a substantial fighting force' (Hanami, 1993: 595).

Aurelia George argues that the traditional view of Japan as a 'free rider' in defence terms is now in need of re-examination: from a weak and dependent American ally in the early postwar period, Japan has evolved into a powerful regional lieutenant with a military role that is edging beyond the boundaries of self-defence. Although it remains dependent on the US security umbrella, Japan has begun the transition to a collective security state with some degree of regional force projection (George, 1993: 237). George sees the Nakasone period as 'the early stages of fundamental structural change in Japan's defence posture' (1993: 290). The old dependency relationship with the United States is being redefined.

Takashi Inoguchi argues that there is a 'functional disparity' between the USA and Japan which clouds relations between the two (Inoguchi, 1993: 58–60). Both countries have considerable vested interests that incline towards protectionism, and a tendency to put domestic political considerations before foreign policy priorities. According to Inoguchi:

> what appears to one side as the adversary's lack of transparency and over reliance on foreign pressure (the American view of Japanese politics), or to the other side as unpredictability, arbitrariness and a self-congratulatory system (the Japanese view of American politics), seems to disturb and irritate the other nation immensely. (1993: 59)

One important debate concerns the extent to which Japan's policy changes are driven by external pressures: is Japan simply a reactive state? Japan tends to be seen in this way by outsiders, but Inoguchi argues that this does not do justice to the complexities of Japanese politics, where even the LDP had to build up a consensus before effecting a policy shift. Thus the security policy which successive LDP governments wanted to pursue was always at variance with its actual policy.

Japan and the USA issued new 'Guidelines for US–Japan Security Defense Cooperation' in September 1997 (see Katahara, 1998: 70–3). This was not a revision of the 1960 Security Treaty, and did not directly address specific regional tensions such as the North Korean situation. However, the new guidelines did contain several important points, including greater sharing of intelligence information (Japan was now receiving 'real-time' defence intelligence direct from US agencies), collaboration between US and Japanese forces when taking part in UN peace-keeping operations or international humanitarian operations, and an increased emphasis on bilateral defence planning and exercises. Significantly, the guidelines noted that 'Japan will have primary responsibility to take action and repel an armed attack as soon as possible'; the main US role would be a supporting one, such as providing strike power in the event of an airborne attack on Japan.

The US–Japan security relationship continues to attract criticism. Analysts such as Shunji Taoka of the *Asahi Shimbun* argued that the changes seen in the new guidelines were an example of 'making the house heavier when it is already located on soft ground' (Taoka, 1997). The presence of substantial US bases in Japan (especially the island of Okinawa) seems increasingly problematic in the post-Cold War world. Prominent politicians, including former Prime Minister Hosokawa, have called for a new policy of a 'US–Japan alliance without bases'. Public opinion polls give some support to this proposal, since around two-thirds of those Japanese polled express support for the US–Japan alliance, but about two-thirds also want to see American bases reduced. Some supporters of this argument suggest that bases should revert to the formal control of the Japanese government, but could still be used by US forces. Critics, however, argue that a reduction in the size or status of US forces in Japan would 'give the wrong signal', perhaps encouraging aggressive moves by North Korea.

One net effect of American withdrawal from the Philippine bases and the switch from a policy of permanent presence to one of collective security could be to encourage Japan to switch from its traditional emphasis on the bilateral relationship with the United States to a new regional stance, in which it identifies more closely with Southeast Asia and other Asia-Pacific countries.

Japan and Asia

Is Japan best seen as a source of inspiration for Asia, an ally in the economic and political development of the region? Or is Japan actually seeking to play on the idea of a shared Asian identity for the purpose of dominating and exploiting Asia? This was an ambiguity clearly apparent during the 1931–45 period, when the Japanese invaded and occupied much of Southeast and East Asia, claiming that they had come to liberate Asia for the Asians, but in practice setting up puppet governments to do their bidding in the region.

One paradox that must be addressed at the outset is Japan's own ambivalence about its Asian identity. From an external perspective, Japan is clearly an Asian country; yet this is not a view with which all Japanese people would find themselves in sympathy. Japan has long regarded itself as an honorary member of the western club of industrialized nations. As an island country not directly connected with the continent of Asia, Japan tends to regard itself as a distinct and separate entity. In 1885, the Japanese intellectual Yukichi Fukuzawa wrote a book called *The Break Free from Asia Theory,* in which he said:

> Although Japan lies close to the eastern edge of Asia, the spirit of its people has transcended Asian conservatism and moved to-wards western civilisation . . . Japan cannot afford to wait for the

enlightenment of its neighbours, in the hope of working with them for the betterment of all Asia. It should break formation and move forward along with the civilised countries of the West. (Quoted in Rowley and do Rosario, 1991: 17)

In practice, this emulation of the West and sense of superiority to Asia was to lead to Japanese imperialism in the region, as Japan first annexed Korea, then Manchuria, and eventually invaded Southeast Asia.

Once Japan had succeeded in 'moving forward' to the extent of overtaking many western powers economically, there was a general recognition, at least in theory, that Japan needed to rejoin Asia in order to play a global role commensurate with its position. But negative stereotypes of Asia remain common in Japanese thinking and behaviour, as evidenced by the poor treatment received by some guest workers in Japan. There is a tendency for the Japanese to see the rest of Asia simply as a ready source of raw materials, despite the considerable changes in the nature of Japan's trade with the region as industrialization spreads from the original NICs (newly-industrialized countries) to the new dragons of Southeast Asia.

In part, the Japanese leaning towards the West was a direct outcome of the international conditions following the Pacific War. Japanese adventurism in Southeast Asia and elsewhere had left a lasting legacy of distrust, whilst the American Occupation marked the beginning of a close political and economic relationship with the United States which was to take precedence over any Asian entanglements. One Japanese scholar, Masahide Shibusawa, has gone so far as to argue that:

> In fact, after the war, Japan was literally banished from continental Asia, and had to survive virtually on its own resources, with little prospect of being able to take part in any regional system that might develop. With wartime memories still fresh, few countries in either Northeast or Southeast Asia wanted its involvement in the region in any form or context. (Shibusawa, 1984: 158)

He contrasts this with the situation of postwar Germany, which was incorporated into a new European order by its western neighbours in the postwar period. During the 1950s and 1960s, Japan was preoccupied with the pursuit of economic reconstruction, and sought to protect and subsidize its agriculture. The only major

Japanese investment in the Southeast Asian region was in securing supplies of raw materials, primarily oil supplies from Indonesia. In the early 1960s, Prime Minister Ikeda called for Japan to establish its international status through economic development, setting the tone for the 'economism' which followed.

By the late 1960s, Japan had become the primary trading partner of most of the Southeast Asian states, and during the 1970s Japan began making substantial investments in the newly-industrialising countries (South Korea, Taiwan, Hong Kong and Singapore) as it sought to enter their markets and transfer some production there. Yet in the early 1970s there were virulent anti-Japanese protests in Thailand and Indonesia, demonstrating that economic success does not necessarily lead to a more positive international image. Japanese premier Tanaka had a disastrous visit to Southeast Asia in 1974, when he was widely heckled by hostile crowds.

When the Association of Southeast Asian Nations (ASEAN) was first formed in 1967, the Japanese were not terribly impressed. Indonesia had been a prime mover in the formation of the Association, but at the time was in a parlous economic condition. Japan's attitude towards ASEAN changed after the fall of Saigon in 1975. The Japanese realized that they could no longer rely upon the Americans to take charge of the Southeast Asia connection, and Japanese markets and sources of raw materials would have to be secured by a new diplomatic line. There was a significant change of tone by Japan, which began to talk in terms of mutual understanding and *nemawashi,* laying the groundwork for business and trade deals. The ASEAN countries also recognized the importance of Japan; now that the Americans had been defeated over Vietnam, they started to look elsewhere for models of success and development.

In 1977 Japanese premier Fukuda visited Southeast Asia, promising $1.55 billion in economic assistance, and calling for an new framework of Japan-Southeast Asian relations. He promised a 'heart-to-heart' relationship based on mutual understanding, and pledged that Japan had no intention of re-militarizing. This became known as the Fukuda Doctrine, and remains substantially intact today. Although a good rapport between Japan and the ASEAN countries was central to the Fukuda doctrine, it was also true that the Japanese sought good trading relations with the countries of Indochina, and indeed with Burma. Japan hoped to promote cooperation between ASEAN and communist Indochina. The aim was to use economic means to ensure the stability of Southeast Asia, thereby obviating the need for military power to be used. The contrast between Tanaka's failed visit to the region in 1974 and Fukuda's very successful visit of 1977 was abundantly clear.

Thai political scientist Chaiwat Khamchoo has quoted one Japanese scholar as saying that the Fukuda doctrine was 'a trader's diplomacy: of the economy, by the economy and for the economy' (Chaiwat, 1991: 8). There was nothing inherently new about the Fukuda doctrine; it was essentially a restatement of the position Japan already held. He saw Japanese policy towards Southeast Asia as a 'declaration of enlightened self-interest' (Chaiwat, 1991: 10); the idea was to forge a link between Japan's economic interests and the development of Southeast Asia in such a way as to make sure that such development depended upon Japan. The Fukuda doctrine was part-and-parcel of an 'omnidirectional foreign policy' that reached out to each side of any potential conflict. Richard Cronin is one of many scholars who disagrees, seeing the Fukuda doctrine as a turning point when: 'For the first time since World War II, Japan began to consciously articulate its interests in Southeast Asia' (Cronin, 1991: 60). One example of this change was that Japan did not remain impartial over vexed matters such as the Cambodia conflict during the 1980s. Despite some pressure from the business sector, the Japanese did act to suspend aid to Vietnam following the Vietnamese invasion of Cambodia. In doing so, Japan supported the position taken by the ASEAN countries.

In the 1980s the Japanese began investing heavily in ASEAN countries, particularly Thailand, Indonesia, and Malaysia. This time, cheap and docile labour was a major attraction. For example, in 1989 manufacturing wages in Jakarta were only 4 per cent of those in Japan; in Bangkok the figure was 10 per cent. Although the gap later closed somewhat, moving production to Southeast Asia remained an extremely attractive financial proposition. The rise in the value of the yen (known as *endaka*) in the mid-1980s led the Japanese to shift away from a primary concern with oil and other natural resources, and an increasing emphasis on manufacturing and retailing. This was accompanied by a shift towards Singapore, Thailand and Malaysia at the expense of Indonesia, though later on investment returned to Indonesia in the wake of government liberalization of investment regulations. In 1990, the Japanese share of foreign direct investment in ASEAN countries ranged from around 25 per cent in Indonesia to around 53 per cent in Thailand.

Despite the high levels of Japanese investment in Asia, investment in the USA and Europe was even higher. There was also a certain caution about Japanese investment strategies in Southeast Asia. Japanese companies were believed to have an informal understanding among themselves that they should not try to gain more than a 30–40 per cent market share in any one local industry. Nevertheless, this has proved difficult in certain sectors: in the car industry, for example, Japanese models are very dominant throughout the region. The range and pre-eminence of Japanese products in Southeast Asia has to be seen to be believed; not only manufactured goods, but also cultural products such as video games and cartoons are extremely pervasive in the region.

One source of resentment against Japanese concerns has been their reluctance to devolve management responsibility to local staff. In this area they are regarded as decades behind many American and European companies. Many Japanese companies have virtually no locals in key positions other than a token personnel manager. The most severe critics of Japan in Southeast Asia have accused the Japanese of a form of neo-colonialism, what the Filipino nationalist writer Renato Constantino (1989) calls *The Second Invasion*. He notes that the early emphasis of Japanese investment in the Philippines was on 'pollution-causing, extractive, raw-material producing and labor-intensive industries' (1989: 45). He cited as an example a plant built by Kawasaki Steel. Whilst at first glance this looked like the beginnings of a Philippine steel industry, initial impressions were misleading; the plant concentrated on 'sintering' – the most pollution-creating phase of the steel-making process – and all other stages would continue to be carried out in Japan. By moving the sintering out of Japan, the company could escape from environmental protests at home.

Public-opinion polls suggest that an attitude of pacifism remained deeply ingrained in the Japanese consciousness; there was little support for expanding the role of Japan's so-called self-defense forces, and even the decision to send SDF members to participate in non-combative roles in the UN peace-keeping operation in Cambodia was a highly controversial move. Nevertheless, the recent American withdrawal from its substantial bases in the Philippines means that Japan will find it even more difficult than before to present an omnidirectional foreign policy to its neighbours in the Asia-Pacific region; the more tatty the American security umbrella, the more Japan will be caught in the rains and squalls of regional tensions and conflicts.

Chaiwat argued that a greater regional security role for Japan in the region should be welcomed, so long as it did not entail direct military involvement. For example, Japan could provide financial backing for US forces in the region, and cooperate closely with ASEAN in intelligence-gathering and technical support with regard to security matters. Yet even steps of this kind would be viewed with unease by many in Southeast Asia, as the 'thin end of the wedge'. Although the Japanese continue to argue that they are simply misunderstood by their Asian neighbours, whom they hold in the highest fraternal regard, Southeast Asia still looks upon Japan with a curious compound of admiration and distrust. Japan's failure to produce a clearly-articulated response to the economic crisis which beset the region from mid-1997 was a source of great disappointment in Southeast Asia; a golden opportunity to assert leadership in the region was squandered, partly because of Japanese reluctance to make any independent initiatives that might antagonize the United States. The idea of a Japanese-backed 'Asian' crisis fund, briefly mooted in September 1997, was vetoed by Washington. The United States feared that such an initiative would undermine the role of the IMF and the World Bank.

Japan and China

The relationship between Japan and China is an extremely important one. There are numerous parallels between the two civilisations, and many supposedly 'distinctive' features of Japanese culture – such as the tea ceremony, the use of chopsticks, and writing with ideogrammatic characters – were actually imported and adapted from Chinese culture. Both China and Japan have exalted notions of their place in the world: while Japan sees itself as the first Asian society to challenge western hegemony in modern times, China regards itself as the 'middle kingdom', the ancient civilisation around which the world has long revolved. In other words, both China and Japan regard themselves at least as the world's pre-eminent non-western power, if not simply as the world's pre-eminent civilisation. Although most western scholars regarded the main global struggle of the twentieth century as one between the USA and the USSR, for China and Japan their own longstanding rivalry has often loomed much larger.

As Caroline Rose notes, the Chinese leadership believes that Japan owes China a huge cultural debt, since so many features of Japanese civilisation are borrowings from the Chinese (Rose, 1998: 8–10). Relations between the two peoples date back at least to the third century BC. Between the fifth and tenth centuries AD, there were very close ties between China and Japan; it was during this 'China boom' that many Chinese cultural, economic, political and religious ideas were imported into Japan, including Buddhism and Confucianism. Japan was later for a time a tributary state of China, but in due course the tables were turned: Japan relegated China to a lowly status in the world order, a status that was confirmed by the obvious military and political decline of China in the nineteenth century. From 1894 to 1945 ('fifty years that overshadow two thousand'), Japan pursued a policy of imperialist aggression towards China. Japan's overwhelming military superiority allowed for an easy victory in the 1894 Sino–Japanese War, and from then on Japan represented a role model for China to emulate. Beginning with the Manchuria Incident of 1931, Japan sought to subjugate and colonize China, committing numerous atrocities in the process (see Rose, 1998: 14–16).

Following the Chinese Revolution of 1949, Sino–Japanese political relations were largely frozen until 1972, when Prime Minister Kakuei Tanaka (following the lead of the United States under Nixon) initiated steps to normalize diplomatic relations between the two countries (see Mendl, 1995: 80–1). In the period that followed, economic relations between China and Japan began to flourish, and the two countries signed a formal peace treaty in 1978. Some outstanding issues remained unresolved, however, such as the status of the disputed Senkaku Islands.

Sino-Japanese relations received a major setback in 1982 when an intense conflict broke out concerning the way in which Japanese school textbooks dealt with Japan's wartime role in China (for a definitive account, see Rose, 1998). China issued a formal diplomatic protest over the issue, which has clouded relations between the two countries ever since, despite what Mendl refers to as the 'thickening network of ties between the two countries' during the 1980s (Mendl, 1995: 83). Following the end of the Cold War in 1989, relations became even closer as Japanese investment poured into business ventures in a China now committed to operating a marketized economy within a totalitarian political order ('one country, two systems'). Compared with western countries, Japan adopted a 'soft' response to China's bloody repression at Tiananmen Square in June 1989; conscious of Chinese sensitivities concerning the war, Japan has always been reluctant to voice open criticisms of China's human-rights record. For example, NHK (Japan's national public broadcasting agency) is well-known for its low-key treatment of controversial issues such as China's Tibet policy.

Under agreements signed in 1972 and 1978, Japan formally recognized China's claims to Taiwan. Nevertheless, Japan was placed in a difficult position during heightened tensions between China and Taiwan in 1995, especially given the role of American forces in providing symbolic support for the Taiwanese. If armed conflict were ever to break out between China and Taiwan, Japan would face some very difficult decisions concerning the parameters of the US–Japan security alliance. China's tough stance on Taiwan highlighted the extent to which the Peoples' Liberation Army had been acquiring modern military hardware, a process of modernization that might pose a threat to Japan's interests in the future. China protested at the new security guidelines issued by the US and Japan in 1997, viewing the provision for enhanced cooperation in regional crises as an indirect reference to the potentially volatile Taiwan issue.

High-level visits by Chinese and Japanese leaders helped secure improved relations between the two countries in the 1990s. One particularly symbolic visit was that of the Japanese Emperor to China in 1992. During this visit – the first ever by a Japanese monarch – he made a partial apology for Japan's wartime actions, a statement which did not fully satisfy the Chinese but was regarded as excessive by many conservative Japanese politicians. Conflicting views of the past are likely to remain a source of tension between China and Japan. As Japan stumbled economically at the end of the twentieth century, fast-growing China was presented with a real opportunity to gain the upper hand in the China–Japan relationship for the first time in centuries.

Japan and North Korea

Japan is very close geographically to North Korea, and has a lot to lose from political instability on the Korean peninsula. From 1990 onwards, talks between Japan and North Korea began over possible normalization of relations between the two countries. A prominent supporter of a 'soft' line on North Korea was former LDP power-broker Shin Kanemaru, who was a leading figure in initiating talks with the regime. The Japan Socialist Party also had quite close connections with North Korea. In 1993, there were claims that North Korea had tested a medium range missile in the Sea of Japan, leading to increased tension in the bilateral relationship.

The death of Stalinist dictator Kim Il-Sung in July 1994 created considerable uncertainty about the future of North Korea. His death coincided with a confused period in Japanese domestic politics, as Murayama became the fourth prime minister to hold office in the space of 12 months. Since Kim Il-Sung's demise, there have been persistent reports of tensions within the regime; alarms over the country's nuclear programme have been coupled with problems of food shortages and famine. Amongst the Korean community in Japan there is evidence that loyalty to North Korea, and membership of the pro-Pyongyang organization Chongryun is declining, as the North Korean regime appears increasingly isolated and fossilized. To a large extent, Japan has adopted a wait-and-see policy on North Korea, letting the United States take the lead. Nevertheless, the unpredictable and potentially dangerous Pyongyang regime poses the most immediate military threat faced by Japan.

Peace-Keeping Operations

While the Japanese constitution clearly forbids Japan from engaging in offensive military action, does it permit Japan to provide forces for use in United Nations peace-keeping operations (PKOs)? This question has provoked considerable debate in Japan, which despatched members of the self-defence forces to serve in the Cambodian PKO in 1992, following the passage of the Peace-Keeping Operations Bill in June 1992. One reason for the passage of the PKO Bill was a sense of concern among Japanese politicians and policy-makers, about Japan's weak reaction to the Iraqi invasion of Kuwait in 1990. Japan was heavily criticized by the international community for making no practical (rather than financial) contribution to the US-led attacks on Iraq in 1991; by agreeing to join UN PKO operations, Japan made a significant gesture to appease its

Table 8.2   Geographical distribution of Japan's bilateral overseas development aid (US$ millions)

Region	1972	1980	1990	1993	1996
Asia	466	1383	4117	4861	4145
	(97.7)	(70.5)	(59.3)	(59.5)	(49.6)
Middle East	4	204	705	522	561
	(0.8)	(10.4)	(10.2)	(6.4)	(6.7)
Africa	5	223	792	966	1067
	(1.0)	(11.4)	(11.4)	(11.8)	(12.8)
Latin America	3	118	651	737	986
	(0.6)	(6.0)	(8.1)	(9.0)	(11.8)
Oceania	1	12	114	138	198
	(0.3)	(0.6)	(1.6)	(1.7)	(2.4)
Europe (including	n/a	n/a	158	124	200
Eastern Europe)			(2.3)	(1.5)	(2.4)
Unspecified	n/a	23	494	816	1200
		(1.2)	(7.1)	(10)	(14.4)
Total	479	1961	6940	8164	8356

Figures in parentheses are the percentages of the respective totals

Source: Economic Cooperation Bureau, Ministry of Foreign Affairs (1998), *Japan's Official Development Assistance: Annual Report 1997,* Tokyo, Association for Promotion of International Cooperation, p. 135.

critics. Nevertheless, many Japanese people remained uneasy about participation of the SDF in PKOs, while some conservatives undoubtedly saw PKO participation as the beginning of a 'normalization' of the role of the armed forces in Japan.

Aid Policy

Whereas many other international aid programmes target poor countries (the least among less-developed countries, or LLDCs) for the greatest support, Japan has pumped huge amounts of development aid into countries with relatively high living standards, which also happen to be major prospective or actual markets for Japanese goods and services. Japan became a significant aid donor in the 1960s, and a series of 'aid-doubling' plans which began with

Fukuda in 1977 made Japan the world's largest ODA (overseas development aid) provider by 1989. At the same time, these high figures partly reflected the rising value of the yen; Söderberg notes that if Japanese aid is measured as a proportion of GNP, Japan is ranked only number 17 among donor countries. (Söderberg 1996: 35). There are also questions about the quality of Japan's aid, which involves a higher proportion of loans to grants than that of any other donor country. Around half of Japan's aid is funded by government-controlled investments such as Japanese postal savings accounts, investments that require returns (Söderberg 1996: 40).

The Japanese government formerly used an unofficial formula of 7:1:1:1 to assign development aid to Asia, Africa, Latin America and the Middle East (Söderberg 1996: 34), though aid to Asia has recently declined to around 50 per cent of the total aid budget (see Table 8.2 for a geographical summary of Japan's aid). Around half of Japan's Asian aid budget has gone to ASEAN countries. However, the fastest growing category of Japan's ODA budget has been 'unspecified', or non-region specific expenditure, which makes accurate comparisons with earlier figures difficult (Ministry of Foreign Affairs, 1997: 135). Also, much Japanese aid takes the form of loans, which are generally tied to orders for Japanese companies. Indonesia, Thailand and the Philippines are among the top five recipients of Japanese ODA, with Indonesia topping the list (Ministry of Foreign Affairs, 1997: 136).

In summaries of ODA country policy, the Japanese government stresses Indonesia's 'strong historical ties with Japan as a neighbouring country' to account for very high levels of aid, whilst Thailand's position as the third largest ODA recipient is justified in terms of 'traditionally friendly relations' with Japan. Poverty levels are clearly a secondary consideration, and the desire by Japan to foster good political relations with recipient countries looms large (Potter, 1996: 155). Only 14.4 per cent of Japanese aid was directed to LLDCs in 1996 (Ministry of Foreign Affairs, 1997: 139), partly since the capacity of these countries to repay loans was doubtful. Around 40 per cent of ODA was directed into economic infrastructure (notably in the transportation and energy sectors), a much higher proportion than most other donors. Aid has regularly been used as a means of countering criticism of Japan – such as by the Arab world during the 1970s oil crisis – and of reducing 'Japan bashing', in Asia and elsewhere.

Table 8.3   Japan's principal exports and imports by country

Country	Exports (¥ billions)		Country	Imports (¥ billions)	
	1985	*1997*		*1985*	*1997*
United States	15 583	14 169	United States	6 213	9 149
Korea	1 649	3 153	China	1 552	5 062
Taiwan	1 205	3 335	Korea	977	1 763
Hong Kong	1 565	3 298	Indonesia	2 431	1 769
China	2 991	2 631	Taiwan	811	1 511
Singapore	925	2 450	Australia	1 785	1 763
Thailand	488	1 764	Germany	700	1 501
Germany	1 646	2 178	Malaysia	1 035	1 375
Total	41 956	50 938	Total	31 085	40 956

Source: Ministry of Finance, Japan

Compared with other donor countries, Japan is much more inclined to view ODA as an instrument of broader trade and economic policies. Söderberg argues that 'ODA became a tool, not only for promoting the export efforts of recipient countries, but also for restructuring Japanese industry' (Söderberg, 72). The business community exerts significant influence over the disbursement of aid. Projects such as MITI's 1987 'New Asian Industries Development Plan' saw Japan's ODA, private investment and trade as a 'trinity': detailed proposals were drawn up, for example, to help Malaysia become a leading producer of word processors (Pyle, 1996: 135). As Cronin writes:

> The essence of the concept is the co-ordination of ODA, commercial lending and private investment to promote a division of economic labour as envisioned in the Japanese 'flock of geese' metaphor for the respective roles of Japan, the Asian NIEs and the developing countries of Asia. (Cronin, 1991: 54–5)

This scheme envisions a three-tiered division of labour, with Japan on top, followed by the NIEs, and then ASEAN plus China. Aid is used, not simply on specific infrastructure projects, but to help create 'structural complementarities with the Japanese economy' (Pyle, 1996: 135).

In 1991, Japan approved an ODA charter emphasising issues such as the preservation of peace, democratization, human rights, and the environment as criteria for awarding aid, stipulations which have not been uniformly applied. The mixed record of the ODA charter illustrates that aid is not a one-way street, but a complex process which involves negotiations and bargaining between the Japanese agencies and recipient governments.

Trade and Investment

Japan has enormous overseas investments, having shifted much of its manufacturing capacity to Asia, Europe and North America from the 1970s onwards. In areas ranging from car manufacturing to electronics, computer-related technology, and international finance, Japan has gained a powerful global position. At the same time, Japan has come under considerable criticism from trade partners (and particularly from the United States) for creating obstacles to inward investment and trade (a summary of Japan's exports and imports by country is shown in Table 8.3). Japan has been accused of protectionist practices, and the creation of 'invisible tariff barriers' to block imports. Japanese trade negotiators frequently resorted to laughable forms of special pleading; one of the most notorious was a refusal to permit the import of American-made skis, on the grounds that they were not suitable for Japanese snow. Former US trade negotiator Clyde Prestowitz argues that: 'To some extent, Japan's success has been derived from its ability to use the international system without conforming to it or accepting its burdens' (Prestowitz, 1988: 313). Nevertheless, he insisted that viewing Japan's trade practices as 'unfair' was to miss the point: the United States could not persist in trying to change Japan's economy to a free market system. At the same time, the phenomenon of *gaiatsu,* or 'foreign pressure' to alter trade and business practices, became widespread in the 1980s.

US–Japan trade relations reflected the 'mentor' role that the United States had assumed towards Japan since the Occupation. America's foster child in Asia had grown up, and by the 1980s it was widely thought that Japan's economic rise was being matched by a parallel American decline. Nevertheless, successive US administrations adopted a patronizing, quasi-parental tone in their dealings with Japan; Japan's peace constitution and dependence on US military support meant that Japan had not achieved fully-fledged international adulthood. Whereas most American commentators on Japan during the 1970s and early 1980s had offered a very positive portrayal of Japanese successes, by the mid-1980s trade disputes were souring relations. Some politicians in the USA – faced with factory closures and job losses in their home states – seized on the writings of 'revisionist' scholars with a more critical perspective on Japan (including Chalmers Johnson, Karel van Wolferen, and Clyde Prestowitz), calling for tougher treatment of Japanese business. Congressmen began to appear on television, smashing up Japanese appliances with sledge-hammers. Revisionists and their self-proclaimed supporters were labelled by pro-Japan analysts as 'Japan-bashers'.

Mikanagi argues that three changes in the global political economy have forced Japan to change its foreign economic policies since the 1980s: declining American tolerance for countries which exploited the open US market while closing their own markets; increasing pressures for deregulation as a means of sustaining economic growth, without replicating previous inflationary cycles; and faster pace of regional economic integration, as evidenced by developments with NAFTA and the EU (Mikanagi, 1996: 9–12). Under these circumstances, Japan faced three options:

> do nothing, create an exclusive regional arrangement with its Asian neighbours, or increase its openness, either unilaterally or within a multilateral form such as Asian Pacific Economic Cooperation (APEC). (Mikanagi, 1996: 12)

APEC, formed in 1991, brings together Japan, the USA, Canada, Australia, South Korea, China and the ASEAN countries in a grouping of 21 members. Although it aims to promote trade between member states, it is not conceived as a protectionist regional bloc. One motive for establishing APEC was a desire by the USA and Australia to pre-empt Malaysian-backed moves for an East Asian Economic Caucus (EAEC), which would have excluded western countries. Such a bloc would have challenged NAFTA. Whereas an EAEC would have provided Japan with scope to play a leading regional role, APEC's multilateral format offered limited scope for Japanese influence. In other words, while Europe and North America have created strong regional trading blocs, Japan and Asia have much less formalized ties. The USA generally prefers to deal with trade partners on a bilateral basis, since the vast American economy allows it to negotiate with individual countries from a position of strength. Since doing nothing was an untenable option in the face of sustained external pressures, and since an Asian bloc failed to materialize (partly because of Japanese deference to US objections), Japan has been nudged in the direction of increasing openness, partly within the APEC framework. Mikanagi (1996: 114) argues that Japan's trade policy remains broadly 'reactive' rather than active, responding to foreign pressures instead of developing initiatives.

Internationalization

Since the 1980s, Japan has been pursuing an overt policy of 'internationalization', making various efforts to broaden its contacts with the wider world. The internationalization strategy (perhaps most clearly articulated during the 1982–87 Nakasone governments) identified euphemistically-termed deficiencies of 'mutual under-standing' as a weak point in Japan's order, which might undermine the country's international standing and competitiveness. Accordingly, numerous programmes were developed to make the Japanese people more internationally-minded, and to make non-Japanese more familiar with Japan.

These programmes ranged from cultural and research activities organized by bodies such as the Japan Foundation, sister-city schemes, and the establishment of 'international centres' and inter-national student residences in cities all over Japan, to the creation of the Japan Exchange and Teaching programme (JET) to bring large numbers of language assistants (mainly young westerners) to work in Japanese schools. While many of these projects were extremely laudable, some were simply tokenistic. The political impetus behind the policy of internationalization was arguably a nationalistic one, a continuation of the Meiji era objective of learning from foreign countries and thereby strengthening Japan. Many internationaliza-tion programmes, particularly in their early phases, focused more on the USA and other western countries than on Japan's Asian neighbours. Japan's nationalist 'internationalizers' sought to steal the thunder from the pacifist internationalists of the left, but were incompletely successful in doing so.

Other Key Relationships

The Asia–Europe Summit Meeting (ASEM), inaugurated in Bang-kok in 1996, represented the first attempts to create a formalized framework for relations between the European Union and the countries of East and Southeast Asia. Although ASEM has yet to evolve much beyond a talking shop, there are logical reasons for Japan to be interested in forging strong ties with Europe, in order to offset its immense military, political and psychological dependence on the United States. Nuttall argues that Japan is becoming 'more like us' – in other words, more like Europe (Nuttall, 1998: 176) – and that the EU ought to consolidate strong bilateral ties with Japan in order to preserve the multilateral system from American attempts to undermine it. However, the Japanese preoccupation with their relations with the USA makes such a development difficult to implement.

The relationship between Russia and Japan is an important one, which has long been overshadowed by a dispute concerning the 'northern territories' – including islands off the coast of Hokkaido that were seized by the former Soviet Union at the end of the war. The Japanese have long demanded the return of these territories, and since the end of the Cold War have sought to use economic aid for Russia as a bargaining tool to support this demand. To date, however, the issue – which arouses strong nationalist feelings on both sides – remains unresolved.

Conclusion

Mikanagi's view of Japan as a country still in 'response mode' internationally is one frequently echoed both inside and outside Japan. Like Nakasone in the 1980s, prominent conservative politi-cians of the 1990s have called on Japan to play a more assertive international role. In the words of Ichiro Ozawa, they urge Japan to become a 'normal nation', with more conventional military forces and a seat on the UN Security Council, willing where necessary to stand up to America (a view most explicitly expressed by maverick politician Shintaro Ishihara (1991) in his book *The Japan that Can Say No*) and to take on a leading role in Asia. The end of the Cold War (followed by the end of LDP hegemony) coincided with a broader debate over the postwar constitution (see McCormack, 1996: 202–19). In 1994, for example, the *Yomiuri* newspaper (Japan's leading daily) produced detailed and provocative proposals for revising the constitution, including regularizing the position of the armed forces. Karel van Wolferen came out in strong support of the proposal. Meanwhile, various groups on both sides of the political spectrum advocated what McCormack calls 'creative reinterpretation': preserving the constitution in its original form, but endowing it with new meanings (McCormack, 1996: 205). For many Japanese, however, the 'peace constitution' (and the reactive international stance that it implies) remains a sacred defence against the possible resurgence of militarism; why tinker with a formula which has brought lasting security and prosperity in the postwar period?

Many of Japan's allies take an ambivalent view of this debate. The United States would like Japan to broaden its defence roles, becoming an equal rather than a subordinate partner in the 'mutual' security alliance that links the two countries. Some Asian countries (Malaysia, for example) would like to see Japan provide an alternative to US hegemony in the Pacific. Yet a reactive Japan is also very useful to the West, since a passive Japan does not challenge or threaten western interests. Asian countries such as China and South Korea remain deeply wary of Japan for historical reasons. The recession in Japan since the early 1990s, compounded by the wider Asian crisis that began in 1997, raised doubts about the implicit triumphalism of some earlier Japanese views. Assumptions that Japan was inexorably 'rising', as North America and Europe entered a period of terminal decline, were not borne out by unfolding events. Japan – with its state interventionism, powerful bureaucracy, high degree of regulation and all-pervasive hierarchies – no longer looked like an ideal model for other Asian countries to emulate.

The rise of China also posed new challenges to Japan: the remarkable rise of Japan was partly a function of the fog of Maoism that clouded China for several decades. As this fog is lifting and economic liberalization is proceeding apace, Japan faces the prospect of a resurgent China, which could undermine any residual Japanese notions of regional leadership.

Events such as the Gulf War and the Asian currency crisis have provided Japan with ample opportunities to demonstrate a more active role on the international stage – opportunities that Japan has failed to take. In part, the failure of Japan to move beyond a reactive mode reflects Japanese weaknesses, faced with a combination of economic recession and (since 1993) political uncertainties and confusion. Confronted with increasing domestic difficulties, Japan has been forced to look inwards. Paul Kennedy argues that, without sustained political leadership that offers a clear vision for the future, serious question marks remain about Japan's status as a major power (Kennedy, 1994: 199).

9
Conclusion

Evaluating, summarizing, and assessing contemporary Japan is a highly contentious business. At the beginning of the new millennium, Japan seems to have lost the remarkable sense of purpose and direction that characterized its earlier postwar history. From the ashes of the American bombing, and the humiliations of defeat and Occupation, the Japanese successfully recreated themselves as a major nation. By the 1980s, Japan was challenging America's place in the sun, and appeared poised to become the world's 'number one' economic giant. The rest of the world looked on with awe as Japan gained a dominant economic position in the Asia-Pacific region, and began exporting productive capacity to Europe and North America as well. Yet Japan became more than simply an economic superpower. Many features of Japanese society, ranging from world-beating life expectancy to extraordinarily high levels of literacy and exceptionally low incidences of crime, attracted enormous international attention. A whole literature sprang up with a 'learn from Japan' theme, as people sought to discover what 'lessons' could be derived from the Japanese experience, and how far Japan's social and economic successes could be replicated elsewhere.

Interpretations of Japan's remarkable achievements varied widely. Given the country's troublesome terrain and paucity of natural resources, Japan was hardly an obvious candidate for the status of economic superpower. Clearly, the answers had to lie primarily with Japan's people, rather than with the land itself. A review of modern Japanese history reveals a people not given to making a drama out of a crisis. Perhaps more than any other people in the world, the Japanese have succeeded in turning calamities into opportunities, in making the most of bad situations. Faced with seemingly disastrous predicaments in 1853 and 1945, the Japanese won though adversity to assume great power status. While it is possible to offer cultural interpretations for these responses, there was clearly a strong element of political will involved. Central political institutions were able to mould and shape national purpose, manipulating national symbols (such as the Emperor from 1931–45), forging policies which united the public and private sectors (as with MITI during the 1950s), and devising social contracts to ensure the implementation of core agendas (as with Ikeda's income-doubling policy during the early 1960s). Japanese growth was aided by a number of favourable international factors, including the onset of the Cold War, the availability of raw materials, and the existence of ready markets for industrial exports.

Whether or not one accepts the description of early postwar Japan as a 'developmental state', there is little doubt that during this period Japan saw an unusual degree of elite level coordination, which straddled the bureaucracy, the political parties, and the corporate world. This elite collaboration was facilitated by the long one-party reign of the Liberal Democratic Party, from 1955 to 1993; many senior LDP figures had entered politics after bureaucratic careers, and the party was largely funded by big corporate donors. During the high growth decades of the 1950s and 1960s, these alliances were extremely remunerative for all concerned. The LDP and its allies were highly successful in coopting and suppressing opposition and resistance: breaking up or buying off unions, riding roughshod over protest movements such as the 1960 *Anpo* rallies, and pacifying the burgeoning citizens' movements with new legislation on environmental issues.

Japan's period of high growth effectively ended with the 1970s oil shocks, and the boom years of the late 1980s 'bubble economy' were based more on the rising values of Japan's currency, shares and real estate than upon any surge in productivity. Japan's economy seemed to stumble at the very point when the longstanding goal of 'catching up' with western industrialized countries had been surpassed. Having overtaken most of Europe and North America in terms of industrial efficiency, where should Japan go next? Japan had become the world's industrial economy par excellence. Yet, meanwhile, the global economy was shifting away from manufacturing as knowledge and information-based service industries moved centre-stage. Building computers was now less important than devising the software on which they operated. Working practices which had served Japan well during the first and second industrial eras – such as seniority-based pay, reliance on in-house training, and recruiting managers from within an organization, rather than bringing in specialist expertise – were less suited to the faster-changing 'third wave' industrial revolution. Japan lacked workers trained in independent thinking and problem-solving, and lacked the kind of corporate structures within which quick-witted staff could rise rapidly to positions of influence. The corporate culture of most Japanese organizations, with its emphases on hierarchism and deference to superiors, sat uneasily with the ethos of the new knowledge-based society and information economy.

Structural corruption is not new and neither is it unique to Japan. Nevertheless, the economic dynamism that characterized the bubble era generated enormous scope for the misuse of funds and resources. Problems such as bad bank debts (including huge sums owed by *yakuza* front companies), institutionalized payoffs to politicians, and the systematic subversion of financial regulators, created significant weaknesses in the economy. The extent of these weaknesses was clearly revealed after the Southeast Asian economies entered a period of crisis from 1997 onwards. Although it has been argued that corruption had some positive impacts on Japan's economic and political order during the 'catch-up' period, there is growing evidence that institutionalised corruption had begun seriously to undermine Japan's impressive achievements by the 1980s. As the full effects of the banking crisis began to bite in the late 1990s, profitable businesses began to turn in heavy losses, and bankruptcies became endemic (see Tables 9.1 and 9.2).

While these may be temporary setbacks for the Japanese economy, the malaise of Japan's financial system could turn out to be terminal: some estimates suggest that the cost of recapitalizing Japanese banks might be as high as 20 per cent of the country's GDP.

Japanese society clearly has many core strengths which helped sustain and nurture economic growth and transformation during the postwar period, and many observers have commented on the capacity of Japanese people to subordinate individual needs and wishes to the collective good. Whether this capacity derives from inherent cultural qualities (as some argue), or whether 'groupism' was actually an ideology manufactured and fostered by the state for the purposes of social control (as others insist), the end results have been extremely impressive. Divorce rates have been very low, people live longer than elsewhere in the world, and levels of popular satisfaction have been high, with most people seeing themselves as middle class.

Table 9.1   Profits: percentage changes from previous periods

	FY 1995	FY 1996	FY 1997	FY 1998*
Major enterprises (all)	22.1	12.8	−4.9	−21.4
Manufacturing	31.7	18.7	−6.7	−23.8
Non-manufacturing	16.4	9.8	−7.9	−15.5
Small enterprises (all)	6.9	13.7	−18.0	−18.8
Manufacturing	15.2	30.2	−20.4	−34.2
Non-manufacturing	2.9	5.4	−16.6	−9.5
All industries in Japan	19.1	12.0	−7.3	−19.9

* April–September (forecast); FY = fiscal year (12 months beginning 1 April of year stated).

Source: Bank of Japan, http://www.epa.go.jp/geturei/1998sep-7-1.jpg

Table 9.2   Bankruptcies

	FY 1996	FY 1997	FY 1998*
Number of cases of bankruptcy	15 030	17 496	15 390
Liabilities (¥billions)	9 259.4	14 523.6	9 376.9

* January–July 1998 only; FY = fiscal year (12 months beginning 1 April of year stated).

Source: Tokyo Shoukou Research Limited, http://www.epa.go.jp/geturei/1998sep-8.jpg

The postwar period has seen numerous positive social develop-ments in Japan: women have gained more independence and greater career opportunities, the position of minority groups has somewhat improved, peoples' outlooks have become rather more internatio-nalized, and living standards have risen sharply. At the same time, there is a dark side to Japanese society: the falling birthrate, the low quality of family life for many people, preoccupations with futile consumerism, and the apparent alienation of some young people, especially those who are low educational achievers. Social mobility remains limited; there is a big gap between the wealth of Kanto and Kansai, and the relative deprivation of *ura nihon*; discrimination of various kinds flourishes; and disturbing episodes such as the Aum Shinrikyo sect's murderous gas attacks in 1994 and 1995 seem to hint at darker forces stirring beneath the surface of society. Sociologists are expressing growing dissatisfaction with traditional ways of describing and classifying Japanese society, a society which appears to contain both highly successful and acutely dysfunctional elements.

Japan's political order is also difficult to classify. On the one hand Japan has all the formal institutional prerequisites of a modern liberal democracy, yet at the same time there is little doubt that bureaucrats enjoy much greater degrees of formal and informal power in the Japanese system than in most other democracies. Japanese party politicians play an important role, but ministerial authority is weak, and the prime minister has very limited central control over the mechanisms of government. The Japanese model of elite governance is one that entails an exceptional degree of mutual back-scratching by ministers, party grandees, top civil servants, and corporate leaders. Although this cosy elite collaboration may have served Japan well during the high growth era, an unhealthy degree of collusion and cronyism had penetrated the system by the time of Tanaka's premiership in the 1970s. Despite the evident need for greater transparency and self-criticism on the part of the political elite, reforming the lumbering remnants of the 1955 system has so far proved an uphill struggle.

The most significant recent development in Japanese politics was the loss of power by the Liberal Democratic Party in 1993. At the time, the end of the LDP's one party rule seemed to mark the beginning of a reformist era in Japan, to show that Japan was a normal working democracy in which the ruling party could be turned out of office. The old politics, with its pervasive factionalism and clientelism, seemed under threat. Self-proclaimed 'reformers' such as Hosokawa and Ozawa were lionized in the international media, and an electoral reform bill was passed the following year. What followed, however, was acutely disappointing. A ramshackle coalition government, made up of parties united only by their opposition to the LDP, collapsed shortly after passing electoral reform legislation. These 'reformists' were replaced by a curious new coalition, a hybrid alliance of the LDP and the Socialists. By coopting the Socialists, the LDP expedited the demise of their longstanding opponents. The first lower-house elections held under the new rules produced a largely conservative Diet, containing a rough balance between LDP members, and those from right-wing but anti-LDP parties.

The old politics of factionalism plus ideological antagonism were replaced by a new politics of pure and simple factionalism. While some political scientists argued that the LDP had been brought down by the rising costs of corruption and clientelism, the new order seemed unlikely to reduce those costs. Faced with an economic downturn, both LDP and anti-LDP politicians called for more public works spending. Such spending was calculated to satisfy the vociferous demands of the construction industry which continued to bankroll many political actors. One of the root causes of Japan's political and economic woes – clientelism and corrupt relationships between bureaucrats, politicians and business people – remained largely untackled. When the self-styled 'reformists' rejoined forces with their old friends in the LDP at the end of 1998, all hope of seismic political change seemed to have evaporated.

Japan's political elite does not operate in a vacuum, but has to respond to pressures from various elements of civil society. However, many features of Japanese society help to insulate the elite from vociferous public criticism and pressures. Japan's education system tends to encourage obedience and conformity, rather than an attitude of critical questioning. Policing methods and the workings of the criminal justice system, though rarely draconian, broadly privilege the power of the state over the rights of the individual. By the 1990s, the union movement was weak and internally divided, and even once powerful public sector unions such as the teachers' union had become a shadow of their former bolshie selves. The media, despite regularly (perhaps even ritually) exposing juicy scandals, continues to enjoy highly ambiguous relationships with holders of political power. The big five Japanese newspaper groups rarely engage in the kind of adversarial roles played by their counterparts in some Southeast Asian or western countries. Protest movements, both of the radical kind, and of the milder 'citizens' variety, were widespread in Japan during the 1960s and 1970s. Yet these protests seem to have declined greatly in importance during the last two decades of the twentieth century. The economic benefits of the high-growth era and the later 'bubble' period provided the Japanese state with abundant resources to buy off (or co-opt) sources of dissent. Whether public protests will re-emerge in the face of sustained recession remains to be seen. Nevertheless, it could well be argued that elite mismanagement of the economic and political order in the post-catch-up era has been facilitated by a relatively tame (or tamed) civil society.

Japan's main preoccupation at the end of the twentieth century is with domestic concerns. Economic and political problems at home make it difficult for opinion-makers to address long-term questions about Japan's international role. Japan remains an incomplete superpower, hindered from remilitarization by constitutional limitations, and by unpleasant wartime memories. During the 1980s and early 1990s there were signs of a new global assertiveness, as politicians such as Nakasone and Ozawa pushed for the 'normalization' of Japan's nationhood. There was growing talk of amending Article 9 of the constitution, and pressing for a permanent Japanese seat on the UN Security Council. Yet this assertiveness was borne largely from the greater confidence generated by new-found wealth. As that wealth diminished, and supposedly 'declining' competitor economies – such as those of the United States and Europe – demonstrated more resilience than Japanese nationalists had bargained for, projections of a new and more outspoken world role for Japan had to be revised downwards. Japan has thus far failed to assume a clear leadership role even in Asia, let alone globally.

Interpreting Japan

This book has suggested three broad (and very over-simplified) approaches to understanding Japan: a mainstream approach, a revisionist approach, and a culturalist approach. How successfully have these approaches helped answer core questions about the nature of contemporary Japan?

The mainstream approach sees Japan as a modern liberal democracy with a largely free market economy, highly comparable with other industrialized countries, and especially with Japan's old mentor, the United States. Mainstream scholars argued that Japan was outperforming the United States and many other western countries in a variety of fields by the 1970s, including: industrial production, secondary education, health and nutrition, welfare, and crime prevention. As social problems have risen exponentially in the West, and as traditional manufacturing has declined sharply in the 'old' industrial powers, mainstream scholars have seen these trends as vindicating their core arguments. When the LDP lost power in 1993, mainstream political scientists could rejoice. The old accusation that Japan could not be a functioning democracy since power never changed from one party to another seemed to have been decisively rebutted. Mainstream analysts argue that Japan is show-ing every sign of convergence with western models, as markets become more open, women and minorities are improving their standing, and old hierarchies are broken down.

If 1993 was a good year for mainstream analysts, subsequent years have revived the old taunts of the revisionists. Revisionists see Japan as a semi-authoritarian order, with a strong tendency towards centralism. Japan's loss of political direction since 1994 seems to confirm revisionist doubts about the quality and responsiveness of Japan's representative institutions, and about the capacity of leading politicians to determine the policy agenda. Recent 'political econo-my' studies by both academics and journalists specializing on Japan have revealed serious concerns about issues such as the excessive influence of the construction industry, and the questionable compe-tence of the Finance Ministry. These large question marks tend to confirm revisionist views that something is rotten in the state of Japan. The Japanese economic recession, coupled with the 'hollow-ing out' of the manufacturing base, and the difficulties encountered by Japanese firms in the information technology era, support revisionist claims that Japan's economic ascendancy was more fortuitous than miraculous. Growing domestic social problems, like Japan's failure to consolidate a major international role, illustrate that Japan is not an infallible giant rising inexorably to global dominance.

Whilst mainstream and revisionist scholars can find some support for their views from recent developments in contemporary Japan, culturalist views now face serious challenges. The heyday of cultur-alist views of Japan was arguably in the 1970s: cultural explanations were frequently invoked to 'explain' Japan's remarkable recovery from wartime devastation. Features of Japanese culture and society such as groupism, consensus and hierarchy were employed to account for the monumental collective efforts made by the Japanese people to reconstruct their economy and society in the postwar period. In other words, most culturalist explanations have been one-sided, setting out to describe and account for the positive features of Japan. When Japan was seen as highly successful, culturalist ex-planations appeared extremely persuasive. However, recent devel-opments seem to illustrate that Japan's social, economic and political order has serious shortcomings. Can cultural readings account for the weaknesses of Japan, as well as Japan's strengths? Might hierarchy and consensus actually become obstacles to economic success, instead of positive factors? Or do we need to question whether Japanese culture was ever genuinely characterized by features such as group identity in the first place? Clearly, scholars using cultural approaches to account for Japanese society need now to ask some new questions, and probably to engage in some new research.

Conclusion

Contemporary Japan is the great success story of the twentieth century. The country's postwar resurgence transformed the nature of international capitalism, overturning the received wisdom about economic development in the process. In numerous social and economic fields, Japan challenged western hegemony, and set world-beating standards. Japan was admired and applauded, envied and feared, both in Asia and beyond. Across the globe, people were captivated by the ingenuity of Japanese products, and by Japan's wondrous cultural artifacts. For a brief spell in the 1980s it seemed that Japan was becoming 'number one', poised to dislodge the United States from some of its global leadership positions. At the end of the twentieth century, however, Japan is an ailing samurai, 'alone and palely loitering', suffering from a dual economic and political sclerosis. The fleeting mirage of a Japanese-led 'Pacific Century' has vanished. Japan is struggling to reinvent itself as a nation, and to regain its formerly vigorous sense of national purpose.

Understanding how Japan reached its present position is very difficult; and envisaging how Japan can rise above the current impasse is even harder. There is a rich and ever-expanding literature on Japan in English, but a lot of this literature is quite partisan. To make sense of it requires a familiarity with some of the main debates and disagreements among those who have produced it. This book has tried to reduce those debates to three core positions: mainstream, revisionist, and culturalist. In practice, however, many Japan specialists would reject these labels. Such terms as 'revisionist' actually describe trends or tendencies in the literature, rather than offering fully accurate descriptions of the positions adopted by particular authors. Above all, though, students of Japan should understand something of the intellectual minefield they are entering when they set foot in the contested territory of contemporary Japanese studies.

Recommended Reading

1 Introduction: Themes and Debates

A general overview with a mainstream perspective can be found in Reischauer (1988); for revisionist antidotes to Reischauer, read Karel van Wolferen's iconoclastic classic (1989), and the collection of articles by Johnson (1995). Other useful general books include Horsley and Buckley (1990), Buckley (1999), and Smith (1997). A good introduction to the culturalist perspective is Benedict (1967), while Dale (1986) examines the issue of Japanese uniqueness.

2 Historical Background

Two recent surveys, Pyle (1996) and Allinson (1997), are the definitive introductory accounts of modern Japanese history. Waswo (1994) is another useful book. On the Tokugawa period, see Nakane and Oisho (eds) (1990); on the Meiji period, see Gluck (1985). For more detail on nineteenth-century Japanese history, see Jansen (ed.) (1989). Nakamura (1998) is a well-regarded Japanese acount of the Showa period; a good overview of Showa appears in Gluck (1992), and other essays in the same volume. On the origins of constitutionalism, see Banno (1992). For discussions of the war, see Ienaga (1978) and Dower (1992). On the H-bomb decision, read Bernstein (1995), and other articles in the same issue of *Diplomatic History*.

3 The Changing Political Economy

On Japan's economic development, see Francks (1999); for a general account of the economy, Ito (1992) is excellent, while Argy and Stein (1997) have some more recent data. For discussions of the 'developmental state' model, and the nature of Japanese capitalism, start with Johnson (1982); then see responses to Johnson by Okimoto (1989) and Callon (1995), and Calder's attempts to suggest an alternative model (1993). On 'economism' see McCormack (1986). Hartcher (1997) offers a gripping if rather journalistic account of the Finance Ministry, while Nakatani (1998) provides a critical analysis of Japan's economic woes.

4 Social Structure and Policy

A good general text is Hendry (1995); for a revisionist perspective which views Japan in a more critical light, see Sugimoto (1997). A very influential culturalist account of Japanese society can be found in Nakane (1970). An illustrated tourist manual (Japan National Tourist Board, 1986) offers a remarkably frank account from a Japanese perspective, as does Miyamoto (1994). The best account of Japanese consumerism is Clammer (1997). Knight (1994) and Smith (1997) deal with the urban–rural divide, and Ishida (1993) is the definitive account of social mobility. On Japanese women, see Lock (1996), and other essays in the same volume. Religion is incisively analysed by Davis (1991).

5 Governing Structures

A good overview of Japan's political institutions is Bingham (1989); Abe *et al.* (1994) is also useful. More up-to-date information describing the new electoral system appears in the relevant Foreign Press Center booklets (1995, 1997). For local and regional government, see Steiner (1965) and Reed (1986). On the political elite, see Rothacher (1993) (whose work is partly a response to Wolferen 1989); on the bureaucratic elite, see Koh (1989). The best account of the policy process is Nakano (1997).

6 Politics and Society

An excellent general text is Stockwin (1999). On political parties, the best account is Hrebenar (1992); see also Baerwald (1986), Curtis (1988), and Abe *et al.* (1994). The classic discussion of electoral campaigning is Curtis (1971). To get the 'feel' of Japanese politics – with its constant backroom wheeler-dealing – see the first part of Masumi (1995), whose narrative quotes extensively from the memoirs of leading political figures. On Tanaka, see Johnson (1986) and Hunziker and Kamimura (1996); for discussion of Ozawa, see Schlesinger (1997), as well as Ozawa himself (1994). Woodall (1996) provides a remarkable insight into the politics of construction, which should be read in conjunction with McCormack (1996). For explanations of the end of LDP dominance in 1993, see Johnson (1994), and Kohno (1997).

7 Socialization and Civil Society

For discussions of the education system, see Schoppa (1991), Goodman (1989), and McVeigh (1997). The Japanese media is examined in Farley (1996) and other articles in the same volume, Feldman (1993), and McCargo (1996). Issues of social control are discussed in Mouer and Sugimoto (1989), while Ames (1981), Bayley (1991), and McCormack (1986) offer contrasting views on policing and the criminal justice system. Sato (1991) is a superb study of an anti-social subculture. The most detailed discussion of the citizens' movements is McKean (1981), while Smith (1986) adopts a different perspective. The best account of radical protest is Apter and Sawa (1984), a classic discussion of Sanrizuka.

8   Japan's External Relations

For a general account of Japanese international relations, see Inoguchi
(1993). George (1988) provides a very thorough discussion of the US–Japan
relationship, whilst Pyle (1996) is superb on the options and dilemmas
facing Japan in the international arena. On Japan's relations with the rest of
Asia, see Shibusawa (1984), Cronin (1991), Khamchoo (1991), and Rose
(1998). For a discussion of the changing defence position, see Katahara
(1998). Soderberg (1996) and Potter (1996) contain useful case studies of
Japan's development aid policy. Prestowitz (1988) and Mikanagi (1996)
offer insights into the vexed question of US–Japan trade relations. On Japan
and Europe, see Nuttall (1998).

9   Conclusion

To follow unfolding developments in Japan, the two main relevant journals
are the *Journal of Japanese Studies,* and *Japan Forum,* both of which
regularly carry articles on contemporary social, political and economic
issues. *Japan Quarterly,* published by the Asahi newspaper group in Tokyo,
carries shorter, more journalistic articles than a conventional academic
publication. Japan coverage is poor in most UK and US daily newspapers,
but much better in the *Financial Times, The Economist,* and the Hong Kong-
based magazine *Far Eastern Economic Review.* Also useful are two weekly
publications produced in Japan: the *Nikkei Weekly,* and the *Japan Times
Weekly.*

Japan on the Internet

Perhaps the most useful site of all is:
http://fuji.stanford.edu/jguide/

which has links to sites covering all aspects of contemporary Japan.

If you want to go straight to the top, check out the Japanese prime minister's pages at:
http://www.kantei.go.jp/index-e.html

For an excellent Japanese politics newsletter site, see:
http://www.bekkoame.or.jp/~jneuffer/

For views of Japan from a broadly 'revisionist' perspective, see the many articles posted at the Japan Policy Research Institute website:
http://www.nmjc.org/jpri/

The Japanese Embassy in Washington, DC, has a very informative site with a useful country profile:
http://www.embjapan.org/profile/index.htm

For news and recent developments from Japan, see the following newspaper sites:
http://www.nni.nikkei.co.jp/

http://www.asahi.com/english/english.html

http://www.japantimes.co.jp/

http://www.yomiuri.co.jp/index-e.htm

Bibliography

Abe, H., M. Shindo and S. Kawato (1994), *The Government and Politics of Japan*, Tokyo: University of Tokyo Press.

Abegglen, J. (1958), *The Japanese Factory*, Glencoe, Illinois: The Free Press.

Allinson, G. D. (1997), *Japan's Postwar History*, Ithaca: Cornell University Press.

Ames, W. L. (1981), *Police and Community in Japan*, Berkeley: University of California Press.

Angel, R. C. (1989), 'Prime Ministerial Leadership in Japan: Recent Changes in Personal Style and Administrative Organization', *Pacific Affairs*, 61 (4), Winter, 583–602.

Apter, D. E. and N. Sawa (1984), *Against the State: Politics and Social Protest in Japan*, Cambridge: Harvard University Press.

Argy, V. and L. Stein (1997), *The Japanese Economy*, Basingstoke: Macmillan.

Baerwald, H. H. (1986), *Party Politics in Japan*, Boston: Allen & Unwin.

Banno, J. (1992), *The Establishment of the Japanese Constitutional System*, Routledge: London.

Bayley, D. H. (1991), *Forces of Order: Policing Modern Japan*, Berkeley: University of California Press.

Befu, H. (1980), 'A Critique of the Group Model of Japanese Society', *Social Analysis*, 5/6, 29–43.

Benedict, R. (1967), *The Chrysanthemum and the Sword: Patterns of Japanese Culture*, New York: World Publishing.

Bernstein, B. J. (1995), 'Understanding the Atomic Bomb and the Japanese Surrender: Missed Opportunities, Little-known Near Disasters and Modern Memory', *Diplomatic History*, 19 (2), Spring, 227–73.

Bingham, C. F. (1989), *Japanese Government Leadership and Management*, Basingtoke: Macmillan.

Bix, H. P. (1995), 'Japan's Delayed Surrender: A Reinterpretation', *Diplomatic History*, 19 (2), Spring, 197–225.

Buckley, R. (1999), *Japan Today*, Cambridge: Cambridge University Press.

Calder, K. E. (1993), *Strategic Capitalism*, Princeton: Princeton University Press.

Callon, S. (1995), *Divided Sun: MITI and the Breakdown of Japanese High-tech Industrial Policy 1975–93*, Stanford: Stanford University Press.

Clammer, J. (1997), *Contemporary Urban Japan: A Sociology of Consumption*, Oxford: Blackwell.

Constantino, R. (1989), *The Second Invasion: Japan in the Philippines*, Quezon City: Karrel.

Cronin, R. P. (1991), 'Changing Dynamics of Japan's Interaction with Southeast Asia', *Southeast Asian Affairs 1991*, Singapore: Institute of Southeast Asian Studies, 49–68.

Curtis, G. (1971), *Election Campaigning Japanese Style*, New York: Columbia University Press.

Curtis, G. (1988), *The Japanese Way of Politics*, New York: Columbia University Press.

Dale, P. (1986), *The Myth of Japanese Uniqueness*, London: Croom Helm.

Davis, W. (1991), 'Fundamentalism in Japan: Religious and Political', in M. E. Marty and R. S. Appleby (eds), *Fundamentalisms Observed*, Chicago: University of Chicago Press, 782–813.

Defense Agency, Japan (1997), *Defense of Japan 1997*, Tokyo: Japan Times.

Dower, J. W. (1992), 'The Useful War', in Carol Gluck and Stephen R. Graubard (eds), *Showa: the Japan of Hirohito*, New York: Norton, 49–70.

Dower, J. W. (1995), 'The Bombed: Hiroshimas and Nagasakis in Japanese Memory', *Diplomatic History*, 19 (2), Spring, 275–95.

Egami, T. (1994), 'Politics in Okinawa since the Reversion of Sovereignty', *Asian Survey*, 34 (9), 828–40.

Farley, M. (1996), 'Japan's Press and the Politics of Scandal', in E. Krauss and S. Pharr (eds), *Politics and Media in Japan*, Honolulu: University of Hawaii Press, 133–63.

Feldman, O. (1993), *Politics and the News Media in Japan*, Ann Arbor: University of Michian Press.

Flanagan, S. C. (1991), 'Mechanisms of Social Network Influence in Japanese Voting Behavior', in S. C. Flanagan *et al.*, *The Japanese Voter*, New Haven: Yale, 143–97.

Flanagan, S. C. (1991), 'The Changing Japanese Voter and the 1989 and 1990 Elections', in S. C. Flanagan *et al.*, *The Japanese Voter*, New Haven: Yale, pp. 431–68.

Foreign Press Center (1995), *The Diet, Elections and Political Parties*, Tokyo: Foreign Press Center; supplement, 1997.

Foreign Press Center (1994), *Japan's Mass Media*, Tokyo: Foreign Press Center.

Francks, P. (1999), *Japanese Economic Development: Theory and Practice*, 2nd edn, London: Routledge.

Francks, P. (1998), 'The East Asian Crisis: the Japanese Dimension', *Centre for Industrial Policy and Performance Bulletin*, 13, University of Leeds, 9–11.

Friman, H. R. (1996), 'Gaijinhanzai: Immigrants and Drugs in Contemporary Japan', *Asian Survey*, 36 (10), 964–77.

Fukatsu, M. (1995), 'Whither Goes the 1955 System?' *Japan Quarterly*, April–June, 163–9.

Garon, S. (1997), *Molding Japanese Minds; The State in Everyday Life*, Princeton: Princeton University Press.

George, A. (1988), 'Japan and the United States: Dependent Ally or Equal Partner?' in J. A. A. Stockwin *et al.*, *Dynamic and Immobilist Politics in Japan*, Basingstoke: Macmillan, 237–98.

Gibney, F. (1998), 'Politics and Governance in Japan', in R. Maidment, D. Goldblatt and J. Mitchell (eds), *Governance in the Asia-Pacific*, London: Routledge, pp. 51–78.

Gluck, C. (1985), *Japan's Modern Myths*, Princeton: Princeton University Press.

Gluck, C. (1992), 'The Idea of Showa', in C. Gluck and S. R. Graubard (eds), *Showa: The Japan of Hirohito*, New York: Norton, 1–26.

Goodman, R. (1989), 'Japanese Education: A Model to Emulate?' *The Pacific Review*, 2 (1), 24–37.

Goodman, R. (1998), 'The "Japanese-Style Welfare State" and the Delivery of Personal Social Services', in R. Goodman *et al.* (eds), *The East Asian Welfare Model*, London: Routledge, 139–58.

Haley, J. O. (1987), 'Governance by Negotiation: A Reappraisal of Bureaucratic Power in Japan', *Journal of Japanese Studies*, 13, Summer, 343–57.

Hanami, A. K. (1993), 'The Emerging Military–Industrial Relationship in Japan and the US Connection', *Asian Survey*, 33 (6), 592–609.

Hane, Mikiso (1996), *Eastern Phoenix: Japan Since 1945*, Boulder Col.: Westview.

Hartcher, P. (1997), *The Ministry: The Inside Story of Japan's Ministry of Finance*, London: HarperCollins.

Hayes, L. (1992), *Introduction to Japanese Politics*, New York: Paragon.

Hayes, L. (1995), *Introduction to Japanese Politics*, 2nd edn, New York: Marlowe.

Helton, W. (1966), 'Political Prospects of Soka Gakkai', *Pacific Affairs*, 37: 231–44.

Hendry, J. (1995), *Understanding Japanese Society*, London: Routledge.

Herzog, P. J. (1993), *Japan's Pseudo-democracy*, Folkestone: Japan Library.

Hoffman, D. M. (1992), 'Changing Faces, Changing Places: The New Koreans in Japan', *Japan Quarterly*, October–December, 479–89.

Horsley, W. and R. Buckley (1990), *Nippon, New Superpower: Japan Since 1945*, London: BBC Books.

Hrebenar, R. *et al.* (1992), *The Japanese Party System*, Boulder, Col.: Westview, 1992.

Hunziker, S. and I. Kamimura (1996), *Kakuei Tanaka: A Political Biography of Modern Japan*, Singapore: Times.

Ienaga, S. (1978), *The Pacific War, 1931–1945: A Critical Perspective on Japan's Role in World War II*, New York: Random House.

Immigration Bureau (1997), *Immigration Control 1997*, Tokyo: Ministry of Justice.

Inoguchi, T. (1993), *Japan's International Relations*, London: Pinter.

Ishida, H. (1993), *Social Mobility in Contemporary Japan*, Basingstoke: Macmillan.

Ishihara, S. (1991), *The Japan That Can Say No*, New York: Simon and Schuster.

Ito, T. (1992), *The Japanese Economy*, Cambridge, Mass.: MIT Press.

Iwao N. (1998), 'Reforming the Catch-up Economy', in F. Gibney (ed.), *Unlocking the Bureaucrat's Kingdom: Deregulation and the Japanese Economy*, Washington DC: Brookings Institution, 30–40.

Jain, P. C. (1991), 'Green Politics and Citizen Power in Japan: the Zushi Movement', *Asian Survey*, 31 (6), 559–75.

Jansen, M. B. (ed.) (1989), *The Cambridge History of Japan, vol. 5, The Nineteenth Century*, Cambridge: Cambridge University Press.

Japan External Trade Organization (1998), *Nippon Business Facts and Figures 1998*, Tokyo: JETRO.

Japan Institute of Labour (1997), *Japanese Working Life Profile 1996–97: Labor Statistics*, Tokyo: JIL.

Japan National Tourist Organization (1986), *Salaryman in Japan*, Tokyo: JNTO.

Johnson, C. (1982), *MITI and the Japanese Miracle: The Growth of Industrial Policy, 1925–1975*, Stanford: Stanford University Press.

Johnson, C. (1986), 'Tanaka Kakuei, Structural Corruption and the Advent of Machine Politics in Japan', *Journal of Japanese Studies*, 12 (1) 1–28.

Johnson, C. (1987), 'Political Institutions and Economic Performance: The Government–Business Relationship in Japan, South Korea and Taiwan, in F. C. Deyo (ed.), *The Political Economy of the New Asian Industrialism*, Ithaca: Cornell University Press.

Johnson, C. (1994), *Japan: Who Governs? The Rise of the Developmental State*, New York: Norton.

Johnson, C. (1995), *Japan: Who Governs? The Rise of the Developmental State*, New York: Norton.

Johnson, S. (1994), Continuity and Change in Japanese Electoral Patterns: the 1993 General Election in Yamanashi, *Japan Forum*, 6 (1) 8–20.

Jolivet, M. (1997), *Japan: The Childless Society?* London: Routledge.

Jones, R. S. (1988), 'The Economic Implications of Japan's Aging Population, *Asian Survey*, 28 (9) 958–69.

Kamata, S. (1982), *Japan in the Passing Lane: An Insider's Account of Life in a Japanese Auto Factory*, London: Counterpoint.

Kaplan, D. E. and A. Marshall (1996), *The Cult at the End of the World: The Incredible Story of Aum*, London: Hutchinson.

Katahara, E. (1998), 'Japan', in C. E. Morrison (ed.), *Asia Pacific Security Outlook 1998*, Tokyo: Japan Center for International Exchange, 65–76.

Kawai, K. (1960), *Japan's American Interlude*, Chicago: University of Chicago Press.

Kawanishi, H. (1986), 'The Reality of Enterprise Unionism', in G. McCormack and Y. Sugimoto (eds), *Democracy in Contemporary Japan*, New York: M.E. Sharpe, 138–56.

Keehn E. B. (1990), 'Managing Interests in the Japanese Bureaucracy: Informality and Discretion', *Asian Survey*, 30 (11), 1021–37.

Kennedy, P. (1994), 'Conclusion – Japan: A Twenty-First-Century Power?', in C. C. Garby and M. Brown Bullock (eds), *Japan: A New Kind of Superpower?* Washington DC: Woodrow Wilson Center Press, 193–9.

Khamchoo, C. (1991), 'Japan's Role in Southeast Asian Security: Plus ça Change . . .', *Pacific Affairs*, 64 (1), 7–22.

Knight, J. (1994), 'Rural Revitalization in Japan: Spirit of the Village and Taste of the Country', *Asian Survey*, 34 (7) 34–46.

Koh, B. C. (1989), *Japan's Administrative Elite*, Berkeley: University of California Press.

Kohno, M. (1997), *Japan's Postwar Party Politics*, Princeton: Princeton University Press.

Krauss, E. S. (1988), 'The 1960's Japanese Student Movement in Retrospect', in G. Bernstein and H. Fukui (eds), *Japan and the World*, London: Macmillan, 95–115.

Krauss, E. S. and M. Muramatsu (1988), 'The Japanese Political Economy Today: The Patterned Pluralist Model', in D. I. Okimoto and T. P.

Rohlen (eds), *Inside the Japanese System*, Stanford: Stanford University Press, 208–10.

Krauss, E. S. and B. L. Simcock (1980), 'Citizens' Movements: the Growth and Impact of Environmental Protests in Japan', in K. Steiner, E. S. Krauss and S. C. Flanagan (eds), *Political Opposition and Local Politics in Japan*, Princeton: Princeton University Press, 1980, 187–227.

Large, S. S. (1992), *Emperor Hirohito and Showa Japan: A Political Biography*, London: Routledge.

Lincoln, E. J. (1988), *Japan: Facing Economic Maturity*, Washington DC: Brookings Institution.

Lock, M. (1996), 'Centering the Household: The Remaking of Female Maturity in Japan', in A. E. Imamura (ed.), *Re-imaging Japanese Women*, Berkeley: University of California Press, 73–103.

MacDougall, T. (1988), 'The Lockheed Scandal and the High Cost of Politics in Japan', in A. Markovits and M. Silverstein, *The Politics of Scandal*, New York: Holmes and Meier, 193–229.

Mansfield, M. (1989), 'Japan and the US: Sharing the Destinies', *Foreign Affairs*, 38 (2), 3–15.

Masumi, J. (1995), *Contemporary Politics in Japan*, Berkeley: University of California Press.

McCargo, D. (1996), 'The Political Role of the Japanese Media', *Pacific Review*, 9 (2).

McCargo, D. (1998), 'Elite Governance: Business, Bureaucrats and the Military', in R. Maidment, D. Goldblatt and J. Mitchell (eds), *Governance in the Asia-Pacific*, London: Routledge, 126–49.

McCormack, Gavan (1986), 'Beyond Economism: Japan in a State of Transition', in G. McCormack and Y. Sugimoto (eds), *Democracy in Contemporary Japan*, New York: M.E. Sharpe, 39–64.

McCormack, G. (1986), 'Crime, Confession and Control in Contemporary Japan', in G. McCormack and Y. Sugimoto (eds), *Democracy in Contemporary Japan*, New York: M.E. Sharpe, 186–94.

McCormack, G. (1996), *The Emptiness of Japanese Affluence*, Armonk, New York: M.E. Sharpe.

McKean, M. A. (1980), 'Political Socialization Through Citizens' Movements', in K. Steiner, E. S. Krauss and S. C. Flanagan (eds), *Political Opposition and Local Politics in Japan*, Princeton: Princeton University Press, 228–73.

McKean, M. A. (1981), *Environmental Protest and Citizen Politics in Japan*, Berkeley: University of California Press.

McVeigh, B. J. (1997), *Life in a Japanese Women's College: Learning to be Ladylike*, London: Routledge.

McVeigh, B. J. (1998), *The Nature of the Japanese State: Rationality and Rituality*, London: Routledge.

Metraux, D. A. (1995), Religious Terrorism in Japan: The Fatal Appeal of Aum Shinrikyo, *Asian Survey*, 35 (12), 1140–54.

Mikanagi, Y. (1996), *Japan's Trade Policy: Action or Reaction?* London: Routledge.

Ministry of Foreign Affairs (1998), *Japan's Official Development Assistance Annual Report 1997*, Tokyo: Association for Promotion of International Cooperation.

Miyamoto, M. (1994), *Straightjacket Society: An Insider's Irreverent View of Bureaucratic Japan*, Tokyo: Kodansha.

Mouer, R. and Y. Sugimoto (1989), *Images of Japanese Society*, London: Kegan Paul International.

Nakamura, T. (1998), *A History of Showa Japan, 1926–1989*, Tokyo: University of Tokyo Press.

Nakane, Chie (1970), *Japanese Society*, Berkeley: University of California Press.

Nakane, C. and O. Shinzaburo (eds) (1990), *Tokugawa Japan*, Tokyo: University of Tokyo Press.

Nakano, M. (1997), *The Policy-making Process in Contemporary Japan*, Basingstoke: Macmillan.

Neary, I. (1997), 'Burakumin in Contemporary Japan', in Michael Weiner (ed.), *Japan's Minorities: The Illusion of Homogeneity*, London: Routledge: 50–78.

Nuttall, S., 'Europe and Northeast Asia' (1998), in H. Maull, G. Segal and J. Wanandi (eds), *Europe and the Asia Pacific*, London: Routledge, 174–83.

Oka, T. (1994), *Prying Open the Door: Foreign Workers in Japan*, Washington DC: Carnegie Endowment for International Peace.

Okimoto, D. I. (1989), *Between MITI and the Market*, Stanford: Stanford University Press.

Ozawa, I. (1994), *Blueprint for a New Japan: The Rethinking of a Nation*, New York: Kodansha.

Parker Jr, L Craig (1984), *The Japanese Police System Today: An American Perspective*, Tokyo: Kodansha.

Passin, H. (1982) *Society and Education in Japan*, Tokyo: Kodansha.

Pempel, T. J. (1987), 'The Tar Baby Target: 'Reform' of the Japanese Bureaucracy', in R. E. Ward and S. Yoshikazu (eds), *Democratizing Japan: The Allied Occupation*, Honolulu: University of Hawaii Press.

Pharr, S. J. (1990), *Losing Face: Status Politics in Japan*, Berkeley: University of California Press.

Potter, D. M. (1996), *Japan's Foreign Aid to Thailand and the Philippines*, Basingstoke: Macmillan.

Prestowitz, C. V. (1988), *Trading Places: How America Allowed Japan to Take the Lead*, Tokyo: Tuttle.

Pyle, K. B. (1996), *The Japanese Question: Purpose and Power in a New Era*, 2nd edn, Washington DC: AEI Press.

Pyle, K. B. (1996), *The Making of Modern Japan*, 2nd edn, Lexington, MA: D.C. Heath.

Reed, S. R. (1981), 'Environmental Politics: Some Reflections Based on the Japanese Case', *Comparative Politics*, April, 235–70.

Reed, S. R. (1986), *Japanese Prefectures and Policymaking*, Pittsburgh: University of Pittsburgh Press.

Reischauer, E. O. (1977), *The Japanese*, Cambridge: Harvard University Press.

Religion in Japan Today (1992), Tokyo: Foreign Press Center, Japan.

Rothacher, A. (1993), *The Japanese Power Elite*, Basingtoke and New York: Macmillan/St Martin's Press.

Rothacher, Albrecht (1993), *The Japanese Power Elite*, Basingtoke: Macmillan.

Rouff, K. J. (1993), 'Mr Tomino goes to City Hall: Grassroots Democracy in Zushi City, Japan', *Bulletin of Concerned Asian Scholars*, 25 (3), July–September, 22–32.

Rose, Caroline (1998), *Interpreting History in Sino-Japanese Relations: A Case Study in Political Decision-making*, London: Routledge.

Rowley, A. and L. do Rosario (1991), 'Japan's View of Asia: Empire of the Sun', in N. Holloway (ed.), *Japan in Asia*, Hong Kong: Far Eastern Economic Review, 7–20.

Ryang, Sonia (1997), *North Koreans in Japan: Language, Ideology and Identity*, Boulder CO: Westview.

Sato, I. (1991), *Kamikaze Biker: Parody and Anomy in Affluent Japan*, Chicago: University of Chicago Press.

Sato, T. (1990), 'Tokugawa Villages and Agriculture', in Nakane, Chie and Shinzaburo Oishi (eds), *Tokugawa Japan*, Tokyo: University of Tokyo Press: 37–80.

Schlesinger, J. M. (1997), *Shadow Shoguns: The Rise of Fall of Japan's Postwar Political Machine*, New York: Simon and Schuster.

Schoppa, L. J. (1991), *Education Reform in Japan: Case of Immobilist Politics*, London: Routledge.

Shibusawa, M. (1984), *Japan and the Asian Pacific Region*, London: Croom Helm and Royal Institute of International Affairs.

Siddle, R. (1996), *Race, Resistance and the Ainu of Japan*, London: Routledge.

Smith, B. (1986), 'Democracy Derailed: Citizens' Movements in Historical Perspective', in G. McCormack and Y. Sugimoto (eds), *Democracy in Contemporary Japan*, New York: M.E. Sharpe, 157–72.

Smith, P. (1997), *Japan: a Reinterpretation*, New York: Random House.

Smith, R. J. (1987), 'Gender Inequality in Contemporary Japan', *Journal of Japanese Studies*, 13 (1), 1–25.

Söderberg, M. (ed.) (1996), *The Business of Japanese Foreign Aid*, London: Routledge.

Steiner, K. (1965), *Local Government in Japan*, Stanford: Stanford University Press.

Steinhoff, P. G. (1989), 'Protest and Democracy', in Takeshi Ishida and Ellis S. Krauss (eds), *Democracy in Japan*, Pittsburgh: University of Pittsburgh Press, 171–98.

Stockwin, J. A. A. (1992), 'The Japan Socialist Party: Resurgence After Long Decline', in R. Hrebenar *et al.*, *The Japanese Party System*, Boulder, CO: Westview, 81–115.

Stockwin, J. A. A. (1996), 'New Directions in Japanese Politics', in Ian Neary (ed.), *Leaders and Leadership in Japan*, Richmond: Japan Library, 265–75.

Stockwin, J. A. A. (1999), *Governing Japan*, Oxford: Blackwell.

Sugimoto, Y. (1986), 'The Manipulative Basis of "Consensus" in Contemporary Japan', in G. McCormack and Y. Sugimoto (eds), *Democracy in Contemporary Japan*, New York: M.E. Sharpe, 65–75.

Sugimoto, Y. (1997), *An Introduction to Japanese Society*, Cambridge: Cambridge University Press.

Suzuki, K. (1995), 'Women Rebuff the Call for More Babies', *Japan Quarterly*, January-March, 14–20.

Taira, K. (1997), 'Troubled National Identity: the Ryukuans/Okinawans', in M. Weiner (ed.), *Japan's Minorities: The Illusion of Homogeneity*, London: Routledge, 140–77.

Takagi, M. (1991), 'A Living Legacy of Discrimination', *Japan Quarterly*, July–September, 283–90.

Tanaka, Y. (1996), *Hidden Horrors: Japanese War Crimes in World War II*, Boulder: Westview.

Taoka, S. (1997), *The Japanese-American Security Treaty without a US Military Presence*, Japan Policy Research Institute, Working Paper 31, March.

Taro, Y. (1990), 'The Recruit Scandal: Learning from the Causes of Corruption', *Journal of Japanese Studies*, 93–114.

Thurston, D. (1973), *Teachers and Politics in Japan*, Princeton: Princeton University Press.

Thurston, D. R. (1989), 'The Decline of the Japan Teachers Union', *Journal of Contemporary Asia*, 19 (2), 186–205.

Tomita, N., *et al.* (1992), 'The Liberal Democratic Party: The Ruling Party of Japan', in R. Hrebenar *et al.*, *The Japanese Party System*, Boulder, Col.: Westview, 237–84.

Tsunoda, T. (1985), *The Japanese Brain: Uniqueness and Universality*, Tokyo: Taishukan.

Ui, J. (1992), 'Minamata Disease', in Jun Ui (ed.), *Industrial Pollution in Japan*, Tokyo: United Nations University Press.

Upham, F. K. (1987), *Law and Social Change in Postwar Japan*, Cambridge: Harvard University Press.

Vogel, E. F. (1979), *Japan as Number One: Lessons for America*, Cambridge: Harvard University Press.

Waswo, A. (1996), *Modern Japanese Society, 1868–1994*, Oxford: Oxford University Press.

Watanuki, J. (1991), 'Social Structure and Voting Behavior', in Flanagan *et al.*, *The Japanese Voter*, New Haven: Yale, 49–83.

Weiner, M. (1997), 'Introduction', in Michael Weiner (ed.), *Japan's Minorities: The Illusion of Homogeneity*, London: Routledge, x–xviii.

Westney, D. E. (1996), 'Mass Media as Business Organisations: a U.S.–Japanese Comparison', in S. J. Pharr and E. S. Krauss (eds), *Media and Politics in Japan*, Honolulu: University of Hawaii Press, 47–88.

Williams, D. (1996), 'Ozawa Ichiro: The Making of a Japanese Kingmaker', in I. Neary (ed.), *Leaders and Leadership in Japan*, Richmond: Japan Library, 276–97.

Wolferen, Karel van (1989), *The Enigma of Japanese Power*, London: Papermac.

Wolferen, Karel van (1993), 'Japan's Non-revolution', *Foreign Affairs*, 72 (4), 54–65.

Woodall, B. (1996), *Japan Under Construction: Corruption, Politics and Public Works*, Berkeley: University of California Press.

World Bank (1993), *The East Asian Miracle: Economic Growth and Public Policy*, New York: Oxford University Press.

Yamamoto, H. (1993), 'The Lifetime Employment System Unravels' *Japan Quarterly*, October–December, 381–94.

Yayama, T. (1998), 'Who Has Obstructed Reform?', in F. Gibney (ed.), *Unlocking the Bureaucrat's Kingdom: Deregulation and the Japanese Economy*, Washington DC: Brookings Institution, 91–115.

Index